GUATEMALA

GUATEMALA

Eternal Spring · Eternal Tyranny

Jean-Marie Simon

W.W. Norton & Company   New York · London

Cover photo: Ixil schoolgirls on Independence Day, Nebaj, Quiché.

The Nebaj *huipil* (blouse) is embroidered with the legend of the hummingbird, depicting the triumph of love over jealousy.

Opposite title page: Ixil couple, Nebaj, Quiché.

The average life span in Guatemala is fifty-nine years for urban dwellers, forty-nine years for rural peasants. Poor nutrition, harsh physical labor, and years of unrelieved misery have a pronounced effect on physical appearance. While a twelve-year-old Indian is the size of a seven-year-old in the United States, by contrast middle-aged Guatemalans look decades older. Their faces are a map of wrinkles, their bodies doubled over from years of bending to pick coffee and cardamon from four-foot high bushes. Few Guatemalan Indians live to old age, and sixty-year-old peasants often look as old as the couple in this photo.

Book design by Katy Homans and Jody Hanson, Homans Design, Inc.
The text of this book is composed in Syntax
Composition by Trufont Typographers, Inc.
Manufacturing by Dai Nippon Printing, Ltd.

Copyright © 1987, by Jean-Marie Simon

All Rights Reserved

Published simultaneously in Canada by Penguin Books Canada Ltd.,
2801 John Street, Markam, Ontario L3R 1B4

First Edition

ISBN 0-393-02488-1
ISBN 0-393-30506-6 PPK

W.W. Norton & Company, Inc., 500 Fifth Avenue, New York N.Y. 10110

W.W. Norton & Company, Inc., 37 Great Russell Street, London WC1B 3NU

1 2 3 4 5 6 7 8 9 0

Contents

Ana Lucrecia Orellana Stormont.

For my parents, Frederick W. Simon and Violet Santos Simon,
and for
Luckie Orellana, one of Guatemala's "disappeared."

Preface

In 1980, the idea of doing a book on Guatemala was a vague thought. I have spent half of the past six years there, returning to follow events largely ignored in the news, and out of growing respect and affection for friends and acquaintances. Their testimonies, and what I saw, compelled me to record a situation that changed daily, but not for the better. Scorched earth was overgrown with new corn six months later; refugee camps where helicopters dumped grieving widows and children were renamed and reconstructed over razed huts; and model villages were built on top of these camps, often over the ashes of the dead. I believe that these events were part of a larger cycle of repression and resistance destined to be repeated in the near future unless basic economic and social changes occur. In the meantime, a way of life is being lost.

The Cerezo government is well into its second year, yet those responsible for Guatemala's atrocities are promoted rather than punished, and its leaders and legislators refuse to challenge the structures that protect those who will not compromise even a little. Yet while Guatemala's tragedy must be mourned and protested, its people must be honored as well, for Guatemala is a nation of prisoners, but it is also a nation of survivors. In the end, it is my hope that one day the Guatemalans who see this book will not be confronted with a scene from their present, but only with a nightmare from their past.

Jean-Marie Simon
New York City
August 1987

Acknowledgments

An author's gratitude is small thanks for collaboration rendered, and it is with particular regret that I cannot name most of the dozens of Guatemalans who helped with this book. Guatemalan army intelligence files continue to proliferate under the current civilian government and to thank those who helped me would be a breach of trust rather than a tribute to their generosity and courage. They are as much a part of this book as I am, and they have my deepest respect and admiration. Others who were pivotal to my understanding and love of Guatemala are now dead or "disappeared"—victims of the Guatemalan army's ongoing counterinsurgency doctrine. One, Ana Lucrecia Orellana Stormont, is always present in my thoughts.

I wish to thank a friend whose comments and additions were vital to the text; his encyclopedic knowledge of events in Guatemala is worthy of a book in itself. I am also grateful to Desiderio Menchú Escobar, a lawyer whose integrity and tenacity truly saved me from cynicism; several local journalists whose insights and honesty were inspiration in my own endeavors; and Silvia and Juan, two friends from the Quiché. Members of the Mutual Support Group (GAM) for the families of the "disappeared" were especially helpful in allowing me to record accounts of their personal searches for missing family members, always told with patience, pain, and love. Raymond Petit of the French diplomatic service facilitated my work despite his own overburdened schedule. I owe a special debt of gratitude to Myrna Ponce and her family, for objectivity and support, and for friendship.

My interest in Guatemala began in the United States. Cynthia Grinde Nassim introduced me to Latin America, while Robert Maurer and Janet Johnstone, formerly of Amnesty International USA, pointed me toward Guatemala. Tracy Ulltveit-Moe of AI's International Secretariat offered encouragement and assistance from the start. I am indebted to Angie Berryman, Mike Goldwater, Chuck Harper, Patti Hassler, Dan Jensen, Stephen Kass, Judy LaBelle, Susan Oristaglio, Ingrid Ouchi, Jim Towey, and Bill Wipfler, for friendship and different kinds of generosity. I also wish to thank Dr. Benjamin Colby and Lore Colby, whose material on Guatemala during the 1960s was important not just as historical reference, but as poignant counterpoint to the violence that followed.

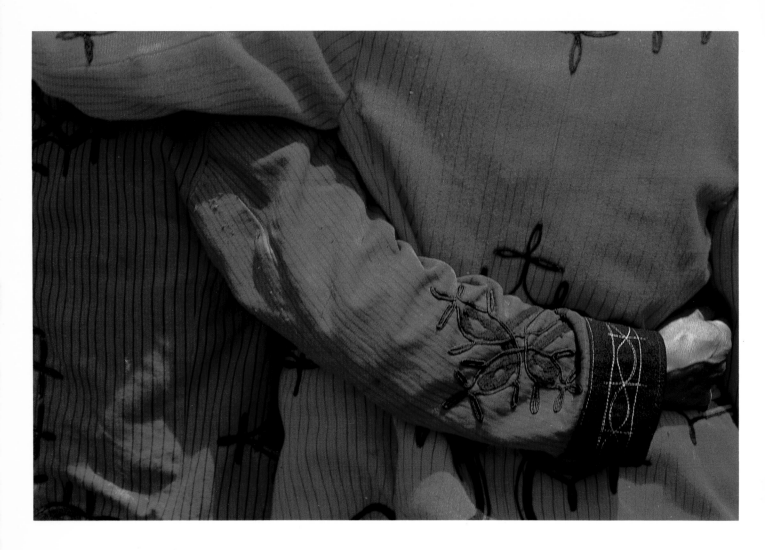

Traditional Ixil men's jackets,
Nebaj, Quiché.

The U.S. and London staffs of Amnesty International, and Americas Watch in New York were consistently helpful.

Ricardo Chavira, Peter Kellner, and Robert Stevens, all of *Time* magazine, lent support far beyond the limits of their responsibilities. Leslie Goldman provided a keen editorial eye.

Katy Schlesinger, a good friend and good editor, brought commitment to the book at a time when my own lagged.

Ken Anderson, Frank Goldman, and Heather Wiley gave hours of careful attention to this book and were its invisible editors.

Additional thanks to Maya Miller for a more specific type of encouragement early on, when the book was still an idea, and to David Haas, Sally Lilienthal, Stanley Sheinbaum, and Jim Wake of *Humanitas*.

My agent, Deborah Karl, and my editor at W.W. Norton, Jim Mairs, turned an idea into a book; their commitment to such a venture is rare.

I would also like to thank Amy Silin, assistant editor at W.W. Norton, and designer Jody Hanson, for help in the book's final stages.

In many ways, this book began with my parents, always supportive, always an example, as well as my sister, Nancy, the first person to tell me that photography as a profession was possible.

Two other individuals deserve special mention. Philip Jones Griffiths, thoroughly generous, taught me much about photojournalism; he is responsible for many of the good photos and none of the bad ones. Aryeh Neier, more a mentor than an employer, encouraged my endeavors and helped this book to become a reality. I will always be grateful.

I owe particular gratitude to Allan Nairn who supported my initial reasons for going to Guatemala and the reasons that developed with time.

Finally, my deepest thanks to the people of Guatemala, who were the most powerful reason for staying on.

Festival at Gumarcaaj, former capital of Quiché, which was destroyed by the Spaniards.

"I find myself always torn between two beliefs:
the belief that life should be better than it is and
the belief that when it appears better it is really worse."

—Graham Greene, *Journey Without Maps*

Introduction

The most spectacular view of the Pacaya volcano is at night, from the air, on the last leg of the Miami–Guatemala flight, twenty-one miles outside Guatemala City. When active, a deep orange ribbon of mercury-bright lava snakes its way down Pacaya's slope, fading into molten ash at the base. First-time visitors are fortunate for this introduction to the country, and Guatemalans themselves are not jaded by the sight.

In the mid-1960s, the Guatemalan government had begun a program of systematic repression against its own citizens, and by 1970 Pacaya was an undeclared dumping site for hundreds of victims, whose tortured bodies were dropped, sometimes alive, into its crater. Since then, tens of thousands of men, women, and children have been killed by government security forces. Some corpses were recovered, while many others decomposed in hundreds of secret cemeteries throughout the country.

Government repression in Guatemala reached its peak in the 1980s. It has been the most unrelenting yet the least acknowledged in the Western Hemisphere. Those responsible have covered up the truth with a barrage of rhetoric as predictable as the violence they have caused. According to the Guatemalan government, violence is caused by "communist subversives," "common delinquents," or "heat waves." In 1984, Guatemala's head-of-state defined violence as "a folkloric problem that began with Cain and Abel." The U.S. government has been no more honest, even though it introduced systematic repression there in the form of Green Berets and police aid in the 1960s. When the U.S. State Department does not directly blame "foreign-supported radical Marxists" and "phantom leftist and rightist" groups for what is simply wholesale government killing, it cites "difficulty in assigning responsibility." Even at its most benign, the State Department uses a jargon so sanitized that these definitions of repression are more an obfuscation of reality than a clarification; the "perpetrators" of torture, it is said, "can be determined only inferentially."

If the Guatemalan government and the U.S. State Department encounter "difficulty in assigning responsibility" for Guatemala's atrocities, then they are alone.

Guatemalans know who kills, and of the 1,500 members of the committee of the families of the "disappeared," not one has charged the guerrillas with a relative's abduction. Guatemala's president, Vinicio Cerezo Arévalo, also knows: he spent the five years prior to his election in hiding or seclusion at urban safehouses, and not once has anyone, including President Cerezo, suggested that it was the guerrillas he was hiding from. And, from time to time, the Guatemalan military has acknowledged its own brutality. In December 1984, when confronted with allegations of continuing army violence in the Guatemalan highlands, then head-of-state, General Mejía Víctores, replied, "Isn't the killing of three hundred, five hundred Indians worth it to save the country?"

Statistics now rote on the Guatemalan scholar circuit indicate that thirty-nine percent of all "disappearances" throughout Latin America since 1966 have taken place in Guatemala. According to the American Association for the Advancement of Science (AAAS), over the past two decades there have been at least 100,000 political killings and 38,000 "disappearances" carried out by army, police, and paramilitary government forces. The term *desaparecido* (literally "disappeared," referring to government kidnappings), acquired its grammatical versatility as both a verb and participle ("to be disappeared," "he was disappeared") in Guatemala almost a decade before the term was exported to Chile and Argentina. As a result, there is hardly a Guatemalan alive who cannot name at least a dozen friends, relatives or colleagues killed or "disappeared" over the past decade.

The continuing instability of the Guatemalan government has been, in itself, cause for amazement. Since 1982 Guatemala has lived through two presidential elections, two military coups, two states of alert, two Constitutions, an eleven-month state of siege, a three-month state of emergency, at least four amnesty periods, and four heads of state—three of them army generals.

There is more. Since the early 1980s the Guatemalan government has developed the most efficient rural counterinsurgency program in Latin America, perhaps in the world. The program is remarkably similar to the civic-action blueprint developed by the United States in Vietnam in the late 1960s. The tactics that finally defined U.S. involvement in Vietnam—"scorched earth," "strategic hamlets," "civil guards"—have all had their counterparts in Guatemala. By incorporating one million peasants into a civil patrol system—unarmed, unremunerated patrol duty required of all rural males—and corralling some seventy thousand internal refugees into "model" villages (permanent containment areas under military control), the Guatemalan military has ensured its domination over every facet of daily life.

This has had disastrous consequences for Guatemala's Mayan Indian population, which, after Bolivia, constitutes the highest concentration of indigenous peoples in Latin America. Where there is a military presence, religious rites and local festivals have been curtailed if not prohibited, and Guatemala's Indians are more impoverished now than ten years ago. Precious work time is forfeited for civil patrol duty, and many villagers are required to betray their neighbors by becoming army informants in order to put food on their own families' tables, or simply to save their lives. Present-day counterinsurgency has probably done as much to alter Indian life as the Spanish Conquest and its aftermath did in four centuries, and one cannot help but wonder if the culture that the Mayans have sustained since the sixteenth century will endure even fifty more years.

The media, however, have largely ignored Guatemala. Between 1978 and 1980, when the State Department issued its first *Country Reports on Human Rights*, a series of events occurred which would have provoked foreign press coverage in other countries: massive coastal strikes; the murder of a dozen priests; the killing of almost forty people inside the Spanish Embassy; the daylight mass abduction of twenty-seven union leaders in Guatemala City, and the abduction of seventeen others two months later; a European boycott of Coca-Cola sparked by government repression against union leaders at Coke's Guatemala City plant; systematic massive repression at the state-run University of San Carlos; a growing list of large-scale rural massacres; the assassination of two promising presidential candidates within two months of each other; blatant corruption that later paralyzed the country; and the lightning growth of four guerrilla groups. These were all compelling reasons for the media to cover Guatemala. When similar events occurred in El Salvador shortly afterwards, they were reported in all their minutiae by a now-permanent press corps that believed Guatemala unworthy of public attention.

Why, then, was Guatemala ignored? At first it wasn't just Guatemala. Until the late 1970s Central America as a region made the news only sporadically. In part, at least, this reflected the way news was defined by editors back home: the U.S. public maintains a provincial attitude about events outside its borders; what doesn't make the news must not be crucial, and this is often determined by some link to the United States. The definition was driven home in 1979, when the murder of ABC-TV correspondent, Bill Stewart, by Nicaraguan National Guardsmen, was filmed by his own crew and shown hours later in time for the evening news. Even though the Nicaraguan civil war against dictator General Anastasio Somoza had been raging for years, the killing of this one U.S. citizen finally focused outside attention there, one month before the final Sandinista victory. Similarly, foreigners routinely confused El Salvador the nation with San Salvador the capital, until the rape and murder of four U.S. religious workers in December 1980. By then, however, the regional die had been cast. What little attention Guatemala did receive was, by 1980, even further diminished when foreign editors deemed that resources should next be directed toward El Salvador; reporters themselves, now part of a stationary press corps, believed that Guatemala would eventually fall into place on the Central American media agenda. While some journalists did cover Guatemala during the early 1980s, there was still little coverage at a time when government rural counterinsurgency was changing the country's landscape from one month to the next.

Paradoxically, had there been U.S. military aid to Guatemala, brutality would have received more attention. By 1977, however, the Guatemalan government was furious with President Jimmy Carter's human rights policy, since it was now being told to uphold human rights by the same government that had instructed it in abuse twenty years before. (Back door military aid—millions of dollars' worth—has been sent to Guatemala throughout the Reagan administration.) The Guatemalan army's own chauvinism prompted it to reject U.S. aid in 1977 before the State Department could subject it to human rights conditions. In short: no aid, no news, no human rights.

Finally, Guatemala is not an easy country to report on. Guatemala is small, no larger than Ohio, but the highland villages where repression takes place are remote, and communication is minimal. Hundreds of towns located an hour or two from Guatemala City depend on a telegraph office as their sole communication link, and that office is controlled by the local military garrison or by a paid informer.

January 14, 1986 marked the inauguration of President Vinicio Cerezo Arévalo, Guatemala's first civilian president in sixteen years, and its sixth since 1898. This transition has been hailed as the signal of a new era, as Guatemala takes its place on the map of the nine Latin American nations "democratized" since 1979. Many of those who now travel there will be hard-pressed to imagine the enormity of its tragedy. For most, there is nothing to remember because Guatemala's brutality was never known to begin with, except by the Guatemalan military, the U.S. State Department, and a people whose collective suffering has made them a nation of prisoners. Today, repression continues. In April 1987, Archbishop Próspero Penados del Barrio stated, "There has been a change in government but not of those who control it. The army is the same. They keep killing many people."

In 1966, Uruguayan writer Eduardo Galeano traveled to Guatemala. In a statement that says as much about Guatemala's present as it does about its past, Galeano wrote:

"In Guatemala things are more easily seen and felt than elsewhere. This is a regime that violently imposes the law of survival of the strongest; this is a society that condemns most people to live as if in a concentration camp; this is an occupied country where the imperium shows and uses its claws and teeth. Dreams fade inevitably into nightmares and one can no longer love without hating, fight for life without killing, say *Yes* without also implying *No*."[1]

This, in the end, is the reason for the greatest outrage, the keenest indignation. Guatemala is a place where the political, economic, and social panorama is unfairly skewed in every possible way. In Guatemala, no one outside the charmed circle of the army and the very rich is safe, almost everyone is a victim in one way or another, and even those privileged few who remain

1. Eduardo Galeano, *Guatemala: Occupied Country* (New York: Monthly Review Press, 1969), p. 115.

immune from repression are conditioned by cowardice or greed. Guatemala is a place where coups are plotted after minimal attempts at land reform, and where even talk of land redistribution is deemed "subversive" or communist. Guatemala is a place where those who have nothing offer the only chair in the house, while those who have everything will often not pay minimum wage. In Guatemala, life gets better for a minority, at the expense of millions of others.

In Guatemala, one doesn't have to carry a gun to be considered a "subversive." It is enough simply to want a better life for your children. Its citizens are abducted from downtown streets at midday before dozens of witnesses who dare not speak for fear of becoming victims themselves. Sometimes their tortured bodies are found, often unrecognizable. In the countryside, men are shot for carrying a dozen tortillas, since that much food in one man's hand must be destined for the "subversives," and those children who witness their parents' deaths grow up with a bitterness and resentment that will not ever be forgotten.

Dawn, Nebaj, Quiché.

Guatemala has the most uneven land distribution in Latin America; seventy percent is owned by two percent of the population. Beginning with the Spanish Conquest, the Catholic Church imposed *reducciones*, literally, "reductions," on the Indians' land, facilitating the Spaniards' takeover of huge areas. In the late 1800s five million acres of land were expropriated and redistributed by the Liberal government to encourage private foreign investment in the lucrative coffee business. In 1954 Guatemala's only decade of democracy was ended by a CIA coup sparked by modest land reform.

Not only have Guatemala's peasants had their land taken from them, but they also have been forced to live according to arbitrary dictums. In the late 1500s the Catholic Church required peasants to live within 560 yards of the church bell tower, so they could hear the call to Mass. Four hundred years later, the Guatemalan military claimed that the proximity of model villages—part of its civic action counterinsurgency program—to the town square was necessary and beneficial to inhabitants because it "makes it easier for children to get to school and for families to attend fiestas," according to one government official.

Chapter 1

Background

In the 1800s a European visitor called Guatemala the "land of the eternal spring." A century later, Guatemalan essayist and politician Manuel Galich called his country the "land of eternal tyranny." For a few, Guatemala is paradise. For most, it is not.

After Nicaragua and Honduras, Guatemala is Central America's third-largest country. With an area of 42,042 square miles, Guatemala is no larger than Tennessee and one-sixth the size of Texas. Its population of 8.5 million people, the largest of the Central American nations, is slightly more than that of New York City. Fifty-five percent of Guatemala's people are Mayan Indians belonging to twenty-two language and ethnic groups; the largest are Quiché, Cakchiquel, Kekchí, Mam, and Pocomam. Guatemala's Indian population is largely concentrated in the rural highlands, or *altiplano*, where sixty-four percent of the population lives, while *ladinos*, or non-Indians (people of mixed Indian and Spanish or European ancestry) live in Guatemala City, the capital, and coastal and eastern lowlands. Guatemala is divided into twenty-two *departamentos*, "departments," or provinces, and 329 municipalities. Each municipality contains several dozen villages; the majority of the population lives outside the village or on its perimeters, on small plots of land.

Guatemala's geography is one of the most compactly varied in Latin America, containing ten-thousand-foot mountain ranges and over two dozen volcanic peaks; extensive jungles to the north; fertile coastlands to the south, and arid flatlands to the east. Coffee, cotton, beef, bananas, and sugar are Guatemala's chief export crops, petroleum and nickel its leading natural resources. In resources, Guatemala is Central America's wealthiest nation; with over three hundred firms with U.S. interests operating there, it has traditionally been a goldmine for foreign investment and for hundreds of Guatemalan families, some of whom control entire industries.[1] Until the early 1980s, Guatemala's currency, the *quetzal*, was on par with the U.S. dollar.

Despite its real wealth, however, Guatemala also presents some of the most appalling statistics in the Western Hemisphere. Seventy-nine percent of its population is considered "poor" or "extremely poor." Over half of them earn less than U.S. $150 per year, while one

1. *El Gráfico*, February 16, 1982, cited in "Guatemala: The Roots of Revolution," Special Update (Washington, D.C.: Washington Office on Latin America, WOLA, February 1983), p. 5.

2. *Inforpress 1982*, p. 131, cited in "Guatemala: The Roots of Revolution," p. 6.
3. *El Gráfico*, February 16, 1982, cited in "Guatemala: The Roots of Revolution," p. 5.
4. Richard Hough et al., *Land and Labor in Guatemala: An Assessment* (Washington, D.C.: Agency for International Development, 1982), p. 1–2.

percent earns over U.S. $1200 annually.[2] Between 1970 and the early 1980s, Guatemala's per capita GNP increased by 27 percent—more than that of any other Central American nation—yet the percentage of the GNP shared by the poorest 50 percent of the population dropped by 20 percent, and that of the wealthiest 20 percent rose from 46.5 percent to 57 percent.[3] According to World Bank figures, 5 percent of the rural population has access to electricity, and 14 percent has access to potable water. Only 15 percent of Guatemala's rural population has access to medical care, while the national social security system, IGSS, covers 7 percent of the working population. Currently under- and unemployment figures hover between 45 and 60 percent, the highest in Guatemalan history.

Many of Guatemala's political and economic problems have originated in its land distribution. Since the Spanish Conquest in 1524, Indians have systematically been denied their land, then forced to work it, for pitiful wages, by Spanish landowners, the Catholic clergy, eighteenth-century coffee barons, and later, by the Guatemalan army, who transformed the military into a lucrative business in the 1960s. In Guatemala, instead of economic progress one sees growing impoverishment and constant forced labor or denial of land. The *encomienda* and *repartimiento* laws of the sixteenth century, which drafted up to one-quarter of the male population of an entire village for unpaid gang labor on vast fincas, has its counterpart in today's civil patrol, "PAC" system, which extracts roadwork from the rural population in addition to enforced patrol duty. The agrarian transformation laws enacted by the government at the turn of the nineteenth century, which expropriated 2.5 million acres of land, and turned them over to German immigrants for profitable coffee production, have their modern-day counterpart in the *Franja Transversal del Norte*, colloquially known as the "Generals' Strip." Thousands of peasants were forcibly removed, and sometimes killed, as part of the expropriation plan.

A study on land distribution carried out by the Agency for International Development (AID) in 1982, *Land and Labor*, stated that Guatemala had the worst figures in all Latin America. Using the Gini index which measures land distribution on a scale of zero to one hundred—zero being perfectly equal distribution, and the one hundred the worst—the AID study concluded that Guatemala's Gini index was higher than figures for pre-reform Nicaragua or El Salvador. The study also noted that between 1964 and 1979, in sixteen of twenty-two departments, Guatemala's Gini index deteriorated.[4] Predictably, the government called the AID study communist, and several weeks later, copies of the report abruptly became unavailable in Guatemala. (A government land study carried out in the 1960s had fared no better; President Peralta Azurdia ordered it thrown into the sea.)

There was one decade when land and other reforms were carried out in Guatemala, during the democratically elected governments of Presidents Juan José Arévalo (1945–51) and Army Colonel Jacobo Arbenz Guzmán (1951–54), two governments referred to by Manuel Galich as "ten years of spring" in the land of the eternal tyranny. President Arévalo abolished the Vagrancy Law imposed by his predecessor, President Jorge Ubico. (Until 1944, peasants possessing less than ten acres of land were required to perform one hundred days of unpaid labor per year, to be officially registered in passbooks signed by the landowners. Well into the 1900s, peasants, in a particularly feudal ritual of obeisance, were required to transport the wives of landowners and military men on their backs.) He also introduced a Work Code, a system of social security, and the 1945 Constitution that allowed for the legalization of unions and the Communist Workers' Party (PGT). Special emphasis was given to education and literacy programs in the form of low-budget rural schools reaching even the most remote rural sectors. Under President Arbenz, popular movements and unions were consolidated, more emphasis was placed on cooperatives, and courts were established to try unfair landowners.

President Arbenz's most important reform, and one which set the stage for future U.S. intervention in Guatemala, was his agrarian reform law, Decree 900, enacted in 1952, which called for expropriation of all idle lands exceeding 223 acres in size. Cultivated land was not touched, and expropriated land was reimbursed for its value with government bonds. Arbenz's land reform program was by no means radical and was mainly intended to do away with rural feudalism. Under Decree 900, half a million Guatemalans—one-tenth the population— benefited from redistribution.

Under Arbenz, 60 percent of the economically active population, some 300,000 to 400,000 workers, were unionized as well, the highest number in Guatemala's history.

The strongest opposition to land reform came from the United States—from United Fruit Company (UFCO), which had enjoyed tax-exempt export privileges on its banana monopoly since 1901, and also controlled one-tenth of the Guatemalan economy through exclusive rights on the Guatemalan railroad and telegraph systems, and a monopoly of its ports. UFCO, which possessed some 555,000 acres of land, was Guatemala's largest landowner.[5] Appropriately, it was dubbed El Pulpo, "The Octopus." When Arbenz offered UFCO compensation based on UFCO's own tax statements—U.S. $1.2 million—UFCO demanded sixteen million dollars instead. When Arbenz refused, UFCO enlisted the aid of two close contacts, U.S. Secretary of State John Foster Dulles and his brother, CIA director Allen Dulles, and the U.S. State Department embarked on destabilization campaign and propaganda blitz to convince the public that President Arbenz was a Soviet sympathizer. In June 1954 the CIA led a rag-tag army of exiled "Liberation Forces" into Guatemala; on June 27, 1954 President Arbenz resigned, telling the Guatemalan people that the country was under attack by agents of the United States and UFCO.[6] The next President, hand-picked by the United States, was Col. Carlos Castillo Armas, a furniture salesman in Tegucigalpa since his exile there in 1952, after having plotted to overthrow President Arbenz. Castillo Armas was flown into Guatemala in the U.S. Ambassador's plane and

5. Michael McClintock, *The American Connection: Volume Two: State Terror and Popular Resistance in Guatemala* (London: Zed Books, 1985), p. 25.
6. Richard H. Immerman, *The CIA in Guatemala: The Foreign Policy of Intervention* (Austin: University of Texas Press, 1982), p. 4.

Rural countryside, Quiché.

Corn is essential to Indian life: their primary food is the corn-based tortilla, which furnishes one-half the calories in the average daily diet. A family of six consumes 150 tortillas daily.

Corn is so vital to Guatemalans that the army's own Democratic Institutional Party (PID) uses an ear of corn as its symbol. Peasants say that for years, some people voted for the PID, believing that it would increase their annual corn crop. A guerrilla group, the Popular Revolutionary Movement (MRP), used an ear of corn as its logo as well—with a grenade sprouting from its center.

Although Guatemala produces over 500,000 tons of corn each year, the Guatemalan American Society announced in its June 1985 newsletter that the annual Fourth of July picnic would include "traditional hamburgers, hot dogs . . . and fresh sweet corn flown in direct from the USA. . . ."

the coup marked the beginning of systematic repression in Guatemala. (Years later, the sentiments of U.S. State Department officials and guerrilla leader Ernesto "Che" Guevara would be surprisingly similar in evoking nostalgia for Guatemala's ten sweet years of "spring." In 1962, at a meeting of the Alliance for Progress in Punta del Este, Uruguay, Guevara noted the irony of the situation, asking how it was possible that eight years before, Arbenz's government was overthrown by the U.S. over the issue of land reform, "and now they come here proposing the same thing?" And by 1980, the modest reforms proposed by conservative Washington legislators were indistinguishable from those that had been the U.S. government's rationale, thirty years before, for Arbenz's overthrow. "What we'd give to have an Arbenz now," one of them remarked.)[7]

7. Alan Riding, "Guatemala: Revolution and Reaction in Central America," *The New York Times Magazine*, August 24, 1980, p. 67.
8. Author interview, Guatemala City, April 1987.

Although large-scale killings did not begin until the mid-1960s, systematic collection of intelligence on government opponents started barely two months after the 1954 coup, when CIA operatives and the "Committee Against Communism" drew up a black list of 70,000 political suspects taken from rosters of Arbenz sympathizers, political parties, and urban and rural organizations. (One CIA operative, David Atlee Phillips, recalled his participation in the Guatemala clean-up, calling the black lists "pearls to be fondled for years.") During this period, thousands of Guatemalans fled into exile, and hundreds of others were assassinated; at a meeting of over two hundred union leaders at an UFCO-owned farm in Tiquisate all the participants were killed, and UFCO ordered that their bodies be buried on the spot.[8]

While the U.S. government and the Guatemalan military claim that the counterinsurgency campaign arose in response to the guerrilla movement, this was not the case. The guerrilla movement in Guatemala grew out of the November 13, 1960 officers' rebellion. The rebellion began as an army protest over widespread corruption under the government of President Miguel Ydígoras Fuentes, and the officers' outrage upon learning that Ydígoras had failed to inform them that the Finca Helvetia was being used to train troops for the U.S. Bay of Pigs invasion. Two of the young officers at the army's Politécnica Military Academy, Luis Turcios Lima and Marco Antonio Yon Sosa, became the country's foremost guerrilla leaders. "Weekend" guerrillas—university students—for example, would leave on Friday and be back in time for classes on Monday, after having received two days of arms training. The first guerrilla cadres, based in the eastern regions of Izabal and Zacapa, would regularly come down from the mountains to play billiards and guitar in town. While the Guatemalan guerrillas never numbered more than 500 in the 1960s, they provided the rationale for killing thousands of unarmed civilians.

Since the 1960s, Guatemala has received over U.S. $66 million in military aid. Between 1957 and 1972, some 2,000 Guatemalan army officers were trained in U.S. schools while over 425 police officers received antiterrorist training at the International Police Academy (IPA) in

9. Allan Nairn, *With Friends Like These*, edited by Cynthia Brown (New York: Pantheon books, 1985), p. 191.
10. Michael McClintock, *The American Connection*, p. 74.
11. *"Disappearances": A Workbook*, (New York: Amnesty International, U.S.A., 1981), p. 17.
12. Ibid., p. 18.
13. *The American Connection*, p. 85.

Washington, D.C. Between 1962 and 1969 Guatemala received U.S. $2 million annual military aid, and even into the 1970s, when U.S. military advisors were being pulled out of most of Latin America, Guatemala still retained a large contingent. Throughout the 1960s and 1970s twelve percent of Guatemala's defense budget came from U.S. aid.[9]

Those who say that someday Guatemala will "become" an El Salvador are mistaken. Guatemala was the regional guinea pig for U.S.–style counterinsurgency; according to author Michael McClintock, some of the U.S. Special Forces Advisors who helped to set up the clandestine Regional Telecommunications Center in the National Palace (the headquarters for organizing and directing "disappearances" and assassinations since 1966) "subsequently turned up in Vietnam's CORDS (Civil Operations and Rural Development Support) program between 1967 and 1970."[10]

It was not by coincidence either that the emergence of the term *desaparecido* ("to be disappeared") coincided with the U.S. military's decision to make Guatemala its regional experiment in counterinsurgency, and was used for the first time in Latin America by the Guatemalan press. According to Amnesty International, "The Guatemalan case is among the most serious in terms of the number of victims. It is also unique, because in no other country have 'disappearances' occurred so regularly for such a long period of time."[11] AI attributed one of the reasons for massive "disappearances" in Guatemala to "the counterinsurgency activities which were originally developed with the assistance of foreign military advisers in the 1960s . . ."[12]

Central America's "death squads" originated in Guatemala City—a joint effort by the Guatemalan military and the National Liberation Movement (MLN). One of the first, the "White Hand" (*Mano Blanca*) death squad, was organized by the government and by right-wing political leader Mario Sandoval Alarcón, who was later Vice President of Guatemala (1974–78), and one of the four leading political contenders in the 1985 Presidential elections. Sandoval publicly announced that the *Mano Blanca* had been formed by his party, MLN, proclaiming in 1966 that it would "eradicate national renegades and traitors to the fatherland."[13] By August, *Mano Blanca* flyers were being spilled from small planes over Guatemala City, and by 1967 some twenty death squads were operating there. In 1967 alone, over 500 names appeared on the lists.

The advent of "disappearances," large-scale U.S. military involvement, and the appearance of so-called "death squads" did not begin under a military dictatorship, however; they began under the civilian government of university professor Julio César Méndez Montenegro, who took office in July 1966. While Méndez called his the "third revolutionary government," it is best referred to as the chronological watershed for the start of massive repression in Guatemala, beginning just before Méndez took office—and just after he signed a nine-point pact with the army, relinquishing all real powers of government—with the March 3 and 5, 1966, abductions of 28 unionists and Communist Party leaders following two government raids on homes in Guatemala City. While government-directed death squads began targeting hundreds of victims in Guatemala City, and provoking the first of dozens of states of siege, lasting into 1967, in the countryside, Guatemala's next president, Gen. Carlos Arana Osorio, gained the nickname of the "Jackal of Zacapa" for his ruthless counterinsurgency tactics in the provinces of Zacapa and Chiquimula. Between 1966 and 1970, on the pretext of eliminating communism, some 10,000 non-combatants were killed in order to assassinate an estimated 300 to 500 guerrillas, who retreated to the northern Petén jungle to recover and regroup. In the countryside, the presence of U.S. advisors was admitted even by the U.S. government. In 1966, when a U.S. reporter described the presence of U.S. Army Special Forces Green Berets in northern Guatemala, the U.S. State Department confirmed her report just before the U.S. Embassy in Guatemala scrambled to deny it.[14]

By 1970, when President Arana took office, the Guatemalan guerrilla movement had been largely decimated, yet according to Amnesty International the actual number of "disappearances" in Guatemala was greatest in the 1970s.[15] On inauguration day, President Arana baptized repression under his government, saying that "anyone who does not abide by the law will be broken in two."[16] Between 1970 and 1974, 15,325 Guatemalans "disappeared." According to the Committee of Relatives of Disappeared Persons, security forces were involved in about 75 percent of the cases. By 1971 the U.S.-based Latin American Studies Association (LASA) estimated that between 1963 and 1971, Guatemala had spent 48 of the past 108 months under a stage of siege.

During the mid-1970s, however, peasant organizations began to organize. The main catalysts of the cooperative movement were two conservative sectors: the Christian Democrat party, formed in 1955, and the Catholic Church hierarchy, both eager to support groups that might discourage more radical social change. By 1967 there were 145 cooperatives with 27,000 members; by 1976, there were 510 with over 132,000 members.[17] Some of the Church's most important work during this period was the formation of "catechist" movements, groups of men, usually local rural leaders, to carry out community religious work, especially in areas not usually reached by priests; and second, through Catholic Action, a movement started by Spanish priests in Guatemala, and carried out along the lines of Vatican II liberation theology, as a means of increasing social awareness.

Two important union coalitions also emerged: the National Workers Confederation (*Confederación Nacional de Trabajadores*, CNT), which included some 20,000 urban and rural members, and the Autonomous Trade Union Federation of Guatemala (*Federación Autónoma Sindical de Guatemala*, FASGUA). Since yearly coastal harvests required the annual migration of

14. Ibid., p. 102.
15. *"Disappearances": A Workbook*, p. 18.
16. *Latinamerica Press*, March 19, 1970, quoted in "Guatemala: The Roots of Revolution," p. 11.
17. Philip Berryman, *Christians in Guatemala's Struggle* (London: Catholic Institute for International Relations, 1984), p. 17.

**Market scene,
Chichicastenango, Quiché.**

Guatemala used to be entirely Mayan Indian. After the Spanish Conquest, Guatemala's population dropped by eighty-five percent and brutal massacres often claimed the lives of entire communities. According to one Quiché legend, so many Indians were killed "that they made a river of blood." Massacres were not the only cause for the population decline: along with guns and cannons, the Spaniards also introduced syphilis, measles, and yellow fevers. Pandemics throughout the 1500s and into the 1700s occurred with almost the same frequency as twentieth-century states of siege.

Rabinal, Baja Verapaz.

"One of the surest indices of the poverty . . . is the almost complete absence of paper as refuse. True, the streets are kept very clean, though all unpaved, and they are regularly swept. But even after the market, while the ground is littered with leaves used in wrapping, hardly a scrap of paper is visible. Paper simply is not refuse here."

—Pierre van den Berghe, an anthropologist who lived in Guatemala during the 1960s some 250,000 peasants, these labor coalitions provided the link between rural protest and later opposition movements.

By the time General Eugenio Kjell Laugerud García was inaugurated on July 1, 1974, the guerrilla movement had grown as well: in addition to the regrouped FAR and PGT, the Guerrilla Army of the Poor (EGP) began its actions, and for the first time, large numbers of Indians were incorporated into the guerrilla movement. In June 1975, the EGP gained notoriety following its killing of landowner Luis Arenas, known as the "Tiger of Ixcán." Workers reportedly responded to Arenas' death with two days of celebration in a neighboring village, including a marimba band. Immediately afterward, army paratroopers responded by kidnapping thirty-seven men from the Xalbal cooperatives in Ixcán Grande, taking them away in helicopters.[18] Under the Laugerud García government (1974–78), army penetration of the rural countryside began, establishing in many areas the groundwork for later occupation.

According to the State Department *Area Handbook*, "compared with Arana, Laugerud was a liberal."[19] In some ways, the political climate under Laugerud García resembled the current situation under President Cerezo. According to WOLA, "[A]ssassinations, massacres, and kidnappings dropped off [to] . . . about twenty per month [and] Laugerud tolerated the formation of unions and permitted public demonstrations. He even encouraged the organization of cooperatives."[20] In part, this organizing was hastened by relief efforts following the February 4, 1976 earthquake that registered 7.5 on the Richter scale, killed 22,000 people, injured 77,000, and left one million peasants homeless.

In April 1976, eight labor federations, including FASGUA and the CNT, formed a broader coalition, the National Committee of Trade Union Unity (*Comité Nacional de Unidad Sindical*, CNUS). On May 18, 1976 CNUS helped to organize a strike at Guatemala's largest sugar refinery, the *Ingenio Pantaleón*. In addition, the Committee for Peasant Unity, CUC, drew increasing numbers of supporters, especially as rural violence increased during the second half of Laugerud's government. CUC first announced its existence publicly at the May 1, 1978 Workers Day demonstration in Guatemala City. Two years later, in April 1980, the CUC would lead a one-month strike of tens of thousands of peasants, paralyzing harvesting. Workers gained increases in daily wages, from 1.19 to 3.20 *quetzales*—although CUC had demanded twice as much, claiming six *quetzales* was the minimum subsistence allowance. CUC was not an armed organization, and its methods were, according to leaders, "not clandestine, just secretive." CUC used unusual but effective methods to spread its propaganda: when it realized that landowners were slaughtering the cattle whose hides they used to spray-paint their slogans, they used stray dogs instead as mobile billboards.[21]

Guatemala's four guerrilla organizations grew in tandem with repression. By the late 1970s the four groups had some two dozen fronts throughout the rural countryside and Guatemala

18. Ibid., p. 28.
19. Richard F. Nyrop, *Guatemala: A Country Study*, Area Handbook Series (Washington, D.C.: The American University), p. 133.
20. "Guatemala: The Roots of Revolution," p. 11.
21. George Black, *Garrison: Guatemala* (New York: Monthly Review Press, 1984), p. 98.

City. And for the first time, ninety percent of the guerrillas were highland Indians (although the leadership remained largely *ladino*). The PGT (Guatemalan Workers Party) functioned largely in Guatemala City and on the southern coast; the FAR (Rebel Armed Forces) was spread throughout the northern Petén jungle; the EGP (Guerrilla Army of the Poor) had seven fronts in the northwestern regions of Quiché, Huehuetenango, and the Verapaces; and ORPA (Organization of the People in Arms), which had announced its existence in 1978, functioned principally in San Marcos, Sololá, and Quezaltenango. By 1979, there were almost two thousand armed combatants; by 1980, there were 5,600.

And repression continued. From July 1974 until April 1976, Amnesty International recorded 379 deaths and "disappearances."[22] Between February 1976 and the end of 1977, 168 cooperative leaders were killed in northern Quiché; in the weeks after the earthquake, 150 employees of the Coca-Cola bottling plant, plus 120 workers in one textile factory, were dismissed.[23] By 1976, Amnesty International stated that 20,000 Guatemalans had been killed in the previous decade.

While the Lucas García government (1978–82) is generally considered the chronological marker for the onset of mass repression of the past decade, massive violence began during the last year of the Laugerud García government, with mounting selective assassinations in Guatemala City and large-scale army repression in the countryside. Amnesty International recorded over 300 cases of "disappeared" Guatemalans between July 1977 and June 1978, most of them murdered shortly after their abductions, including 61 government-directed death squad killings in August 1977 alone.[24] Specific urban sectors were targeted. Dr. Mario López Larrave, ex-Dean of the San Carlos Law School and a prominent labor lawyer, was machine-gunned on June 8, 1977; student leaders Robin García and Aníbal Leonel Caballeros, during the same month; Father Hermógenes López, a fifty-year-old priest, machine-gunned to death one day before Lucas García's inauguration. In the countryside, on May 29, 1978, over one hundred Kekchí Indians were machine-gunned by army soldiers in the town of Panzós, after the peasants had publicly announced that they would travel there to protest the expropriation of their land in the province of Alta Verapaz. One day before the massacre, bulldozers had excavated two mass graves on the outskirts of town.

Popular protest quickly grew in response. Massive urban marches to protest the assassinations of Robin García and Mario Mujía drew some 200,000 mourners. Over 100,000 persons staged a similar demonstration in Guatemala City following the Panzós massacre. And in October 1978, one month after President Lucas García took office, tens of thousands of citizens took to the streets to protest bus fare increases announced by the government. Although the proposed increase was rescinded, forty people were killed and four hundred were wounded during the riots.[25] In February 1979, 140 labor, political, religious, and student

22. "Guatemala: The Roots of Revolution," p. 11.

23. Shelton H. Davis and Julie Hodson, *Witnesses to Political Violence in Guatemala: The Suppression of a Rural Development Movement,* (Boston: Oxfam America, 1982), p. 15; *The American Connection*, p. 137; Roger Plant, *Guatemala: Unnatural Disaster,* (London: Latin America Bureau, 1979), p. 6.

24. *Amnesty International Report 1978* (London: Amnesty International Publications, 1979), p. 123.

25. "Guatemala: The Roots of Revolution," p. 12.

Lake Atitlán, Santiago Atitlán, Sololá.

"Relations were quite formal. The boy would go down to the water fountain, he would kind of look over who he liked and then he would try to talk to the girl and she would either reject him if she didn't like him, or she would give him a signal that yes, she would like to talk to him again. But it was a very public thing.

"He would then give her a present—some money, coins—and if she accepted it, this meant that she was willing to accept him. Then he would have to go to the parents. The first time they might refuse to talk to him, and then, the second time, they would start talking to him, and by the third time they would hear him out, and he would bring presents and it was all arranged."

—Anthropologist Benjamin Colby

Seventeen-year-old coffee picker and her child, Jocotenango, Sacatepéquez.

Over half of Guatemala's income earners are agricultural workers. As a result of inflation they work for even less than they did a decade ago. Six years ago, a pound of corn cost seven cents; by 1987 it cost twenty-four cents. Ten years ago, rural families could afford the luxury of eggs once a week, along with their beans and rice; today many of them eat only tortillas. Some migrant plantation workers were able to save a part of their earnings. Today, saving money is not considered.

26. "Democratic Front Against Repression—FDCR: Proclamation," February 24, 1979, p. 2.

organizations formed the Democratic Front Against Repression (FDCR), whose five principles included "unity . . . of all sectors of the Guatemalan people which are affected by repression and . . . are disposed to struggle against it without discrimination."[26]

The Parrot and the Goldfish

Until the 1944 revolution forced labor was legal in Guatemala—failure to comply led to fine or imprisonment, or both. The following description of forced labor was given by the grandson of a Quiché Indian. According to the grandfather, the one advantage of forced labor in his day was that he only had to transport goods or animals, while *his* father had carried women on his back. The grandson recalled:

"My grandfather would be sent to Cobán [Alta Verapaz] by foot. He would have to carry gourds: they say that he would have to carry something like 125 pounds with his *mecapal* [leather band used with ropes to carry heavy loads on one's back] all the way to San Miguel Uspantán [forty miles from Quiché]. Sometimes he would carry pottery or corn, but this was before they put in the road. My grandfather said he had the easiest route—imagine what the harder ones were like.

"Every citizen had to do this several times a year. I remember one time my grandfather told me that this man, Gerardo Pereira, had given him a parrot to carry. He said that the old man gave it to him, and he put it in one of those string bags they use. He was told to carry it from Salamá [sixty miles on a direct route from Quiché]. But that parrot was hungry and it began to eat the net and escaped. And since my grandfather knew that any mistake you made would be paid for with two weeks of unpaid labor, he began to run—he spent half a day running after that parrot. But he couldn't wear it out. Gerardo [Pereira] was so angry that he told my grandfather that 'for being disobedient, for not carrying out orders, you will have to return to Salamá and bring back some fish, little fish, but alive.' My grandfather says he had those fish in a big clay jug filled with water and Pereira told him, 'Now you're going to carry them and bring them for my pool.' And my grandfather had to carry them back from Salamá to Santa Cruz del Quiché.

"One time one of the big plantation owners was carrying some valuable coins; he was traveling ahead of my grandfather. When they stopped for the night, the ranchers lost the coins. Well, my grandfather was so dirt poor that he picked them up. But the ranchers knew my grandfather was the messenger boy and they came to the house and told him to give them back. But since my grandfather had debts, he had already spent the money.

Bus passengers at roadblock
outside Chiantla,
Huehuetenango.

"There is a custom: If you want to destroy someone, you go to a Mayan altar and pray. The ranchers went and lit candle after candle and asked God to punish my grandfather, and my parents think that is why he went blind."

Nebaj

For foreigners who lived in Guatemala's rural areas twenty years ago, the changes since wrought in those communities are astounding. While technology and outside cultural influences have done little to alter the rural landscape—one can still drive for miles, on unpaved roads, without seeing a single billboard—they are amazed by the extent of army penetration in these areas. Two individuals, a U.S. citizen and a Guatemalan, described the towns of Nebaj and Chajul, in the Ixil triangle, during the 1960s and 1970s:

"When we first arrived in Nebaj, I had the feeling that it was a fairly idyllic place. Nebaj was beautifully set: green pastures, and sheep, and mountains, and smoke rising out of the huts in the morning. When you woke up, you would hear the laughter of the people going down to the fountain for water, and the animals and roosters.

"The men would go out to their *milpas* [cornfields]; usually they would call on a friend and they would work together and go out and clear the *milpa* or plough it. The women who were really good weavers were sometimes commissioned by other women who didn't know how to weave for a very special fiesta. It was just a normal life of working—getting water to the house, collecting firewood, and, for women, weaving *huipiles* [embroidered blouses worn by women, denoting one's place of origin; there are over 200 styles of *huipiles*]. I had the feeling that people were concerned with having a family and somehow getting land if not to buy, then to rent, and developing a herd of livestock—maybe some sheep, a cow, or even a horse. That used to be a ladino privilege, to ride on a horse. People don't know anything but their land; they suffer if they're being moved half a block from where they lived before.

"You knew that people had problems, but how different they were from those they have now. There were always the problems of disease and not enough food and people having to go to the lowlands [to work]. Those were perpetual problems, but somehow there were always *answers* to those problems, even the long-term ones. There were just always answers.

"To resolve a dispute, you would usually go to the mayor, and you would try to get some help from the Indian mayor and try to get it straightened out. The police were never involved.

"There was a *ronda* , a nightly patrol . . . [I]t was an office, part of the Indian government, you were asked to do it. Three or four men would walk around town at night; from time to time they would blow a whistle. They did this as a service to Nebaj.

"At night, after a certain hour, there was a real change; it was very quiet. I remember, because I always looked forward to the morning. There was some electricity, but you could turn it on for just a couple of hours, and at that time, very few Ixil [people] had electricity. It just quieted down, the fires would go out, and people went to sleep. In the morning, when the roosters started crowing, life started again."

Chajul

"Before the army came in, there was very little need for a market because people grew their own food. What you would find in the market was just what couldn't be grown there: coffee, bananas, fruit, chile, and so on. People had enough to eat then. They complemented their diet with wild plants—that was women's work and sometimes children's as well, to go out and find plants and mushrooms or little animals. People would eat meat at least once a month. People would also grow vegetables in their patios. They would grow squash and eat every part of the plant; they would also mix the squash with honey and refill the gourd. Nothing was wasted.

"Some families had cows and they would sell the milk to other families, but that was considered a luxury; only those with money could afford milk, eggs, and meat. Other families raised pigs, hens, ducks, rabbits—usually to sell. They would go to the market in Nebaj."

Tortillas

Corn-based tortillas are essential food in an Indian's diet. An Indian man described planting season and tortilla-making:

"We were born learning how to plant: our survival depended on the harvests. When my father would chop down a tree, he would ask the world to forgive him because he knew that the tree had done nothing to the man. And when he asked for forgiveness, he would say that he was not doing it thoughtlessly, but out of necessity. My father would pray to God, and ask him for forgiveness since, each year, he had to wound the earth, but he would say that he did it only to survive. At the same time, he would give thanks, because the land is so good, and one knows it will not seek vengeance.

"We were born learning how to plant corn. In the countryside, you don't go to school after the age of nine or ten. The corn was always more important. Our survival depended on the harvests. Tortillas begin with the rain, after our yearly fair. On the last night of our yearly

Indian wedding near Chimaltenango.

Although the bride and groom are both Indians, the woman has bought a western bridal gown for the occasion. The only accommodation to traditional dress is the groom's *cadena*, a string of silver beads around his neck, symbolizing unity. The elderly man behind the couple wears Indian dress. In traditional Mayan ceremony the couple is married by other family members. Afterwards, the bride retreats to her bedroom where her godparents and grandparents undress her and put her to bed, while her groom drinks and dances in the next room with his parents. When she is ready, the groom enters and he is undressed as well. The couple is tucked into bed, flowers are tossed on top, and candles are lit. Guests then depart. This blessing is still practiced in some areas.

Ixil couple dancing at local
festival, Nebaj, Quiché.

festival, the rains come, and then the celebrating ends, and the next day we begin to plant.

"When you plant, you throw four seeds into the ground, no more, no less. It looks ugly if you throw two here, three here, and six in another. Each group of corn has four stalks, four plants. We take advantage of the rain, we cut down any other plant growing next to the corn, because it robs it of its strength. When the stalk turns out rickety, the land is not to blame; it's the farmer who doesn't know how to plant.

"The women are in charge of planting beans. You do it with a stick. The women had an incredible rhythm for planting beans. But they do not plant corn; they prepare the *atol* [hot corn-based drink with water and salt added, or sugar]. Women don't work with hoes—just the women in those concentration camps [model villages]. Or widows.

"Some girls learn to make tortillas when they are nine, others when they're eleven. The mother hands down the art of making tortillas, but in our society, it's not like a ladino's, where they expect their children to be doing certain things by a given age. I remember my little sister would go out to look for clay and she would mold it; she was only six or seven. Then my mother would give her some dough and she would begin to practice. Finally, something comes out resembling a tortilla; I remember that if one of my sisters had made tortillas, they looked like shoes or bells. We would joke and my mother would tell my sister not to cry. By the time you're fourteen, though, you can make good tortillas."

The Courtship

An excerpt from a conversation between an Ixil Indian couple during their courtship, recorded by a U.S. graduate student in 1970:

Boy: I know you don't have a husband, and I don't have a wife, so I want to marry you.

Girl: You just want to take advantage because you found me alone in the street.

Boy: It's true but even if you don't love me, you are my love now.

Girl: Don't you know that people are watching? They are going to tell my mother and she will scold me.

Boy: Maybe they would punish you if I already had a wife. But since I don't and you are not married, I have to win you over even though you may fight it. I love only you. What's wrong?

Girl: They told me you were with another woman.

Boy: People lie. Don't believe them. Anyway, who is the woman they saw me with?

Girl: You already know who you were talking to. You already know it.

Boy: Well, if they told you, tell me who the woman is.

Girl: I already know it and you know it too.

Boy: I'm not going out with any other woman. People are telling you that so you will become disenchanted with me. You have to love me.

Girl: I don't want to. It's better if you go off with that other girl.

Boy: Don't think that and don't believe it because I love you a lot. At least tell me that I have the hope of being able to see you.

Girl: No, because maybe they won't let me in your house. They've told me that your mother is saying that I don't know how to work and that I'm just wasting time. Maybe they won't put up the money.

Boy: Don't worry about the expenses. We'll take care of all the expenses and thirty *quetzales* besides. There's no problem because my father hasn't spent the allowance for me yet. If I had been with another woman there wouldn't be any money.

Girl: Maybe they won't let me in because I don't know how to cook well and I don't know how to weave well and your mother will say, 'Why is she coming here if she doesn't know how to work?' That's not good.

Boy: Don't worry about that because my mother can teach you to work. Don't worry because my mother will treat you like a daughter because you're mine. I don't know how to work either, but I do know how to save my pennies.

Religion

When the Spaniards conquered Guatemala in 1524 their domination over the Guatemalan population was fortified by the Catholic clergy, who sent Franciscan friars and Dominican priests to carry out the task of containing scattered villages through *reducciones*, "reductions," of the population into some seven hundred settlements. Mayan religion was suppressed but not quashed by the imposition of Catholicism, and Catholicism and native *costumbre* (rituals) fused. Names of Guatemalan towns, for example, were joined with the names of saints—Nebaj, Cotzal, and Chajul became Santa María Nebaj, San Juan Cotzal, and San Gaspar Chajul. The Church's attitude of racial superiority did not change until Vatican II, in 1963. A Catholic priest explained:

"Until Vatican II, the Guatemalan church had been a traditional church: external practices and traditions mixed with superstition. Medellín [Catholic conference held in Colombia in 1968] and Puebla [a similar conference held in Mexico in 1979] had a big impact. Foreign missionaries and religious leaders tried to apply these principles [a reference to liberation theology, a term loosely defined as the Catholic Church's identification with the poor's economic and social needs]; from 1973 to 1975, nobody realized what was going on. It took the government until 1980 to realize that the quality of changes in Guatemala was due to the Catholic Church. Before, the Church had been a pyramid: God on top, you go to heaven or hell, and it was something private and you performed acts of charity for the poor. You collected merits, which would serve you well later. It was easier to be a Catholic before than it is now."[27]

Between 1950 and 1970 the number of foreign missionaries in Guatemala more than quintupled. Lay assistants—"catechists" or "Delegates of the Word"—as well as Catholic Action, proliferated in rural areas. Catholic Action, while religious in theory, offered concrete aid, although not always unconditional in nature; in Nebaj, it distributed free radios, permanently tuned to a Catholic radio station. A former resident of Chajul explained:

"In 1975 and 1976 . . . Catholic Action was a strong movement. They won over converts by offering them benefits. You could only get your cows vaccinated if you belonged to Catholic Action, and it was the only way to get fertilizer. Almost everyone who participated was younger than thirty-five, because they didn't worry about becoming modernized. It didn't bother them if you said, 'Don't go off and perform your rituals,' as long as you were getting your cows vaccinated."[28]

Protestantism did not exist in Guatemala until 1882. Today, at least thirty-five percent of the population is Protestant. In Guatemala City alone there are some five hundred Protestant churches. The rise of Protestantism in Guatemala had little if anything to do with (Protestant) Ríos Montt's ascent to power in 1982—even after his overthrow, his evangelical "Church of the Word" continued to grow so rapidly that in 1985 it moved to a former roller rink.

The growth of Protestantism, in general terms, is partly owed to its hands-on, unified . approach. "Since there is a permanent ambiance of incertitude in Guatemala," one analyst explained, "people look for something to participate in." In addition, the persecution of the Catholic Church in Guatemala resulted in a mass exodus of its congregation. In the late 1970s

27. Author interview, Guatemala City, December 1985.
28. Author interview, Guatemala City, August 1984.

Annual festival, Nebaj, Quiché.

"The evening of November 27 . . . represented the end of the 260-day cycle of the native calendar. Right next to the town hall was the main center of Indian worship, which consisted of five crosses with a thatched roof. I could see a fire in front of the crosses, clouds of incense smoke, and a group of men praying. I knew that important *costumbre* (Mayan worship) was going on . . . I saw clearly the people standing up outlined by the fire, praying at the crosses and strongly suspected that a sacrifice was going on. . . . I saw through a procession of women carrying pine torches and I ran outside, but I was too late. The fire in front of the crosses was out and all was over except for the fire seen on all sides at the mountain crosses.

"I went up the street in the rain and mud with my flashlight to the store to try to find out exactly what was going on. I found out that the *brujo* was following me in the dark. . . . I got lost in a black side street and what seemed like a hundred screaming dogs rushed at me. . . . I finally got back and the *Padre* couldn't understand my behavior at all. I didn't even bother to explain. I later found out from my manservant that a bird or other animal had been sacrificed that night, but he would not tell me any details."

—Anthropologist Jackson Steward Lincoln, Ixil triangle, Quiché, 1940s

Funeral procession for two-month-old infant, Jacaltenango, Huehuetenango.

Back in the 1960s, President Ydígoras Fuentes (1958–63) blocked the publication of a government document citing 50,000 infant deaths per year, on the charge the information was "communistic." Today, with 79 deaths per 1,000 live births, Guatemala still has one of the highest infant mortality rates in the Western Hemisphere, second only to Haiti, an infinitely poorer country.

Catholic penitents carrying three-ton *anda* (float) during Holy Week procession, Guatemala City.

The majority of Guatemalans are nominally Roman Catholics. These men are doing their annual penance—an Easter Week tradition imported from Spain—carrying heavy wooden religious floats, some half a block long, through Guatemala City streets, often until dawn the next day. Penitents pay anywhere from five to fifty *quetzales* for the privilege of carrying the float the distance of several blocks. The number of cards pinned to their robes represent the number of *turnos*, or "turns" they have paid for. Only the middle-class and the wealthy can afford such penance. Some of Guatemala's most fervent participants in this Holy Week tradition, after sweating away a year of sins under a swaying statue, return to their homes and businesses and continue abusing their maids and workers. For the poor the gesture is not only unaffordable but gratuitous as well, since they know better than any penitent the burden of a hundred-pound load.

Indian woman awaiting arrival of Pope John Paul II, Campo de Marte (Mars, the God of War) army field, Guatemala City.

Some of Guatemala's first foreign missionaries arrived at the invitation of its wealthy class who were anxious for their children to have a proper Catholic education. Between 1950 and 1965 the number of foreign missionaries—mostly U.S., Spanish, and Belgian—grew from 132 to 483. Their presence, together with the Guatemalan religious community influenced by liberation theology and Vatican II, had an enormous impact on grassroots peasant organizing, which was largely responsible for the mass mobilization that followed. By the late 1970s the Guatemalan military defined any type of organizing as tantamount to subversion: in 1982, Colonel Roberto Mata Gálvez, now President Cerezo's Presidential Chief of Staff said, "We [the army] make no distinction between the Catholic Church and communist subversion."

and early 1980s hundreds of catechists were killed and thousands of Catholics either converted to Protestantism or no longer practiced their religion, since Catholicism was now considered subversive for having "organized" people in the first place. As one Guatemalan explained:

"Back in 1975 and 1976 there were only four or five families in town who were Protestants. They weren't looked upon well by Indians, who would say that they were getting 'mixed up in gringo things.' By 1978 and 1979, however, people were realizing that the Protestants were much safer, and that was when Catholic Action declined and the Protestants became much more numerous. In 1978, people began asking for letters of recommendation from a local Protestant institute, to prove that they had worked there, so the army wouldn't bother them. One of my friends told me that he had converted to Protestantism so that the army wouldn't come to kill him and he could go to the capital to sell his *huipiles*."[29]

Contrary to popular belief, however, Protestants were not categorically conservative. President Arbenz, for example, grew up Protestant. Several guerrilla leaders were Protestants as well, including one of the founders of the Communist Workers Party (PGT) in Chiquimula and the second-in-command of the Rebel Armed Forces (FAR), Emilio Román López, "Comandante Pascual," a Protestant pastor.

A Protestant journalist in Guatemala City recalled that in the 1950s, in his Protestant high school, out of thirty students "twenty were leftists, three were right-wingers and seven were indifferent."[30]

Conscription

Although military service is formally obligatory, the law is almost never applied in Guatemala City, or to those who can bribe their way out of service. On the other hand, virtually any young male who is a poor peasant is a target of forced conscription. Peasants, usually young Indian boys, are forcibly rounded up after leaving church service, on market day, or during local festivals—wherever the army knows there will be a large crowd. This practice continues today: in 1984 the army swept into Livingston, Izabal, and hauled off a dozen construction-site workers; in 1986 the army rounded up soccer players, still in uniform, during half-time. On May 2, 1986 I was leaving a banana plantation for Entre Ríos, when the army attached an animal cage to our trolley and filled it with thirty young boys, captured on their way to a local dance.

A foreigner described army conscription under the Lucas García government:

"An Indian project associate was going to the capital with me. We stopped to change buses in one town. An army bus came by and a soldier got out and shoved a machine gun into my

29. Ibid.
30. Author interview, Guatemala City, March 1985.

31. Shelton H. Davis and Julie Hodson, *Witnesses to Political Violence in Guatemala . . .*, p. 31.

32. U.S. Department of State, *Country Reports on Human Rights Practices for 1980* (Washington, D.C., February 1981), p. 441.

33. "Guatemala: A Government Program of Political Murder" (London: Amnesty International Publications, February 1981), pp. 3–5.

friend's belly, and, without saying a word, pointed to the bus, where more soldiers were waiting. I accompanied him on the bus ride to the local military base where hundreds of men had been abducted in a similar manner. I spoke with the local colonel and he agreed to "hand him over" to me. While waiting I saw a young boy from town who had been abducted. I appealed to the colonel but he replied, 'You can only have one.' At the time, he was rolling dice with one man over the fate of his three sons."[31]

The U.S. State Department

Since the 1970s the United States government has provided legislation making foreign assistance conditional upon maintaining certain human rights standards in those countries (in accordance with Sections 166(d) and 502(b) of the Foreign Assistance Acts of 1961 and 1974). In 1977 the State Department released its first *Country Reports on Human Rights Practices*: annual compendiums of the human rights situation, usually written by Embassy staff in the given country.

Just how accurately an embassy details its reports depends on how the embassy chooses its sources, and its own political agenda for that country; that is, how anxious it is to continue or resume military and economic aid, and the real or imagined threat it perceives from anti-government forces in friendly countries. Nowhere was State Department rhetoric more opaque at best and untruthful at worst than in its yearly descriptions of Guatemala—apologist resumés of each successive military regime since 1977. Governments were criticized only after they were overthrown, as in the case of generals Lucas García and Ríos Montt, and even then this *post facto* clarity was less a stab at honesty than an attempt to bulwark their praises of each current regime. Between 1980 and 1986 descriptions by the State Department in their *Country Reports* were in direct counterpoint to reporting by Amnesty International:

State Department: "Violence has plagued Guatemalan history. . . . It is frequently impossible to differentiate politically-inspired from privately-inspired violence."[32]

Amnesty International: "Amnesty International believes that abuses attributed by the Government of Guatemala to independent 'death squads' are perpetrated by the regular forces of the civil and military services. . . . [T]argets for detention and murder . . . can be pin-pointed to secret offices in an annex of the National Palace, under the control of the President of the Republic."[33]

Dance of the Spanish
Conquerors, Nebaj, Quiché.

34. *Country Reports . . . for 1980*, p. 442.

35. "Guatemala: A Government Program . . . ," p. 3.

36. *Country Reports . . . for 1981*, p. 442.

37. "Guatemala: A Government Program . . . ," pp. 5–6.

38. Statement made by Stephen Bosworth, Principal Deputy Assistant Secretary of State for Inter-American Affairs, July 30, 1981 before the Subcommittee on Inter-American Affairs House Committee on Foreign Affairs, Washington D.C.

39. "Guatemala: A Government Program . . . ," p. 4.

40. *Country Reports . . . for 1982*, pp. 516–517.

41. Testimony on Guatemala submitted by AI/USA to the Subcommittee on International Development Institutions and Finance of the Banking Committee of the U.S. House of Representatives, Washington Office of AI/USA, August 5, 1982, p. 8.

42. *Country Reports . . . for 1982*, p. 516.

State Department: "Anti-criminal 'death squad' killings averaged about thirteen a month, according to press articles."[34]

Amnesty International: "Between January and November 1980 alone some 3,000 people described by government representatives as 'subversives' and 'criminals' were either shot on the spot in political assassinations or seized and murdered later. . . ."[35]

State Department: "In most instances it has not been possible to establish who the perpetrators [of torture] were."[36]

Amnesty International: "Nearly 5,000 Guatemalans have been seized without warrant and killed since General Lucas García became President of Guatemala in 1978 . . . Thousands bore the scars of torture. . . ."[37]

State Department: "There have been some positive developments in the past several weeks. The Guatemalan security forces have made inroads in guerrilla operations. And they have done it while taking care to protect innocent bystanders."[38]

Amnesty International: "The prisoner [interviewed in the AI report] was brutally tortured and escaped only the day before he was due to be executed . . . [he] believes that a neighbor denounced him as a 'subversive' because of a dispute over the village basketball court—a good enough reason, as far as officers of the Guatemalan army were concerned, for him to be tortured and put to death."[39]

State Department: "Since Ríos Montt came to power in March 1982, there has been a decrease in the level of killing. . . . The Government publicly committed itself to ending the abuses of the Lucas García government."[40]

Amnesty International: "[Following the Ríos Montt coup] the pace of rural massacres increased. . . . [C]ontinued reports were received of the raiding and burning of villages and the murder of Indian[s] in large numbers. In each of these areas, members of the junta had visited strategic local counter-insurgency bases by helicopter within one week of the coup. . . ."[41]

State Department: "The situation in the countryside . . . remained unclear for several months. . . ."[42]

Amnesty International: "In the aftermath of the [Ríos Montt] coup, between April and late June 1982, Amnesty International reported the deaths of some 2,186 individuals in large scale extrajudicial executions. . . . Testimony was presented to AI, from a seventeen-year-old Indian woman from Alta Verapaz who survived an April army attack on her village: 'A group of soldiers came. . . . They seized three . . . they took them to the mountains; they tied them up in the

Young girl lifting coffee in orange grove, Jocotenango, Sacatepéquez.

Guatemala is one of the world's largest coffee producers: it is inexpensive to grow and so profitable that the expression *es agradecido* is applied to the crop, since coffee harvests are "generous" to the planters. The peasants who work on coffee plantations are not as fortunate: they cannot afford to drink the coffee they pick, since one pound of coffee costs more than their total daily wages.

Weighing scales at the El Potrero finca in Ciudad Vieja, Sacatepéquez.

Minimum rural wage is 3.20 *quetzales*—less than $1.25 per day. At these farms workers were paid one cent per pound of coffee picked. A fast worker might pick one hundred pounds of coffee in a day. Even then, the scales are often deliberately tipped in the owner's favor, diminishing the worker's daily pay by twenty to thirty percent.

Younger *finqueros* (plantation owners) are not much more enlightened than their fathers or grandfathers. One 29-year-old plantation owner in Antigua who paid his workers one cent per pound said, "On my farm, minimum wage is not a problem. My workers and I understand each other." Much of the day-to-day functioning of his plantation was left to an overseer, while the young owner spent his time breeding eighty varieties of orchids and sculpting clay heads, half bird, half human. He collected Cape Cod bone china and kept his cache of marijuana in a chocolate box. At night, a young boy would wave an incense burner through his room to ward off mosquitoes, while automatic hoses watered the lawn.

Children and teenager picking coffee, Jocotenango, Sacatepéquez.

Most children never make it past the third or fourth grade, since their labor is vital to a family's income. Government statistics released in early 1987 stated that 2.3 million children—one quarter of Guatemala's total population—do not attend school.

In 1987 the Cerezo government introduced the *Plan de Reordenamiento Económico y Social*, the "Economic and Social Reordering Plan": one goal was to provide a third-grade education to 80% of all Guatemalans by 1988.

Man carrying firewood and sick child being carried to a local health clinic five miles away, San Martín Jilotepeque, Chimaltenango.

The child in this photo is more fortunate than most: not only is he spared his daily task of carrying almost as much wood as the grown man next to him, but his family can also afford the luxury of medical care, even if it means being transported in the same manner that his grandfather and his great-grandfather carried the wives of wealthy ladinos fifty years before. Most children receive no health care at all: they are delivered at home by midwives with no possibility of medical attention in case of complications. Guatemala has the highest maternal mortality rate in Central America. Forty percent of all children—sixty percent in rural areas— do not survive to the age of five: most die either from malnutrition while being weaned, or from diarrheal diseases.

Man hauling one hundred-pound bags of refined sugar, Puerto Barrios, Izabal.

"People definitely had the feeling that something was not fair, that their land would get smaller and smaller, and maybe their children would not survive, and people had to leave all the time because there was not enough to go around. They had to go down to the lowlands and, of course, they really noticed that other people lived better there. I mean, the riches really were concentrated in two to four percent of the population. I think they sensed that something was not right."

—Foreigner who lived in Guatemala during the 1960s

Literacy campaign under the Lucas García government (1978–82), Comalapa, Chimaltenango.

There was a certain irony to the $300 million government literacy program—more an exercise in corruption than in education—carried out in Comalapa and throughout Guatemala during the last years of the Lucas García regime: an apparent government effort to improve by day the lot of those whose relatives were abducted at night by men on the same government payroll as those assigned to teach the ABCs. Literacy figures given after the program ended were no higher than those before.

Literacy programs are far more successful when administered privately. The "STECSA" Coca-Cola union's own program has achieved 98% worker literacy—more than twice the national average.

Sololá Indian and tourist on Pan American highway.

Even when word did begin to spread that the army had occupied villages once considered requisite stops on the gringo trail, the Guatemalan government and local business groups rallied to produce an eight-page illustrated advertising supplement in *Time* magazine's October 20, 1980 edition: "Guatemala: There's Strength under its Majestic Beauty":

"There is native joy in everything from the marimba music that greets the guest at the airport to the bargain struck in a village marketplace. *Bienvenidos*. In Guatemala, the word is loaded with the power to please."

Late afternoon, downtown
Huehuetenango.

Outdoor photo studio,
Sacapulas, Quiché.

Portable photograph stands are mounted everywhere throughout Guatemala. Some men earn a living as itinerant Polaroid vendors traveling from one village fair to the next, setting up their painted paradises for the duration of the fair, then moving on.

Other photographers moonlight on weekends: an army officer in Guatemala City spends Sundays out of uniform positioning children in front of one-dimensional castles and Disneylands. He turned up at a rally for presidential candidate Vinicio Cerezo one week before the 1985 elections, carrying a party flag and looking as happy as I had ever seen anyone in Guatemala. "I'm working for Vinicio," he said in conspiratorial tones. "But please don't tell anyone."

Vendor reading newspaper to citizens in Chichicastenango, Quiché.

In the 1960s Guatemala's own literacy program worked in tandem with similar efforts directed by AID (Agency for International Development) in the United States, and the Guatemalan army's "Civic Action" office. The Guatemalan government provided a "Department of Literacy" with its own stationery, printing equipment, and vehicles. According to *The New York Times* , the efficacy of AID's program had been undermined by the State Department itself; *The New York Times* magazine, in 1965, wrote that "a powerful group which includes many people in the State Department . . . views literacy primarily as a dangerously volatile element extremely difficult to control, and thus, in the interest of stability, to be avoided." Today, national literacy stands at 47 percent, 20 percent in some rural areas.

**Street scene,
Chichicastenango, Quiché.**

Although Guatemala's Indians constitute over half of its total population and are an attraction to tourists, prejudices against Indians have changed little over the centuries. It is not unusual for Guatemalans to use expressions such as *no seas indio* ("don't be an Indian") or *es más estúpido que un indio* ("he's dumber than an Indian").

In his youth even the Guatemalan Nobel laureate, Miguel Angel Asturias, in his 1923 essay, "The Indian Social Problem," wrote that Guatemalan Indians were "dirty, slow, barbaric and cruel," which could only be offset by massive European immigration. Asturias changed. Today his son, Rodrigo Asturias Amado, commander-in-chief of the ORPA guerrillas, uses the *nom de guerre*, "Gaspar Ilom," a character from his father's novel, *Men of Corn*.

Urban slum, zone three, Guatemala City.

One of the largest U.S. investors in Guatemala is the Bank of America, which opened its first branch in Guatemala City in 1957 and soon became the principal lending institution for agricultural loans in Guatemala, which, by 1970, comprised seventy percent of all loans. In 1980, Bank of America manager, Keith Parker explained his views to a foreign journalist:

"When you've got a situation like you have here, you need the strongest government you can get. If you use human rights in a country with guerrillas, you're not going to get anywhere. . . . What they should do is declare martial law. There you catch somebody; they go to a military court. Three colonels are sitting there; you're guilty, you're shot. It works very well."

Jogging race sponsored by the Camino Real Hotel, Guatemala City.

Most peasants cannot understand why anyone would necessarily expend valuable energy solely to exercise. Jogging is common in Guatemala City, but it is not the safest sport. In 1983 army soldiers suffered several casualties, including one dead, when a bomb planted by guerrillas in a parked car exploded as they jogged by the Morazán Park. An American who lived in Guatemala during the Lucas García years gave up jogging for sport in 1980. He ran daily around a track behind the Camino Real Hotel, driving there in his car and running laps for half an hour. One day, a *judicial* (government informer) caught up with him at the track; when the man realized he was being watched, he bolted into the nearby woods and ran home, leaving his VW behind.

At least one jogger took precautions; he showed up for local races with his bodyguard, who ran behind him, a pistol secured to his running clothes.

Mother and children in
Quezaltenango,
Quezaltenango.

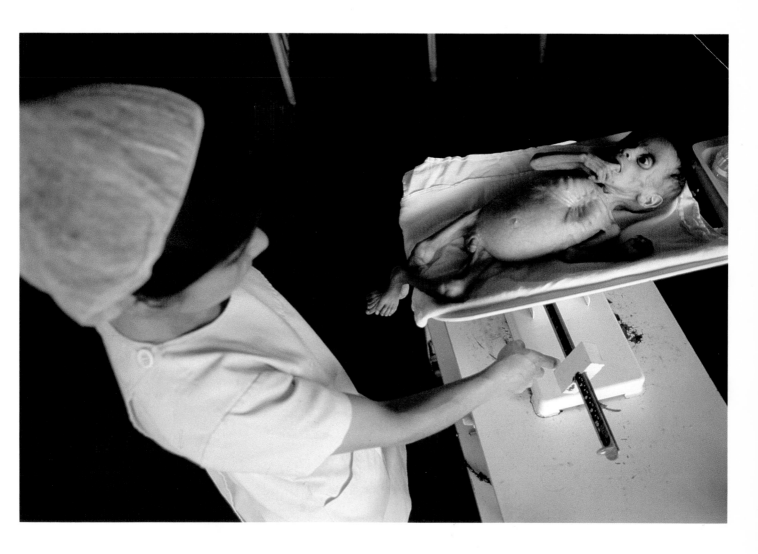

Nine-month-old boy at clinic, Guatemala City. He died the following day.

There is one soldier for every 213 Guatemalans, one medical doctor for every 2,600. According to the *Central America Fact Book*, "The average U.S. cat eats more beef than the average Central American person." In Guatemala, the comparison can be carried further: the average U.S. cat eats beef, while the average Guatemalan family does not.

43. AI/USA, Testimony on Guatemala, pp. 8–9 and 13.

44. Elliott Abrams, U.S. Assistant Secretary of State for Human Rights, at Hearing before the House Foreign Affairs Committee, Washington, D.C., May 16, 1984.

45. "Amnesty International's Human Rights Concerns in Guatemala Since the August 1983 Coup which Brought General Oscar Humberto Mejía Víctores to Power" (London: Amnesty International Publications, December 1983), p. 5.

46. Country Reports . . . for 1984 (February 1985), p. 546.

47. Letter to Patricia L. Rengel, Director, Washington Office, Amnesty International USA, from Thomas O. Enders, Assistant Secretary of State for Inter-American Affairs, September 15, 1982.

48. "Amnesty International's Human Rights Concerns. . . . ," December 1983, p. 7.

49. Country Reports . . . for 1984 (February 1985), pp. 541 and 543.

50. Amnesty International Report 1985, covering January–December 1984, (London: Amnesty International Publications), p. 4.

51. Country Reports . . . for 1985 (February 1986), p. 545.

mountains and killed them with machetes and knives. . . . They raped me; they threw me on the ground and slashed my head with the machete, my breasts, my entire hand. . . .' A second testimony came from a member of the civil patrol: [He] told of seeing a man who tried to escape being recaptured. All his muscles were cut and gunpowder placed in his navel and set on fire. The victim's eye was put out, and his skin was then peeled off. The soldiers joked that they were going to have a barbecue."[43]

State Department: "Now, the Mejía government has somewhat, I would say, to my surprise, continued a large number of [human rights] improvements that Ríos Montt began, rather than slipping back into the Lucas García type of behavior."[44]

Amnesty International: "Since the accession of General Mejía Víctores to power, AI has continued to receive reports of 'death-squad'–style 'disappearances' and extrajudicial executions from Guatemalan cities. By the end of September, the Guatemalan press itself has listed more than eight cases of 'disappearances' since Mejía Víctores came to power. . . ."[45]

State Department: "Forced labor is not practiced. Service in the civilian self-defense patrols in many rural areas takes on the character of a requirement for able-bodied males. . . ."[46] "The very organization and presence of such [civil patrol] units belies the impression that the Government of Guatemala is at war with 'the people.' This may account for the ferocity of some of the guerrilla attacks on such forces or the villages where they have been organized."[47]

Amnesty International: ". . . AI has concluded . . . that villagers are formed into such [civil patrol] squads under military orders, and act under military supervision. . . . AI has also received detailed testimony about killings of individuals who refused to join such squads. . . ."[48]

State Department: "Overall human rights conditions improved in 1984. . . . [I]t is difficult to apportion responsibility for many killings. The guerrillas on occasion use the same weapons, tactics, and uniforms as the army. . . ."[49]

Amnesty International: "Amnesty International continued to be concerned that the regular security and military forces—as well as paramilitary groups acting under government orders . . . were responsible for massive human rights violations. . . ."[50]

State Department: "Students and faculty at the National University of San Carlos continued to be kidnapped in 1985, and some of these cases were attributed to government security forces acting against suspected insurgents or their supporters. . . . Violence affecting university students and faculty is neither unusual nor easily attributable to specific perpetrators or motives. San Carlos has an enrollment of over 50,000 students, many of whom attend on a casual basis for many years. Thus a victim's association with the university may be only coincidental."[51]

**Garbage dump,
Guatemala City.**

Each day, horse-drawn garbage carts pull up to the dump, a swamp of steamy refuse, where they are besieged by hundreds of garbage pickers—women, children, and Indian refugees who work and live there, ferreting pieces of glass, plastic and paper for resale. Children learn to sniff glue at an early age, to numb their hunger and brace themselves against the dump's overwhelming stench, which immediately permeates skin and clothing. The vultures are usually benign: they scavenge for food while people search for a way to survive.

Some people are born in the dump, others never make it out, living in boxes carved into the knee-high garbage. At least twice a year, newspapers describe fruitless searches for people buried alive. In January 1986 an eleven-year-old child died under the wheels of an arriving dump truck when he tried to retrieve a leftover Christmas wreath thrown on top of rotting food. One year earlier, a family of glass collectors, trapped under the garbage, died from suffocation.

Garbage dumps are body dumps as well, where death squad victims decompose into anonymous forms following spontaneous combustion in the dry season and torrential rains later in the year. In September 1983, *Prensa Libre* reported the discovery of a human hand in the dump. "The hand," the paper determined, "in an advanced state of decomposition, has not been identified as male or female . . . It was discovered when a dog picked it from the garbage and was seen carrying it away in his mouth."

Backyard of cattle breeder, Manuel Ralda, La Máquina, Suchitepéquez.

Absent from this photo is the front of the Ralda home, set back from a circular driveway; barely concealed by bougainvillaea shrubs, are dozens of workers' shacks without plumbing, without privacy, without any of the minimal necessities. Manuel Ralda's teenage son said that his father could not pay more than minimum wage—one dollar per day. "If he did, we'd go broke," he explained.

**Debutante and father,
Guatemala Club,
Guatemala City.**

"From what I have seen of the ruling class in Guatemala, they are people without very much in the way of redeeming features. . . . All they can talk about is how much it costs them to have a guard for their daughter, their sister."

—Representative Clarence Long (D-Maryland) New York City, 1983

Ad Astra discotheque during Mardi Gras, Guatemala City.

Ad Astra, the discotheque that looked like a UFO from outside, was one of the last nightspots in Guatemala City to stay open into the Lucas García years, although it too eventually closed. One drink at the Ad Astra cost five dollars in 1981: over one-and-a-half times the minimum daily rural wage.

Some people did not go out at all. One woman, the daughter of a wealthy cotton grower, did not go onto the street at night; instead she always ate at the same French restaurant, accessible through a common patio adjacent to her home.

52. "Memorandum to the Government of Guatemala Following an AI Mission to the Country in April 1985" (London: Amnesty International Publications, January 1986), pp. 8–9.

53. *Country Reports . . . for 1985*, p. 543.

54. "Memorandum . . . ," January 1986, p. 3.

55. *Country Reports . . . for 1985*, p. 554.

56. "Memorandum . . . ," January 1986, p. 15.

57. Letter to Senator Tom Harkin (D-Iowa) from Mark Johnson, Acting Assistant Secretary, Legislative and Intergovernmental Affairs, U.S. Department of State, August 20, 1986.

Amnesty International: "[AI] has been gravely concerned for many years that the academic sector in Guatemala has under successive administrations been the object of human rights violations carried out by the official military and security forces. . . . The Guatemalan press itself reported seventy other members of the university community who were killed or 'disappeared' between January and October 1984 alone. They included . . . almost the entire leadership of the . . . Association of University Students. . . ."[52]

State Department: "There were an estimated 304 civilian noncombatant deaths in Guatemala in 1985, a significant decline from the 491 killings the previous year. . . . Most of the alleged incidents reported in 1985 involved persons in the western highlands, where clashes between insurgents and the army are still frequent and often fierce."[53]

Amnesty International: "In April 1985 an Amnesty International delegation visited Guatemala. . . . The delegation collected further eye-witness accounts concerning such abuses from many departments in Guatemala. . . . In some cases, it was alleged, people, including entire families, were arbitrarily executed by government forces simply on the basis of their place of residence in areas in contention between government troops and the armed opposition."[54]

State Department: "The Government [of Guatemala] maintained an open door to visits by human rights groups during 1985."[55]

Amnesty International: "When the Amnesty International delegation [to Guatemala] attempted to visit a particular military base . . . the delegation was first denied access to the base. . . . [AI] had repeatedly been assured . . . that its delegations would have complete freedom to visit any government office or military installation it wished. When the delegation requested permission to visit the Patzún encampment [for years, residents of Patzún have alleged that the local army garrison regularly tortures peasants inside its garrison there, sometimes burying the bodies in a cemetery directly behind the garrison], however, it was told that authorization was required from the regional military commander at Chimaltenango. The delegation was subsequently told that authorization could not be obtained by radio as radio transmissions were not secure, and the military officials assigned to accompany the delegation said they could not themselves give the authorization. . . . When the delegation eventually gained access to the base at Patzún, it did find a [prisoner] pit in the ground. . . ."[56]

State Department: "We see definite signs that the human rights situation is improving. Our conclusion is based on intelligence information available to us, an analysis of data from all published sources. . . . We also collect case data from . . . Amnesty International. . . ."[57]

Army occupation of La Perla finca, Ixcán, Quiché.

From 1978 on, the army maintained a constant presence in some fifty highland towns. In Santiago Atitlán, soldiers entered by the truckload in what would become a permanent occupation. According to Amnesty International, over the next two months, dozens of residents were abducted, some in broad daylight, in the town square; at the height of occupation, three hundred people took refuge in the local church, fearing that a large-scale massacre would follow. The army established a permanent camp just outside the center of town, next to a small, privately run hospital. The hospital itself was expropriated by the local army commander, who used its precious hot water supply for his daily shower when he wasn't ordering lightning searches of patients' beds for suspected guerrillas.

The Armed Forces finally had something in common with Amnesty International after the Guatemalan Tourist Institute, INGUAT, complained that not only AI, but the army as well were wreaking havoc on the tourist trade; INGUAT demanded that soldiers lay low at least while tourism was in progress. As a result, for the forty-five minutes each morning that the tourist ferry was at the dock, the army would disappear. Sometimes, however, the two coincided. One morning, a U.S. couple came upon a group of soldiers heading back into town. The husband, irate, turned to his wife and said, "I'll sure be glad when Reagan gets elected and gets rid of all these commies!"

Chapter 2

Lucas García

When I first came to Guatemala in December 1980 urban repression was at its peak. Streets were deserted at night, restaurants folded in quick succession, and couples who did venture out sometimes traveled in two cars if they had children. Gunshots were commonplace sounds in downtown Guatemala City after dark, as Cherokee Chief station wagons, the unofficial "death squad" vehicle, pointed machine guns out smoked-glass windows and fired at will on downtown streets. Journalists' interviews with politicians and opposition leaders—those who were left—were conducted in similar vehicles in the twilight anonymity of fast-food parking lots. ("We use Cherokees too—it throws them off.") By day, Guatemala City was little better. A U.S. journalist on his way to the immigration office witnessed the 8 A.M. shooting of two pedestrians a few yards away, while another foreigner became so distraught by mere news of repression that she called a psychologist recommended by a friend, a professor at the University of San Carlos (USAC). The psychologist's secretary answered the phone and apologized, explaining that the professor was not available; she had recently gone into hiding.

President Fernando Romeo Lucas García, an army general and defense minister under Laugerud García (1974–78), hand-picked to continue the reign of military rule in Guatemala, won the 1978 elections, in what the *Washington Post* called "a fraud . . . so transparent that nobody could expect to get away with it." The U.S. State Department defended the elections on grounds of relativity: "The . . . elections were marred by fraud charges . . . but apparently to a significantly lesser degree than in 1974."[1]

On July 1, 1978 General Lucas García took office after receiving the vote of less than seven percent of the population. President Lucas's vice president was Dr. Francisco Villagrán Kramer, a civilian and an expert in international law, who ran with Lucas on the *Frente Amplio* (Broad Front) ticket, a coalition of three conservative parties. Villagrán, a political liberal, hoped to create a wedge of influence within the army. He thought he would be able to assume many of the presidential duties, but he underestimated Lucas García's actual intentions. At a meeting in Tegucigalpa, Honduras, prior to the elections, MLN intellectual Jorge Torres Ocampo, a close friend of Villagrán, told him, "You're mistaken if you think that you can play that role," and

1. U.S. Department of State, *Country Reports on Human Rights Practices for 1979* (Washington, D.C., February 4, 1980), p. 331.

71

2. Philip Berryman, *Christians in Guatemala's Struggle* (London: Catholic Institute for International Relations, 1984), p. 58.

3. Central American Historical Institute, *On the Road to Democracy: A Chronology of Human Rights and U.S.-Guatemala Relations* (Washington, D.C.: Georgetown University, September, 1985), p. 10.

4. *Country Reports . . .* (February 2, 1981), p. 441.

5. Richard F. Nyrop, *Guatemala: A Country Study*, Area Handbook Series (Washington, D.C.: The American University, 1983), p. 165.

6. NISGUA, "The Road to the 1985 Guatemalan Elections," (Washington D.C., 1985).

7. "Guatemala: A Government Program of Political Murder" (London: Amnesty International Publications, 1981), p. 5.

8. Stephen Schlesinger, "Bad News in Guatemala," *The Village Voice*, May 13–19, 1981, p. 34.

recommended that he not participate. Villagrán ran anyway, believing that he would be the intellectual operation behind a paper-tiger president. In 1979 Vice President Villagrán told a visiting reporter that he had spoken with President Lucas García twice so far that year.[2] On September 1, 1980 Villagrán resigned and fled to Washington, D.C., after saying that "death or exile is the fate of those who fight for justice in Guatemala," and that in Guatemala "there are no political prisoners, only political corpses."[3] The 1980 State Department *Country Report* did not record the vice president's resignation, nor his flight, although it did state that violence had "damaged free expression . . ."[4]

In Guatemala City 1979 and 1980 marked the beginning of massive, selective repression—not a contradiction in terms but the definition of government license to carry out urban "disappearances" and killings by the hundreds, then by the thousands.

In 1979 Guatemala's two brightest presidential hopefuls, who were expected to share the 1982 ticket, were gunned down within two months of each other. Alberto Fuentes Mohr, leader of the Social Democrat Party (PSD), was killed on January 25, 1979 on the day his party submitted its request for official recognition; on March 22, 1979, Manuel Colom Argueta, leader of the United Front of the Revolution (FUR), was killed by three cars of armed plainclothesmen just days after having registered the FUR. In an interview one week before his assassination, Colom said that "in exchange [for the party's legal recognition] they may want my head."[5] Colom's funeral was attended by over 200,000 mourners. By 1981, 36 PSD and FUR leaders had been assassinated.[6]

One year after President Lucas García took office, Amnesty International sent a delegation to Guatemala: in one three-day period during their August 1979 visit, AI delegates counted 107 bodies that were reported in the local press. Eighteen months later, AI documented five thousand "disappearances" and extrajudicial killings since Lucas took office.[7]

In 1980 an AI employee privately remarked that the two worst human rights violators in the world were "first, Uganda (under Idi Amin) and then Guatemala"; he then thought twice and said, "No, wait, maybe it's the other way around." Amnesty International estimated that between March and September 1980, 127 teachers, lawyers, and students were murdered by government forces. Fifteen journalists were killed in 1980 and, according to one U.S. journalist, Guatemala had become "one of the most frightening countries in the world to visit," adding that if political violence continued at the same rate, it would become "virtually impossible to get firsthand reporting . . ."[8]

The Guatemalan Tourist Institute (INGUAT) director, Alvaro Arzú Irigoyen, traveled to London and threatened to sue Amnesty International on the grounds that its charges were causing a drop in tourism. Arzú, however, did not need AI denunciations to ruin the tourist industry. AI's own estimates of political human rights violations had been buttressed in 1979

9. "Guatemala: A Government Program of Political Murder," p. 5.
10. *The New York Times*, October 4, 1981.
11. *Country Reports . . . for 1980*, (February 2, 1981), p. 442.
12. Ibid.
13. *Inforpress*, 458, September 3, 1981, pp. 5–6.

from unexpected quarters—the National Police—who announced that between January and June 1979, "1,224 criminals" had been killed by the *Escuadrón de la Muerte* (Death Squad) and that "3,252 subversives" had been murdered by the *Ejército Secreto Anticomunista* (ESA, or Secret Anti-Communist Army) during the first ten months of 1979.[9] According to the Christian Democrat party, 238 of its leaders were assassinated between 1980 and 1981. "In 1980, to be a Christian Democrat was to have your cemetery plot picked out," remarked Congressman Edgar López Straub.

On August 6, 1981 the U.S. State Department, usually eager to promote a positive image of Guatemala, issued a travel advisory recommending that U.S. citizens refrain from traveling to Guatemala except for "essential visits," and even then, to avoid virtually every tourist spot outside Guatemala City. The State Department blamed "leftist terrorist" violence for these reluctant measures. The Guatemalan government, incensed, produced its own response, stating that "the government of Guatemala is taking all necessary precautions to preserve its unblemished record of providing security for American tourists."[10]

At the same time the U.S. Department of State assigned equal responsibility to "armed extremists of the left and right, and official security forces," calling investigations of disappearances "pro forma," that is, nonexistent. When the U.S. Embassy did concede army culpability, the admission was diluted by accusations against "Marxist and military rightist terrorists, and . . . private parties" as well.[11] At times, the State Department simply deferred to the Cowboy and Indian theory, stating that systematic repression was "endemic to Guatemala," or that violence had "plagued Guatemalan history," as if it didn't have a calculated beginning in the twentieth century.

The State Department, in citing "reports" that government security personnel were engaged in torture "and other . . . unjust treatment," was often absurd in its understatement: "The constitution and the criminal procedures code prohibit torture."[12] In Guatemala, one did not have to be literate to interpret the press; on any given day, newspapers were replete with grainy but graphic photographs of bullet-ridden bodies, slashed throats, and gouged eyes. On August 26, 1981 forensic doctors from Suchitepéquez, Huehuetenango, San Marcos, and the Quiché announced a fifty percent increase in the number of corpses during recent months, and asked for an additional doctor in each departmental morgue to accommodate the overflow.[13]

Two of the hardest-hit groups were labor unions and the University of San Carlos (USAC), both of which had been catalysts for massive organizing. In its 1979 *Country Report* the State Department said that "labor unions are free to organize and to bargain collectively and strikes are permitted in the private sector . . ." It cited "beatings" and assassinations of trade union figures, exculpating the Lucas government by saying that "unidentified parties" and "right-wing terrorists" were responsible. In 1980, one thousand unionists were assassinated. In the

Soldier in front of burned house, Nebaj, Quiché.

"It is easy enough to get by truck to Nebaj. . . . Nebaj has *Las Tres Hermanas* [pension]. . . . Alternatively you can get a room in a private house . . . there is also an army camp . . . there are magnificent walks from Nebaj along the river or in the surrounding hills, but North of the town is still not safe. All houses have been burnt between Nebaj, Chajul and Cotzal; no one lives in this area and most traffic is accompanied by military personnel . . . views of the Cuchumatán mountains are spectacular."

—*The 1985 South American Handbook*, Sixty-First Annual Edition, Trade and Travel
    Publications Ltd., November 1984

Prisoner captured by local civil patrol, army barracks, originally the Catholic parish house, Chichicastenango, Quiché.

From 1981 through 1985 the Catholic rectory in Chichicastenango was expropriated by the army and used as their local garrison, as were one dozen other parish houses and convents throughout the Quiché department. In early 1985 the army returned the rectory to the priests who were coming back for the first time in five years. The priests found their telephone lines cut, their electrical lines stripped; this was the obvious damage. The basement contained several rooms that the priests believed were used as torture chambers, while the backyard, which overlooked a ravine, was encircled by six-foot deep pits.

Although parish houses are usually a town's social hub, the people of Chichicastenango were afraid to return to the rectory even after it was restored. "For a few weeks, people wouldn't come inside," one resident priest said. "They would only come up as far as our front gate. We understood what was going on when they started lighting candles and waxing them to stones outside the front door. They were mourning for the people who had been killed inside."

meantime, dozens of foreigners spoke with as many union leaders. Not one union official blamed the guerrillas for the violence.

In 1980, when repression against unions was at its highest in Guatemala City, the State Department made no mention of the abduction and killing of dozens of participants in the May 1, 1980, Workers Day demonstration in Guatemala City. Some estimates say that as many as two hundred participants were abducted and killed. Some bodies were found blocks from the site of the march, including those of three members of one family, two employed by the Duralux battery factory. The next day, their tortured bodies were discovered downtown, covered with the banner they had carried in the march.

The June 21, 1980 kidnapping of twenty-seven union leaders who were planning funeral arrangements for Coca-Cola leader Edgar René Aldana, killed the same day, four blocks from the National Palace, in the presence of uniformed police agents, and the August 24, 1980 abduction of seventeen other unionists in Palín, Escuintla, were described by the U.S. Embassy as "two meetings of left-wing labor activists." The State Department's 1980 *Country Report* described a ban on the film *Norma Rae* by the Guatemalan censorship board, devoting more description to Sally Field's latest box office hit than to the details of the "disappearance" of 44 trade union leaders within seven weeks of each other.

The University of San Carlos (USAC) was the other urban sector singled out by government violence. Scarcely a day would pass without headlines of a professor or student murdered or "disappeared" in Guatemala City or on the grounds of the USAC campus. A medical student who survived described the smoked-glass "death squad" Bronco jeeps that would park outside the medical school to grab students as they left classes. "No one admitted to being an USAC student," she recalled. "We were all scraping the USAC decals off our fenders, and hiding our student I.D.'s inside our shoes." According to former USAC rector, now minister of education, Dr. Eduardo Meyer Maldonado, 300 members of the USAC community were assassinated between 1980 and 1981, while another one thousand "disappeared" or went into exile. During the same period official data indicated that 140 professionals fled the USAC Medical School and the country. One of the most blatant slayings took place on July 14, 1980, when plainclothes security forces opened fire on a busload of young medical and engineering students arriving for classes; when two of the wounded escaped, the gunmen returned and made a second sweep of the USAC entrance, mowing them down as they ran toward the rector's office, leaving eight dead among notebooks and calculators soaked in blood. In June 1981 officials at the Guatemalan Teachers' Pension Fund reported that 70 members had been assassinated since January 1980; in addition, the fund was now paying out more in life insurance claims than it was collecting in payments.[14] It was a time when people changed even their pseudonyms.

Although repression in urban areas was widespread, at least it was palpable and, for what it was worth, reported. In the Guatemalan highlands, on the other hand, where some five million

14. Julia Preston, "Guatemala: The Muffled Scream," *Mother Jones*, November 1981.

Guatemalans live, "selective" killings ballooned into massacres, and sometimes the elimination of entire villages. In late 1985, a conservative Guatemalan congressman recalled a conversation with a friend, an army general, who had told him, "Look, I'm going to give it to you straight. We did kill a lot of people in this area [Quiché]. We would get orders from the Army Chief of Staff to go in and eliminate two or three peasants. We would arrive at the village and if the suspects weren't there, or if the people wouldn't talk, we'd just raze the entire place."[15] Five years later, government officials would confirm these mass killings. In a 1986 interview Interior Minister Juan José Rodil Peralta told a foreign reporter that over 25,000 Guatemalans were killed during the four years of the Lucas regime.[16] An Indian from Xesic II, in southern Quiché, saw five hundred bodies between 1980 and 1982.

The retrieval of bodies was so enormous—sometimes three dozen in one trip—that they were referred to as *leña*, firewood. Sometimes, the overflow had to be transported on the ambulance roof. The "lucky" ones were dropped at local morgues, where, according to the morgue pathologist, the floors were sometimes so full of bodies that there was nowhere to step.

Throughout rural Guatemala, the army had established permanent outposts in virtually every Indian town, occupying convents and parish houses abandoned shortly before by the Catholic clergy, after Bishop Juan Gerardi Conedera had gone into hiding and ordered the Diocese closed in July 1980. Church pews were replaced with army cots, and convent chapels became torture chambers. Four years later, when the army returned the buildings to the Church, clergy found hand prints of blood on the walls and twelve-foot pits in their backyards. During 1980 alone, three priests were killed, another "disappeared," and three Protestant pastors and one evangelical deacon were gunned down. In 1981 five priests and two lay missionaries were "disappeared" or killed, while over 150 nuns and 200 priests, as well as dozens of Protestant pastors, were forced to flee the country. Those who didn't leave were under a constant psychological state of siege. One foreign priest abandoned his rural parish and transferred his files to the shower stall of a fellow priest.

Indiscriminate massacres became commonplace. In April 1980, 36 bodies were found in a mass grave outside Comalapa, Chimaltenango; in August 1980 soldiers rounded up 60 men in Cotzal, Quiché and killed them in front of other villagers; on September 6, 1980 the army dropped four bombs on the convent in Chajul, Quiché, killing 36 peasants. More massacres were reported from 1981 on, reflecting the upscaled counterinsurgency program carried out by the then-President's brother, Army Chief of Staff Gen. Benedicto Lucas García. In early 1981, 17 people were assassinated in Santiago Atitlán; during the first week of February, soldiers killed 168 peasants in the villages of Patzaj and Panimacac, Comalapa; during the first two weeks of March, 171 people were killed and 43 "disappeared" in Chimaltenango, just 35 miles from Guatemala City; in April 1981 Oxfam/America sources estimated that 1500 Indians in

15. Author interview, Quiché, October 1985.
16. Siete Días television program, March 25, 1987.

Hooded guerrilla deserter, outside Chupol army garrison on the Pan American highway, Quiché.

During 1982 and 1983, and throughout the government "amnesty" periods, the local army garrison at Chupol, Chichicastenango posted a hooded army informant to point out guerrilla collaborators. It is not known how many of these individuals fingered by the informant had actually supported the guerrillas, since he had a quota to fill, and failure to do so would result in his own elimination. When asked about the hooded man, Colonel Roberto Mata Gálvez, head of the Quiché military base, replied that Chupol "is not under my jurisdiction." But it was, and always has been: the Quiché department begins at kilometer 100, and Chupol falls on kilometer 110. Chupol is also Chichicastenango's largest canton, and since Chichi is one of Guatemala's three biggest tourist attractions, one wonders what tourists en route to Chichi were told by their guide as they too were inspected by the hooded informant. Tourists, of course, were never at risk of being fingered themselves, only Guatemalans. A resident of Chichicastenango explained:

"You would be taking a bus from the capital to Chichi and everyone would be talking until you got to Tecpán. That was the signal: the bus would fall silent and the driver would become extremely nervous. No one would talk. All the passengers had to get off. With everyone lined up, the hooded man, accompanied by soldiers, would go down the line, looking at all the passengers. If the hooded man pointed someone out, the soldiers would grab him. If he went down the line without pointing anyone out, the passengers felt an indescribable relief, because they had just spent the past few minutes in hell."

Former U.S. military attaché, Colonel George Maynes, observing civil patrol rally in Nebaj, Quiché.

Colonel Maynes attended one of the first massive civil patrol rallies, held in April 1982 at which ten thousand patrollers were present. Maynes stood on the church steps, eating chiles out of a paper bag, and observing the rally while his assistant, a tall American in camouflage moved about the plaza snapping pictures with an Instamatic camera.

The rally itself was a succession of recitations ranging from the emotional to pro-government rhetoric. Miss Civil Patrol, a teenager from one of Nebaj's more affluent families, promised to do everything in her power to help the patrollers. A young Ixil woman said that her brother, a drug addict was now an EGP guerrilla commander, and that all guerrilla commanders were drug addicts as well. A young man said that he had been coerced into joining the guerrillas. An Ixil civil patroller presented the Army with the bloodied clothing and gun of a suspected guerrilla killed by the local patrol. The town mayor presented Nebaj's commander with a traditional red Ixil jacket. It was three sizes too small, but he put it on anyway, and walked away from the ceremony with his arm draped around Colonel Maynes. Several months later, the commander was transferred. According to one government official, he had raped too many women in the area.

17. Shelton H. Davis and Julie Hodson, *Witness to Political Violence in Guatemala: The Suppression of a Rural Development Movement* (Boston: Oxfam America, 1982), pp. 49–50.

18. *Inforpress*, 458, September 3, 1981, p. 6.

19. Michael McClintock, *The American Connection: Volume Two* (London: Zed Books, 1985), p. 226.

20. *The Washington Post*, May 14, 1981, p. A16.

21. "Guatemala: A Government Program of Political Murder," p. 7.

22. *Country Reports . . . for 1981* (February 1982), p. 446.

23. *Guatemala Revised: How the Reagan Administration Finds "Improvements" in Human Rights in Guatemala* (Washington, D.C.: Americas Watch, September 1985), p. 5, citing statement by Stephen W. Bosworth, principal deputy assistant secretary of state for Inter-American Affairs, at hearing before House Foreign Affairs Subcommittee on Western Hemisphere Affairs, July 30, 1981.

Chimaltenango had been murdered by "death squads" and regular army troops in the past two months.[17] In July 1981, 26 bodies were found in Panajxit, Quiché, 15 with their throats slashed. That same month, a local weekly reported the discovery of 100 bodies in a five-day period.[18]

And the lists went on. Church sources put the death toll of victims from government operations at eleven thousand in 1981 alone.[19] By the end of 1981 the news of thirty or forty corpses buried in mass graves was taken for granted by a Guatemalan citizenry now numb to even the most sensational headlines.

In May 1981 Gen. Vernon Walters, special emissary to Guatemala, rationalized violence under Lucas, saying that "there will be human rights problems in the year 3000 with the governments of Mars and the moon. There are some problems that are never resolved."[20] The 1980 *Country Report* stated that "it is frequently impossible to differentiate politically-inspired from privately-inspired violence." Amnesty International, however, had no trouble identifying the origins of violence in Guatemala. In its February 1981 report, "Guatemala: A Government Program of Political Murder," AI charged that government security forces were responsible for most of the violence, and their day-to-day operation was not directed from a nebulous safehouse but an annex of the National Palace:

"This presidential agency is situated in the Presidential Guard annex to the National Palace, near the offices of the President and his principal ministers, and next to the Presidential Residence. . . . Known until recently as the *Centro Regional de Telecomunicaciones* (Regional Telecommunications Center), the agency is situated under two rooftop telecommunications masts on the block-long building."[21]

In its 1981 Country Report the State Department stated, "The [Guatemala] government views Amnesty International's reports as biased and inaccurate,"[22] and praised Lucas security forces, distinguishing their "positive developments [in] taking care to protect innocent bystanders."[23]

Repression, in fact, made guerrilla organizing easy under Lucas; little coaxing was needed to win over a population whose lives and communities were being destroyed daily by uniformed government troops. By late 1981 the Guatemalan insurgency reached its zenith in military strength and civilian support, with an estimated force of six thousand armed combatants and, according to Guatemalan army figures, some 250,000 unarmed collaborators. On January 25, 1982 the four guerrilla groups announced their coalition in the "Guatemalan National Revolutionary Unity," the URNG (*Unidad Revolucionaria Nacional Guatemalteca*).

Throughout the Lucas García government, Guatemala did not officially receive U.S. military aid, and State Department officials claimed, after the fact, that the United States had "carefully refrained" from backing the "murderous" Lucas García regime. This was not the case. Covert aid continued. In late 1981 ten U.S. M-41 tanks, worth 36 million dollars, were sent to

24. Allan Nairn, "The Guatemala Connection," *The Progressive*, May 1986, p. 22.
25. *Inforpress*, 482, February 24, 1982, p. 8.
26. "The Guatemala Connection," p. 22.
27. North American Congress on Latin America, "Guatemala: The War is Not Over," Vol. XVII, No. 2, March/April 1983, p. 11.

Guatemala via Belgium; in early 1982, twenty Guatemalan air-force pilots received training at the Fort Worth, Texas, headquarters of Bell-helicopter manufacturers, after the arrival in Guatemala of 23 Jet-Ranger Bell helicopters.[24]

Presidential elections were scheduled for March 1982. By then, after three fraudulent elections in twelve years, "won" by army defense ministers, Guatemalans had little expectation that the 1982 elections would be honest. Some four hundred foreign journalists covered the 1982 presidential elections, which everyone except the U.S. Embassy had preordained as fraudulent. Weeks before, there were rumors that the official party of Lucas's hand-picked successor, Gen. Angel Aníbal Guevara Rodríguez, had a warehouse filled with false ballots. Guevara's party, the FDP, or Popular Democratic Front, (a coalition of the PR, PID, and FUN parties) called itself, "A New Era,"[25] and promised to eradicate violence and uphold justice. Three weeks after the registration deadline, 235,000 phantom votes had been added to voter lists. A report issued from Guevara headquarters detailed boxes of fake voter-registration slips and tally sheets sent by the army to rural polling places.[26] Several months before the March 7 elections Guevara's supporters had approached a local weekly asking them to run a voter poll. When the weekly refused, the Guevara people explained that they didn't have to *conduct* the poll, they just had to publish Guevara party figures in exchange for five hundred dollars to announce that Guevara was ahead. When the weekly still refused the poll was published in a rival newspaper.

Election day procedures were no less crude. A priest from Chimaltenango said, "Right there, in the plaza where people were voting, we watched from the church as the army switched one ballot box for another." The 1982 State Department *Country Report* called the campaign "hotly contested" among the four presidential candidates, noting a "significant increase" in voter turnout over years before. While the U.S. Embassy refused to concede fraud, Guatemalans displayed no such reticence. Weeks before elections, a joke cropped up in Guatemala City: A little girl was crying, and her aunt asked her why. "Because Daddy didn't come to see me," she replied. 'But he died two years ago." "Yes," the little girl said, "but they told me he voted yesterday."

Predictably, General Guevara "won" the elections, although informal polls ranked him in third place.[27]

Another joke from the Lucas era serves as testimony to the collective feeling of a nation that had lived through its own holocaust. President Lucas decides to make a speech. He steps out onto the balcony of the National Palace to address the crowd below, approaches the podium, clears his throat, and begins, "Dear survivors . . ." By 1987, the adage was, "Well, at least it's not like Lucas."

Soldiers, Nebaj, Quiché.

"They make you sing the national anthem and the army anthem and they tell you that the army guarantees and protects the Guatemalan economy and the rich, and the reason they protect [the rich] is because they are the ones who provide work for Guatemalans, and someone must protect those who provide work. They tell you that the definition of a guerrilla is someone who steals. They never tell you what 'guerrilla' or 'communist' really mean. They tell you that Cuba and Nicaragua have 'communism' but you don't know who your enemy really is."

—Former soldier, Guatemala City

**Army float, Independence
Day, Nebaj, Quiché.**

Nowhere was the Guatemalan army more fierce in its massacres than in the Ixil triangle in
northern Quiché. By September 1982, however, the local garrison, in a surreal attempt at
community outreach, created its own Independence Day float: a huge army helmet atop a
pickup truck, painted and decorated. There was one other incongruity: although Nebaj is
over ninety percent Ixil Indian, the children riding atop the float were chosen from its small
ladino population, parading through the town's muddy streets in candy-box gowns.

83

The Ixil Triangle

The "Ixil triangle" consists of three towns in northern Quiché: Nebaj, Cotzal, and Chajul. Over ninety percent of the inhabitants are Ixil Indians who have retained their dress, language, and customs to a greater extent than most other Indians in Guatemala, primarily due to their relative isolation. The Ixil triangle was one of the first areas targeted by the Guatemalan army for selective repression, then large-scale massacres, and finally, as the pilot for civil patrols and model villages. Although permanent army occupation of the Ixil triangle did not begin until 1978–79, selective repression began in 1975 when landowner Luis Arenas was killed by guerrillas and, in reprisal, the army abducted 37 local cooperative leaders. By the late 1970s anything could be interpreted as subversive: fleeing if the army entered an area, carrying more than two tortillas to work, failing to turn out your light after nightfall, giving a hesitant answer during army interrogation—even though half the Ixil population speaks no Spanish.

An individual who lived in the Ixil triangle described early repression:

"One time I saw three dead peasants dropped off right in the square. The army had killed them. They were out in their cornfield working with their hoes when they heard a helicopter nearby, shooting. So they dropped their hoes and took off running. The army saw them and killed them. Everybody knew that these three peasants had been working out there in their *milpa*. The army put green pants on them so they would look like guerrillas."

Testimony was given by a Guatemalan anthropologist who lived in the Ixil triangle from 1975 until 1979:

"In 1977, the army still wasn't in [my village], but they would come down with the commander; it was a kind of general control at night. They would bring along a *soplón* [government informer], who would tell them who was with the guerrillas, and at night they would dress up in civilian clothes with a straw hat and their machine guns hidden inside their ponchos, and they would go into people's homes at midnight and take the man of the house, and steal what people had, and hit the wife and children. One night, in a house nearby, we heard a woman screaming; the next day we found out there had been a funeral.

"Before, if you had been angry at someone, the first thing you would do would be to go to a *pajorín* (witch doctor) and ask him to put a spell on your enemy so he would die. The *pajorín* would buy special candles to ask that so-and-so die, and he would repeat [the ritual] every three days. If there were no results, you would wait; the *pajorín* said that sometimes you had to wait five years, and then, if the person did get sick, he would say, 'Look, my witchcraft is having results.' But when people started complaining to the army, they didn't have to wait. . . . If someone had his cow stolen, he would go to the army and say, 'Look this guy was giving food to the guerrillas.' And the army wouldn't bother to investigate. Kill first and ask questions later was their motto.

"In 1978 there had been a very bad bean crop; by 1979 both beans and corn were very scarce. People blamed the bad crop in part on the spirits of nature, since they had not been able to go to the mountains to carry out their rituals and to offer the harvest to the spirits. They believe that if they are going to plant, they must be respectful and ask permission, and offer a part of their crop as a gift. There are many sacred hills in the area where they couldn't go anymore because the army didn't accept the excuse that one was going to burn candles on the mountainside—it was that simple.

"By 1979, if a stranger came in, the people were totally close-mouthed because they knew that it could be a guerrilla, who, if they helped him, would get them killed. I remember one time when I went to look for a friend at about seven at night, and as I approached, all he saw was a shadow, since it was dark and he didn't recognize me. The first thing he did was to put his hand out as if he had a pistol. Many people began to do that: people didn't have the first idea about how to use a gun, but they thought it might help if they looked truly aggressive. People weren't intrinsically that way, they did it to survive. After awhile, they got a reputation for being closed and aggressive."

The Soldier

A young Indian from Chimaltenango described army induction:

"As an Indian, you feel inferior. A group of us—about fifteen boys, sixteen, seventeen years old—decided to enroll in the army. We went to the town hall and they had the military commissioner write down our names. That same day they took us to the main military barracks. We stayed there overnight.

"The next day, around 8 A.M., two officers from the *Cuartel General* [the Justo Rufino General Barracks in Guatemala City] came, carrying a radio; they put on marimba music and called us all over, saying 'Okay, *reclutas* [recruits], you're not at home anymore, so look for a partner.' They made us dance together; if someone refused, they would kick him. Next, they began to tell us that we had to answer whatever they asked. They called the first one: 'You, get up.' They grabbed his elbow and rammed it into his stomach, so he couldn't breathe; they asked, 'What's your name?' but he couldn't even talk. They kept saying. 'What's your name?' and they'd ask the guy next to him, 'What did he say?' and they'd do the same thing to him, beating him over and over.

"We went to the *Cuartel General*: it's like going to hell, because you're always hungry; they don't give you much food and if you go out to the store, any soldier can grab you and hit you. And when you go to the mess hall, the soldiers spit or urinate in your food, or they throw

Eleven-year-old mascot, military barracks, Acul, Quiché. His parents were killed by the army.

In 1985 the Juvenile Division of the Guatemalan Supreme Court issued revised numbers of earlier counts of highland orphans who were fatherless, motherless, or both: an estimated 100,000–200,000 in all. While the figures seemed staggering for a country with 8.5 million people, they were supported by statistics from individual communities, where up to forty percent of the entire population consisted of widows and children. Based on these figures, it was estimated that over 45,000 *parents* had been killed since 1978.

**Religious statues,
Guatemala City.**

"You must watch their eyes. No one will talk. You must try and see what they may be trying to tell you with their eyes. . . . If you try to go [to the countryside] . . . the thing that will most move you is the silence. They will not talk to you because to talk would mean risking their very lives, and the people are already terrorized and prefer not to talk. What you'll really notice is that people will do one of two things. Either they will say that the army is very good, or they will not say anything. They are never going to tell you that it's the army that attacks them."

—Priest and nun to Amnesty International delegation, May 1985

in a handful of chile and you have to eat it. If you vomit, you have to vomit into your plate, and eat it. For three months the treatment was like that. They tell you that if you cry, you're a dead man.

"What makes recruits scream the most is when they tie up your feet behind you with a stick and you have to kneel. They ask you questions like whether you're able to withstand interrogation if you fall into the guerrillas' hands, and whether you would give away the name of your superior. A lot of soldiers cry because the punishment is very harsh, especially those sticks. They have snakes too; they are mascots they keep in the water. They take them out and put them around your neck and they say, 'What's your superior's name?' You feel the snake tightening itself around you and if you don't say your officer's name, you at least shout out for your parents. Sometimes they put a hood on you: all the recruits get the hood along with the stick. Most people shout out for their mother or father, and if you still haven't said anything, then they put you in a kind of stockade and they hit your back and keep asking you the same questions.

"You leave the *Cuartel* feeling very macho. You begin to insult people, and you are taught never to take any shit from civilians. They give you talks: the talks are about soldiers defending the land, and they mention patriotic symbols, like the ceiba tree, and the *quetzal* [the national bird and the national currency] and the *monja blanca* [the national flower] and the flag, and the 'coat of arms.' I had to swear to the flag and we all filed under it, but I came out feeling the same. I didn't feel any different afterwards. But they told me that 'now that you have saluted the flag, you can't waver.'

"In your village, the *cuques* [new recruits] who are stronger and who know how to fight, well, the girls admire them more. We all had that idea that once we were in the army, we'd have more girls than we'd know what to do with. After two months, they gave me time off—by then I was in the *Guardia de Honor* [Honor Guard] barracks in zone ten, in Guatemala City. I was given permission by the officers to go out. At the door, one of them said, 'Okay, if you all want to go, that's okay, we want you to have a good time.' And the first thing they said was that everyone should take a lemon. They said, 'A soldier should know what it's like to have a woman and you're not going to get a *traida* [girlfriend] just by talking.' They said that 'the way to do these things is to go to one of the bars.' And they tell you, 'That's where you have to find a woman's underwear.' They're whorehouses, and they tell you that you should use a lemon after you have sex with a woman, so you don't get venereal diseases. The officers who have gone to the *Politécnica* [Military Academy] are the worst: they're very aggressive and they tell you, 'Okay, bring me women's underwear and if you don't I'm going to punish you when you come back.' I was sixteen at the time."

Funeral for Spanish priest Father Juan Alonso Fernández, killed on his way to say Mass, Chichicastenango, Quiché.

"Persecution in the 1980s was part of the price the Church had to pay, the punishment. Nineteen religious—priests, seminarians, a brother and a nun—were killed. The lower church leaders, the catechists and Delegates of the Word, were 'disappeared,' thousands of them between 1978 and 1980."

—Foreign priest living in Guatemala, December 1985

The Raincoats

In its early stages of organization in northern Quiché, the Guerrilla Army of the Poor (EGP) was able to mobilize fairly openly. One U.S. citizen who lived in Nebaj, Quiché during the late 1970s said that the EGP, in uniform, would march by his house in the center of town. "That was very brazen," he said, "because the military had its garrison just two blocks away." He recalled one episode:

"One day, this dear friend came up and said, 'I got these raincoats at army surplus in the States, and I thought they'd be a hot item here.' This was a real harmless guy, just looking for a scam, a way to stay in Guatemala . . . So he brought three or four dozen olive green raincoats to Nebaj.

"I said, 'Get rid of those, you'd better get rid of them right away.' It was very incriminating, having those four dozen army raincoats around. But he was only in Nebaj for a week, and when he left, he still hadn't buried them. I mentioned this to a friend, one of the leaders in the community, laughing about it all the while. 'Oh really?' he says, 'You buried them?' 'Can we dig them up?' 'Why, yes,' I said. 'If you want, come over and dig them up, but when nobody is around.' And the last I saw of the raincoats, they were headed out into the hills, going to the guerrillas."

Pancakes

When tourists were still visiting Nebaj, a foreigner opened a pancake restaurant there that was as popular with the Ixils as it was with tourists. When the army became a permanent presence, however, business fell off. One former resident of Nebaj described the restaurant:

"The pancake restaurant was the social center of town. They made thousands of pancakes there, and they sold like crazy. By that time, there were no tourists to speak of in Nebaj, so the customers were lower-class ladinos and Indians.

"The restaurant was a family place; it was a social center. The kids would come in and hang out, and whole families would come too.

"Business started falling off when the army came to Nebaj. They started hanging out at the pancake restaurant, and nobody showed up because they were afraid they'd be there when the army was around. So hours would go by with nobody there, and all of a sudden, the army would come, about once or twice a week. The army loved the pancake restaurant. They would hang out for hours and the lieutenants would practice their English with the gringos and you

Religious statue dressed as soldier, church altar, Chajul, Quiché.

"The soldiers on the altar have been there since the late 1970s. I think they used to be Roman Centurions next to Christ at the moment of his crucifixion. The people, who believe in a sun god of nature who roams freely in the mountains, associate the government with repression of the sun god. The uniform he used to wear was from President Ubico's time. By 1979 or 1980, I didn't see that uniform on the statue anymore, but the *kaibil* (elite army counterinsurgency troops, similar to U.S. Green Berets) uniform [instead]. The soldiers who 'take care of' the god to prevent his escape are interpreted by the people as the oppressor government."

—Guatemalan anthropologist, 1984

Spray-painting by the Organization of the People in Arms (ORPA): "Fight Repression," Quezaltenango.

No one suffers more than Guatemala's children. In one school in Totonicapán, Quezaltenango, 55 out of 250 children had lost both their parents. All had witnessed their deaths. When a journalist visiting a Chichicastenango orphanage extended his microphone toward a group of children, expecting that they would sing, they recited details of their parents' killing by the army instead.

Even in Guatemala City, there is no immunity. A young boy from Guatemala's middle class answered the door one day, to find a uniformed policeman there. When the policeman asked for his father, a dentist, the boy, five years old, told him that his father "doesn't treat killers." Shortly afterward, his sister asked an army colonel on President Cerezo's staff "why the army kills people."

The director of an orphanage recalled the day she had loaded her car with children for a ride through the suburbs. They were stopped at an army checkpoint in the downtown; when a soldier approached the car, asking for registration papers, the children inside began screaming, "Don't kill us!"

Humanities Department student cafeteria at the University of San Carlos (USAC), Guatemala City.

Each USAC department's cafeteria has its own mural. This one says, "We Swear That Freedom Will Push Its Naked Flower Through the Violated Sand. We Promise To Continue In Your Path Until the People Triumph." Unlike most U.S. campuses, the USAC is a catalyst for Guatemalan political life; it is the one place in Guatemala City where open political opposition is not only evident but unavoidable. Classrooms have been used as meeting places for peasant groups, human rights delegations, and committees of relatives of the "disappeared." Its professors and students were always at the center of rallies, demonstrations, and mass organizing. Some of its students were among those killed in the January 1980 Spanish Embassy massacre. The USAC community paid a price for such commitment— together with labor unions, the USAC student body and faculty was the most heavily targeted urban sector for government killings and "disappearances." Some 200 students and 300 professors were "disappeared" or killed between 1978 and 1985. There were dozens of victims each year, sometimes dozens each month. Logically, survivors are wary: in 1985, an economics professor asked me never to publish his photo. He had been kidnapped three years before, survived and now feared that the next time he would not be so fortunate.

just had to be courteous to them and be buddy-buddy and joke around. The owner got nervous, though; we all thought, 'This place is going to blow up, we've got to get out of Nebaj.' One day he was coming out of his kitchen, carrying pancakes, four plates of them, two on each arm, when a soldier's machine gun fell off the table, onto the floor. It was on 'off,' but it made this clack and the owner was so nervous that he just dove under the table. That was the turning point."

The Identification Card

By 1980 most of rural Guatemala was under direct army control. Soldiers were present everywhere: in the market, in the *cantinas*, in church bell towers. In many areas Guatemalans were required to procure passes before leaving their towns, to be signed by the military or the military commissioner, stating the duration of time to be spent away, one's destination, and the purpose of travel. As one Guatemalan said, "Whenever you wanted to bring in firewood, get water, or leave your village, you had to explain where you were going and why, and everything depended on whether the soldiers believed you or not. It was like a concentration camp." The State Department, however, said that there were "generally no restrictions on . . . emigration."[28]

28. *Country Reports . . . for 1980* (February 2, 1981), p. 447.

A former resident of northern Quiché gave the following account of army distribution of identification cards:

"The army decided that as a way of controlling people, to see who was a guerrilla (the assumption being that anyone who could not produce an I.D. card had been in the mountains with the guerrillas when the army was handing them out), they would distribute identification cards. The army gave you an I.D. card after investigating and confirming your innocence. The I.D. card stated the location of each person's *milpa*—that way, since the *milpas* were outside of town, they could make sure people were only going as far as their plots of land. People had to carry their I.D.'s all the time. If the men were out planting or gathering firewood and they didn't have them, the army could take them away. Sometimes, they would torture them and then let them go when, I suppose, they realized the men were innocent.

"That I.D. card caused a lot of problems for people. Since people were afraid, everyone tried to get his picture taken as quickly as possible. Some went as far as Santa Cruz del Quiché because there were more photo studios there, but it was expensive.

"The problem was that until 1975, there was almost no government control. It had just left people alone to make their own rules, and as a result, very few people had any kind of official identification. The traditional Indians, especially those from the furthest villages, didn't even know what a photograph was. They were the ones who got killed."

**Government "Comando Seis"
SWAT–style teams repelling
protest march following 1982
presidential elections,
Guatemala City.**

To appreciate the breadth of urban repression, the sidewalk is as far as one need look; city
curbs and traffic islands are imprinted with plaques to Guatemala's dead and crosses to its
martyred leaders. In zone one there is a bronze square inscribed with the names of five
students gunned down in 1956 by army and police forces. Three blocks away, there is
another plaque to the student leader Oliverio Castañeda de León, shot down in 1978, a block
from the Palace, in front of hundreds of pedestrians and dozens of uniformed police who
made no attempt to intervene. Two blocks away there is another plaque to the social
democrat politician, Adolfo "Fito" Mijangos López, shot to death in his wheelchair. There is
another plaque outside the former USAC law school to three law students gunned down
during Holy Week 1962, and crosses to politicians, Manuel Colom Argueta and Alberto
Fuentes Mohr, near the Industrial Park and across from the old Politécnica Military Academy.

For many Guatemalans, death brings only anonymity; there is no plaque, no record of the
event, except for family Mass cards or a discreet funeral announcement. In 1986, architecture
student Carlos Manuel Díaz Maza, was killed by two armed men who escaped on foot, the
National Palace, four from police headquarters. The ambulance arrived before the
authorities; there was no police record of his death, nor any press account, even though
three daily newspapers have their offices nearby. The only mention of the death was in a
funeral advertisement placed by the family.

**Opposition spray-painting,
Guatemala City.**

The high-school student is writing "1981: Year of Liberation for the People of El Salvador."
Throughout the Lucas García years, members of the Guatemalan opposition—at least those
in the city—pinned El Salvador as the primary focus of attention, believing that Guatemala
would follow next.

   Anyone found spray-painting could be shot on sight. One was: a fifteen-year-old student,
gunned down in 1980 by an army patrol as he wrote "Freedom . . ." on a wall near the
National Palace.

Visa lines at the U.S. Embassy, Guatemala City.

Most of those who apply for visas are denied them; those who apply for political asylum are even less fortunate. In 1986, seven of 589 asylum petitions were granted. Despite these odds, Guatemalans line up for hours in front of the Embassy, sometimes as early as 4 A.M. Those who have money pay someone to stand in line.

The men with the typewriters fill out visa application forms for one *quetzal*; at night they use flashlights or the low-beams from a car.

The Ceiba and the Cornfield

In the town of Zacualpa, southern Quiché, the army began committing large-scale massacres in 1981, and by 1983 there were only two families left in what had been a town of eighteen thousand inhabitants. The rest had fled to neighboring towns and Guatemala City. According to a resident there, the convent was used as a torture center; when people finally began returning in 1984, they were so afraid of going inside the church that only an eighty-year-old woman showed up for Mass.

A Guatemalan who had lived in the Quiché until 1980 described Zacualpa during that time:

"The Army established a base there. . . . At first they killed people inside the convent, where no one could see. Eventually, however, they began to line them up in front of the ceiba tree in the main square, and simply shot people in plain view of anyone who happened to be there. Once, the army started shooting from the air: there were so many bullets flying that my aunt said it looked like beans raining down.

"In 1984, people began to plant corn again for the first time. One man's field had been used by the army as a body-dumping ground and everyone in Zacualpa knew this. But the people had to plant so they could eat. When the workers planted the corn, they found bones and skeletons in the cornfield. 'What misfortune,' they said, 'that our land is where the dead of the town lie.' The crop, however, was very good that year. They didn't even need fertilizer. The people of Zacualpa knew why, though, and they refused to eat the corn from that piece of land. They told the owner, 'Your land has been fertilized with the dead of Zacualpa.' "

A religious worker described the Quiché department:

"I'll tell you, in these villages around Quiché, people couldn't even sleep at home anymore. As soon as dusk started falling, all of them would go and sleep in the mountains, for fear that the army would come and take them from their homes. In the fields, they felt protected by one another.

"One night, one of the little girls got up to go to the bathroom while everyone else was still sleeping; just from the noise of her feet rustling the leaves, everyone woke up. They sat on the rocks the rest of the night; they couldn't sleep from the anguish they felt. They just sat there until the sun came up. They spent months and months that way.

"There was another family with two children. One of the daughters was eleven years old at the time. At night, they would sleep in their cornfield. One day, they sent their daughter back to the house in the morning to see what she could get to eat, even if it was just a piece of bread. When she had almost reached her house, she was confronted with the sight of their next-door neighbor, lying dead, with his head split open. She went a long time without sleeping; she would just scream."

A man from Rabinal, Baja Verapaz, described an incident in 1980 near his town:

"People flee when the army comes. If they don't, the army kills them. Once, they killed forty-five men in a place near here, La Clínica. It was Christmas time; the army invited everyone from La Clínica to come and receive gifts. They told the people to find a marimba band and to decorate La Clínica, because 'we are going to show up.' The families came, and the army did give out gifts. But afterwards, after the presents had been handed out, the soldiers told the women and children to go home, and they ordered the men to stay. The army took out a list and began calling the men over, one by one. The next day, we went to La Clínica and all we saw were bloodstains, and six ears thrown on the ground."

Sometimes soldiers talk as well. A young Indian served in the army twice, under the governments of Laugerud García (1974–78) and Lucas García (1978–82):

"I was stationed in El Tumbador, San Marcos. In June, the army captured five peasants; they were taken from their homes. Three died quickly; two of them withstood the beatings. I saw it when they put the hoods on them.

"The officers grabbed them and said, 'We know that besides you two, there are others who are communists and guerrillas and if you don't talk, you will die.' Since they had a hood on, I don't even know if they heard what was being said; all you heard was mumbling from inside the hoods. They put them in holes or wells that were about six or nine feet deep.

"I saw all this because it was my turn to watch over the officers' tent. But since it was June 30, Army Day, and the rest of the company had gone to Guatemala City to parade, there was just one officer left with us. He had orders to kill the others, but he had a girlfriend in El Tumbador, so he told a sergeant and a recruit to round up the four most macho [soldiers] and a recruit and kill those two guys near Escuintla.

" 'I'll give you ten *quetzales* for booze,' he said. 'You dump them, not on the highway, but where nobody will see you do it.' They named me and three other soldiers. The four of us and a sergeant and the driver went. We had to drive these prisoners all tied up in a pick-up truck. We put them under a piece of tarpaulin and we sat on top of them. I don't know what part of Escuintla it was, but at about eleven at night, we passed a little village—I don't remember the name. The sergeant said, 'Let's have a drink before we carry this out.' So we had a drink and then we arrived at a spot where we tied them up.

"The driver said, 'I'll take care of one,' and he grabbed the revolver and said, 'Okay, guerrilla, you son-of-a-bitch, now you're going to die because you didn't say where your *compañeros* are.' And he put a bullet in his throat. I saw it happen. He shot him in the throat and it came out the nape of his neck. The guy, he was about thirty-five, just shouted and they kicked him in the stomach and shot him again, in the head, and that was that. They told the other soldier to kill the second guy, but the soldier got frightened, and didn't do it, and the sergeant said, 'Why the hell did you come if you can't do anything?' But the soldier didn't move

Cadets from the Adolfo Hall military academy, Guatemala City.

The thirteen-year-old daughter of law student Hugo de León Palacios, kidnapped on March 12, 1984, explained how her father's abduction had affected her:

"I don't like to look at military men. I feel like they owe me something, something that I have to make them give back to me, because I can't go on like this. Before my father was kidnapped, I didn't think one way or another about the soldiers. Among my classmates, we would gossip about the cadets at the Politécnica, the cadets from the Adolfo Hall. And sometimes we would say, 'This one is cute, this one is ugly . . .' But now . . . a friend of mine is the daughter of an army officer—she told me that her father and her brother are in [the army] to be well off economically. . . . There is one schoolmate who sits in front of me and when she talks about 'the cute guy at the [Adolfo] Hall,' it sounds stupid to me. I don't know why but I feel like they are talking about a person who is my enemy."

Cadets at the Adolfo Hall military academy, Guatemala City.

"Most soldiers aren't aggressive to begin with; you become that way. It's because of the mistreatment you receive in the army. There are always people in my town who haven't been in the army, and we were always comparing our social position; you become so changed that, after awhile, I didn't talk to those people who hadn't been in the army, only those who had, because someone who has served has the same kind of mentality, and you're more *macho*, more of a man. You hang out with people who have been in the army too."

—Former soldier, Guatemala City, 1985

and the sergeant killed the second man. The soldier screamed, because he had never seen anyone be killed."

The Spanish Embassy

The most publicized urban killing under the Lucas García government took place in the Spanish Embassy in Guatemala City on January 31, 1980. That morning, thirty-one Quiché peasants, accompanied by university students, peacefully entered the Spanish Embassy in residential zone nine, less than three miles from the National Palace, in order to draw attention to growing repression in the countryside, which went largely undenounced in the city. Spanish Ambassador Máximo Cajal knew of the repression there; his concern heightened after a trip to the Quiché department, following the killings of several Spanish priests.

The Indians who had entered the Embassy planned to read a list of their grievances at a noon press conference inside. What happened next provoked immediate international outcry. Ignoring the fact that embassies are "foreign soil," the government, according to *Time* magazine, "ordered police to begin an assault." Ambassador Cajal, from an upstairs window, yelled down, "Please don't enter! We have immunity!" When he called the National Palace in a last-ditch protest, no one answered the phone. Police broke down the door; in the ensuing panic, thirty-nine people were burned to death, including Guatemalan ex-Vice President Eduardo Cáceres Lehnhoff. The only survivors were Ambassador Cajal and Quiché peasant Gregorio Yujá Xona, who was taken to a private hospital for treatment of his burns. Although Cajal had insisted that Yujá be given armed police protection, he was abducted from his hospital bed the same night, and his savagely tortured body was dumped on the grounds of the University of San Carlos the following morning.

The U.S. State Department, in its 1980 *Country Report*, dismissed the Embassy massacre, calling some of the occupants "armed members of a radical student organization."[29] *Time* said that security forces were "hacking away at the building to get in and get their hands on the peasants," and called the incident "outright murder."[30] The U.S. Chamber of Commerce in Guatemala produced its own response to the *Time* article in a cable signed by its President Thomas W. Mooney, who said that the article was "inaccurate in fact and misleading in terms of innuendo," calling the peasants "armed terrorist leaders."[31]

Spain broke off diplomatic relations with Guatemala for over five years.

29. *Country Reports . . . for 1980* (February 2, 1981), pp. 141–42.
30. "Outright Murder," *Time* magazine, February 11, 1980.
31. Cable from American Chamber of Commerce, Guatemala, to *Time* magazine, cited in *Monthly Bulletin*, 159, February 15, 1980.

The American Chamber of Commerce

The Guatemala branch of the American Chamber of Commerce ("AmCham") represents dozens of U.S. companies. U.S. investment in Guatemala is higher than in any other Central American nation, including Costa Rica, and is more than double the investment in El Salvador. According to U.S. Embassy figures in 1985, 208 U.S. companies had direct investment or subsidiaries in Guatemala, representing $325,000,000 annual investment there.

The Guatemala branch of AmCham has played an active role in lobbying to influence U.S. congressional policy since 1954, when United Fruit Company engineered Guatemala's military coup. The rhetoric of AmCham leaders is indistinguishable from that of the Guatemalan right-wing, partly because many of those right-wingers are active AmCham members themselves.

On March 19, 1980 AmCham Vice President Ira Lewis, of the Chicago-based Diversey Corporation, wrote to Senator Alan Cranston of California, justifying the acts of government death squads:

"I am a U.S. citizen from Oxnard, California, resident in Central America for the past eighteen years. . . . There seems to be a general misconception in Washington and the rest of the U.S.A. about the situation in Central America. News stories are frequently slanted abroad. Over the past three years our Central American friends feel they have been deserted by the United States. . . . They are fighting and frequently [sic] with methods just as harsh as the terrorists, but we must remember what they are fighting for."[32]

Lewis's justification of government terrorism echoed the sentiments of Mario Sandoval Alarcón, of the self-described "party of organized violence," the National Liberation Movement (MLN). In 1977 he said, "Anything goes when it comes to fighting guerrillas. . . . I might even say that you must be more cruel than they."[33] Lewis concluded his letter saying that his "friends" were fighting for a "stable capitalistic society" and that the Lucas García government merited assistance, "not condemnation." Lewis informed Senator Cranston that other past presidents of AmCham, including Mr. Fred Sherwood, had mailed similar letters to Congressional representatives.

Fred Sherwood, a U.S. resident of Guatemala for over forty years, owns the Prokesa coffee-bag factory in Guatemala. In 1954, he aided CIA forces in carrying out the coup; since then, he has openly espoused his support for government death squads—and offered his definition of Guatemalan Indians as "dumb savages." In September 1980 Sherwood said: "They're [the government death squads] bumping off the commies, our enemies. . . . Hell, I'd give them some cartridges if I could and everyone else would, too. . . . Why should we criticize them? . . . Why the hell should we criticize the death squad or whatever you want to call it? Christ, I'm all for it."[34]

32. American Chamber of Commerce, *Monthly Bulletin*, 160, Guatemala, March 19, 1980.

33. Philippe Labreveux, "Votes Alone Don't Win Elections," *The Guardian*, July 31, 1977.

34. Allan Nairn, "Controversial Reagan Campaign Links with Guatemalan Government and Private Sector leaders," Council on Hemispheric Affairs (Washington, D.C., October 30, 1980), p. 6.

Bodyguard for right-wing political party, the National Liberation Movement (MLN), during campaign kick-off to Esquipulas, Chiquimula.

In 1984 a European diplomat accompanied his friend to a shopping center in downtown Guatemala City. While his friend went inside, the diplomat stayed in the car with the driver, who was also his friend's bodyguard. A few minutes later, the bodyguard turned around and said, "You are a good friend of my boss: if you ever need anybody killed, I'll do it for fifty *quetzales.*"

Political rally for 1982 presidential candidate, General Angel Aníbal Guevara Rodríguez, Guatemala City.

General Guevara was the fourth Defense Minister hand-picked for the presidency since 1963. According to the Guatemalan weekly, *Central America Report*, "The doubts regarding General Guevara's ability to govern Guatemala were best summed up by a reporter's question during the campaign: 'If during the time you were minister of defense, the guerrilla movement was not only not defeated but grew, how can you expect to run the country?' "

The AmCham monthly bulletin provided a steady stream of praise for each successive government, lacking even the U.S. Embassy's sanitized language. In early 1980, during the worst repression, AmCham President Thomas Mooney wrote to U.S. Ambassador Frank Ortiz, complaining that the Embassy was too critical of Lucas García:

"The Government of Guatemala, despite its numerous faults, is better than most governments in the world in terms of the very human rights ground [sic] on which it is so severely attacked, and is infinitely better in these same terms than would be a government formed by those who are determined to overthrow it."[35]

A year later, the AmCham Monthly Bulletin reiterated its support:

"[President Romeo Lucas García] is sagacious and practical . . . and with a very strong determination to afford important and enduring benefits for his people."[36]

In 1981 the Monthly Bulletin began a "Cheerful Facts Sheets" to counteract "rumor-prone visiting writers or legislators [who are] often intent [sic] to make facts fit preconceptions or ideologies," citing the excellent weather, the stable currency, the low incidence of tuberculosis, and the absence of bomb blasts in wealthy residential districts.

35. American Chamber of Commerce, *Monthly Bulletin*, 160, Guatemala, March 19, 1980.
36. American Chamber of Commerce, *Monthly Bulletin*, 173, Guatemala, May 13, 1981.

Guerrillas

There are four guerrilla groups: the Communist Workers Party (PGT), the Guerrilla Army of the Poor (EGP), the Rebel Armed Forces (FAR), and the Organization of the People in Arms (ORPA). An Indian from southern Quiché, described the beginning of rural opposition:

"In 1977 two nuns came to teach us. They really flung themselves into things. At that time there wasn't so much violence. Oppression, yes, because there was a lot of humiliation. The nuns started it—talking about social injustice—but then the Bishop began to talk about it too. And in this way, we became politicized.

"What happened with the nuns was like [getting] soft little blows on your head, like gasoline already spread all over the place, and they just lit a match to it."

In some areas the guerrilla movement was not well known at first, even where it later received the strongest support:

"At first, people didn't even know the difference between the guerrillas and the army. At first, they would call the guerrillas the *militares*, the 'men in the mountains.' They would say, 'The ones who come here are good people, they ask us for something and we give it to them.' In the beginning, there was a certain indifference, and since people were generous, they received the guerrillas in the same way they received foreigners, calling them *gringos*. For them, a gringo was any person who was not from that area and who was not an Indian. For them, the army and the guerrillas were both *militares*. And if one of the *militares*—a guerrilla—would say, 'I'm thirsty, please give me some water,' they would reply, 'Of course, certainly,' because they are very generous.

"At first, people didn't hate the army; they thought that the army was simply picking off guerrilla collaborators. When the soldiers began to rape and steal, and when they began to have free rein over the town, then people began to realize that the army was its enemy, and between those two 'bad' groups, perhaps the others weren't so bad. Then they began to hear that the guerrillas protected people from the army, and from then on, they began to sympathize more with them. That was their interest: that the guerrillas could protect them and even save them from the army. This came way before real solidarity and sympathy for guerrillas."

Originally some people who collaborated with the guerrillas did not have ideology in mind when they began aiding them. An anthropologist who lived in northern Quiché during the late 1970s explained:

"In 1977 we noticed that the people in town were aware that they were in some kind of danger, but they thought nothing would come of it—it was something that happened to so-and-so, it was because he had sold meat to the guerrillas, or because he had talked to them, or that someone else had gone outside when he shouldn't have. They believed that these people had committed some error for having contact with the guerrillas; since they did something risky, they were the ones to whom something would happen. They thought that as long as they stayed away from all that nothing would happen to them, and there wouldn't be any problems. At that time there were so few people collaborating with the guerrillas that you could count them by name. I remember one who was a butcher—he sold them meat—and there were two others who gave them food. Four or five perhaps, and they did it not so much out of ideology but for economic reasons. Even in 1979, when the situation became much worse, the butcher continued helping the guerrillas secretly because they paid him and gave him certain 'advantages.' The butcher knew that in exchange for giving them food, they would give him military protection, which in turn gave him certain power in town. From the time he had started helping the guerrillas, he had been able to buy a bigger house and more cattle."

Brigadier General José Efraín Ríos Montt, flanked by General Horacio Egberto Maldonado Schaad and Colonel Francisco Luis Gordillo Martínez, at first press conference on March 23, 1982, National Palace, Guatemala City.

While the origins of the March 23, 1982 military coup that deposed General Lucas García are disputed, what became clear shortly after the general euphoria dissipated was that far from being a reformist coup, this triumvirate of army officers—all trained in counterinsurgency in U.S. schools—unleashed Guatemala's bloodiest period of rural repression in the twentieth century. While the U.S. State Department claimed that the new government "publicly committed itself to ending the abuses of the Lucas García government," on May 27, 1982, the Guatemalan bishops stated, "Never in our national history have we come to such grave extremes. These murders are . . . genocide." Amnesty International recorded 2,186 killings by security forces during the first three months after the coup; by October, the number had reached 6,000.

Chapter 3

Ríos Montt

1. *Inforpress*, 486, March 25, 1982, p. 1.
2. *Central America Report*, Vol. IX, No. 12, March 26, 1982, p. 90.
3. Decree Law 20–82 established the Department of Technical Investigations (DIT).

General Guevara never took office. On March 7, 1982, Guatemalans went to the polls to vote in elections described by *The New York Times* as "a charade that deserves no further commendation from Washington." On March 23, 1982, less than three weeks after the elections, a military coup was staged by right-wing politicians and 900 dissident officers of the Armed Forces.[1] Throughout the day army helicopters buzzed the National Palace, using major streets as landing strips and posting 105mm. artillery, light tanks, and cannons next to the fountains in the central plaza, aimed at the President's office. By noon the National Police had surrendered; at four P.M., President Lucas García resigned. Brigadier General José Efraín Ríos Montt was installed as the head of an army triumvirate, and a tentative sigh of relief swept through Guatemala City. At the junta's first press conference that afternoon, Ríos Montt, flanked by General Horacio Maldonado Schaad and Colonel Francisco Luis Gordillo Martínez, all in camouflage uniforms, gave a post-coup political sermon, and demonstrated the Protestant evangelical fervor he acquired in 1978, with references to God as "my Lord and King." Ríos Montt's religious beliefs mattered little to Guatemalans that day; his reputation as a Christian Democrat presidential candidate, robbed of the 1974 presidency, gave them fragile cause for hope. Ríos Montt told Guatemalans to "take down your machine gun from your roof, and replace your pistol with a work machete." Ríos Montt declared that there would be no more assassinations—"if someone violates the law, they will be tried, and if convicted of a capital crime, shot. Only the Army will carry guns."[2]

For a short time, urban Guatemalans believed that under Ríos Montt the situation had improved. Kidnapping cars briefly disappeared from downtown streets, padlocked restaurants reopened, and, for the first time in years, tourists and penitents ventured onto the Pan American highway for Holy Week in Antigua. Within weeks of the coup, dozens of government officials—all civilians—were arrested; the feared judicial police corps was renamed, relocated and put under the direction of a former motorcycle policeman;[3] the home of former Interior Minister Donaldo Alvarez Ruíz, who controlled government death squads, was ransacked before television cameras by an angry citizenry; and a "disappearance office" was set up in the

4. *Central America Report*, Vol. IX, No. 16, April 30, 1982, p. 124.

5. Melvyn Levitsky, Deputy Assistant Secretary of State for Human Rights and Humanitarian Affairs, at a hearing before the House Banking Subcommittee, August 5, 1982, and Daniel Southerland, "Administration Defends Plans to Aid Guatemalan Military," *The Christian Science Monitor*, January 10, 1983.

6. Allan Nairn, *With Friends Like These*, edited by Cynthia Brown (New York: Pantheon Books, 1982), p. 198.

7. U.S. Department of State, *Country Reports on Human Rights Practices for 1982* (Washington, D.C., February 1983), p. 517.

8. Ricardo Chavira, "Guatemalan Indians Said Slain," *San Diego Union*, May 5, 1982.

9. Joseph Anfuso and David Scazpanski, *Efraín Ríos Montt: ¿Siervo o Dictador?* (Guatemala: Gospel Outreach, 1984), p. 148

National Police headquarters to investigate petitions of past abductions, receiving hundreds in its first days of operation. On May 22, 1982 the junta decreed a general amnesty law, the first of at least four over the next five years, giving "subversives" thirty days to turn themselves in. (There was no specified time limit for nonsubversives requesting amnesty.) U.S. Ambassador Frederic Chapin presented himself to the Guatemalan business community, assuring his hosts that he was a fighter of communism back to his early diplomatic days in eastern Europe. Ambassador Chapin said, "The killings have stopped. The Guatemalan government has come out of the darkness and into the light."[4] The State Department declared that the Lucas García regime had been one of "horror stories," engaged in "violence against its own people," and Elliott Abrams called the Lucas years "a war against the populace."[5] A senior embassy official confirmed *post facto*, to the Lucas atrocities, saying, "We knew perfectly well that they were raiding villages and taking out all males from fourteen up, tying their hands behind their backs, torturing, and killing them."[6] The State Department, in its 1982 report on human rights, stated that under Ríos Montt "there has been a decrease in the level of killing."[7] U.S. State Department human rights officer, Dale Shaffer, said that "the number of killings are really down. . . . There aren't any massacres in the countryside like we had before."[8]

Rural repression soared immediately after the coup, reaching unprecedented levels. In San Francisco Nentón, Huehuetenango, some 350 villagers were massacred between July 16 and 19; on July 18, 200 villagers from Plan de Sánchez, Rabinal, Baja Verapaz, were killed after the army raped every woman, except one who escaped and lived to tell the story; on September 13, in the village of Agua Fría, Rabinal, army soldiers burned to death over six dozen villagers. Even Ríos Montt sometimes admitted army culpability: after learning of the Nentón massacre, he ordered a full investigation, which concluded that the army had been responsible. No one was punished.[9]

City newspapers ran headlines reminiscent of the Lucas government and graphic photos appeared of the bodies of Indian peasants piled on top of each other in villages an hour from the capital. On May 17 and May 20, 1982 Jorge Carpio Nicolle, conservative publisher of the morning daily, *El Gráfico*, signed his name to two explosive editorials, jolting middle-class Guatemala from its desire to believe that the situation had improved. "How is it possible," Carpio asked, "to behead an eight- or nine-year-old child? How is it possible for a human adult to murder in cold blood a baby of less than a year-and-a-half? . . . [T]his new resurgence of mass murders sends the message that Guatemala is very far from peace . . . [and] does not deserve any aid as long as this keeps happening." *El Gráfico* had reported 584 killings in the first two months after the coup.

Guatemala City's relative tranquility was shattered shortly afterward. On June 9 Ríos Montt dissolved the junta, after reportedly offering to buy off Maldonado Schaad and Gordillo for fifty

10. Amnesty International, *Guatemala: The Human Rights Record*, (London: Amnesty International Publications, 1987), pp. 55–56.

11. Michael McClintock, *The American Connection: Volume Two* (London: Zed Books, 1985), p. 230, originally cited in the *Miami Herald*, June 6, 1982 and the *Eureka Times Standard*, September 9, 1982.

12. Author interview, Guatemala City, June 1985.

13. Richard F. Nyrop, *Guatemala: A Country Study*, Area Handbook Series (Washington, D.C.: The American University, 1983), p. 213.

thousand dollars each (according to Gordillo), and he declared himself president. On June 30, 1982 Ríos Montt imposed a selective state of siege in four departments,[10] followed by a nationwide state of siege on July 1, saying that now the government could "kill legally." He rationalized his statement by claiming that it was "preferable that it be known that twenty people were shot, and not just that twenty bodies have appeared beside the road."[11] Press censorship was imposed. No news on the guerrilla movement could be printed unless it came from government press offices. In addition, "special tribunal" courts were established, empowered to try individuals in clandestine military courts, without lawyers, or even knowledge of the charges brought against them or the laws they had supposedly violated.

By mid-1982 death-squad vehicles had reappeared: a Guatemalan who worked behind the Palace saw the same cars used by Lucas forces resurface under Ríos Montt, months after the coup—with new license plates. The DIT detective corps functioned in the same manner as Lucas' *judiciales*; the mother of twenty-four-year-old Special Tribunal prisoner, Roberto Byron Méndez Luna, alleged in 1983 that her son, who was held in the DIT zone headquarters, was given electric shocks while immersed in a tank of water. The "disappearance" office set up inside the National Police headquarters was dismantled several months later, after failing to resolve a single case. Former National Police Director, Colonel Hernán Orestes Ponce Nitsch, explained its demise, three years later, saying, "We had to phase it out little by little: the information we received would have backfired in our face."[12] Furthermore, the first government amnesty program was an abysmal failure; although government figures cited 1,936 repentant subversives (one week earlier Ríos Montt had cited 240), other reliable estimates counted three hundred at most.[13]

Although Ríos Montt claimed that the special tribunal courts would replace "bodies by the side of the road," "disappearances" began again under his government, barely three months after the coup. While some four hundred individuals were arrested and declared special tribunal prisoners, hundreds of others were simply abducted, never reappearing. In mid-1982 one young woman was abducted from her parents' home four blocks from the National Palace, by armed men. The following day, the only evidence of her "disappearance" was a splintered front door and a living room wall spray-painted by her abductors, who in a token attempt to deflect culpability, wrote the guerrilla acronym, "EGP," which the family later retouched to say, "Emma, Buelva Pronto," a misspelled version of "Emma, Come Back Soon." Emma was fortunate; through her family's influence at Rios Montt's Protestant *Iglesia del Verbo* (Church of the Word), she was released after months of confinement and torture. Most others were not.

Except for occasional press accounts, there was little foreign reporting of this period. The four hundred reporters who had covered Guatemala's 1982 elections were absent for the coup three weeks later. For the most part, post-coup foreign reporting was limited to descriptions of

General Efraín Ríos Montt and Christian Democrat Leader, Vinicio Cerezo Arévalo, at the military junta's first public appearance following the March 23, 1982 coup, Guatemala City. They are flanked by Roberto Carpio Nicolle, now Guatemala's vice president, and the minister for specific affairs, Alfonso Cabrera Hidalgo.

Vinicio Cerezo and General Ríos Montt had known each other since the 1970s, when Cerezo had been a Christian Democrat (DCG) congressman and Ríos Montt had run for president on the DCG ticket, along with Social Democrat leader Alberto Fuentes Mohr. Ríos Montt and the Christian Democrat party received widespread support, more out of general repudiation over President Arana's military repression and his hand-picked successor than out of true fervor for the party or Ríos Montt himself. The day after the elections, radio broadcasts describing Ríos Montt's sweeping victory were abruptly terminated, and only official army information followed. Election results, which were phoned into the national phone company, GUATEL, were altered in passing from one GUATEL office to another in a fraud so obvious that to this day the 1974 elections are referred to as "Guatelgate." As one Guatemalan said, "The United States' Watergate was nothing compared to our 'Guatelgate': you only had your campaign tampered with, we had our presidential elections stolen."

Ríos Montt supporter at first public rally following the March 1982 coup, in front of the National Palace, Guatemala City.

Three days after the military coup which installed Ríos Montt as Guatemala's next leader, the plaza in front of the National Palace was filled with 15,000 enthusiastic supporters of the Ríos Montt army triumvirate, although, that day, jubilant Guatemalans' rejoicing had more to do with the end of the Lucas García regime than it did with Guatemala's immediate future. When a second military coup was staged seventeen months later, there was no cause for celebration: Guatemala had spent almost all of the Ríos Montt government under a stage of siege.

14. Allan Nairn, *With Friends Like These*, edited by Cynthia Brown (New York: Pantheon Books, 1985), p. 204.

15. *Central America Report*, Vol. IX, No. 18, p. 143.

16. Cynthia Brown, *Human Rights in Guatemala: No Neutrals Allowed* (New York: Americas Watch, 1982), p. 109.

17. Allan Nairn and Jean-Marie Simon, "Bureaucracy of Death," *The New Republic*, June 30, 1986, p. 16.

Ríos Montt's interview-sermons and the army's civic action program. For once, the local press was more forthright in covering army atrocities. As headlines screeched the news of massacres in Chichicastenango, San Martín Jilotepeque, and Rabinal, the State Department was still trying hard to convince Congress that Ríos Montt had performed a human rights miracle. Even as news trickled out, the U.S. Embassy continued to insist that human rights violations were down. A senior embassy official dismissed the Embassy's haphazard investigation of reported murders, stating, "We are not a coroner's office. . . . I don't think the numbers matter."[14] Testimonies received from Guatemalans fleeing into Mexico, an exodus that began in August 1981 and increased to tens of thousands under Ríos Montt, provided ample testimony of army atrocities. Less than two months after the coup, the Bishops' office said that some 200,000 Guatemalans had fled to other countries.[15] Yet even when confronted with corroboration of refugees' statements from Mexicans in the border area, Ambassador Chapin retorted that he "wouldn't believe a goddamn thing any Mexican told me."[16] If Ambassador Chapin did not believe Mexicans, one wonders if he placed more credence in the testimonies given by his fellow countrymen. In 1982 Protestant minister Jim Boldenow was seized at gunpoint and taken to an interrogation center, where his captors stripped him and threatened him with torture, showing him a rack, electric cattle prods, and metal-tipped sticks they said were used for breaking bones. Chapin was notified of the kidnapping by a fellow U.S. citizen, and Embassy officials contacted Ríos Montt, who personally ordered Boldenow's release through direct radio contact with his captors.[17]

By July 1982, Amnesty International announced the extrajudicial killing of 2,186 civilians since Ríos Montt had come to power.

While rural massacres were a vital component of Ríos Montt's counterinsurgency program, the new regime also called for a civic action counterpart to repression. Initially outlined in an internal government document dated April 1, 1982 and titled "National Plan for Security and Development," the civic action component was described in specific one-year phases: "Victory 82," "Firmness 83," "Institutional Renewal 84," "Stability 85," and "Consolidation 86." Shortly afterward, a Swedish representative to the United Nations remarked that the Guatemalan government's rhetoric reminded him of George Orwell's novel, *1984*. "When they mean war they speak of peace," he said, "and when they mean repression, they speak of freedom. . . . Guatemala is the same."

There were two general components of the Guatemalans' five-year plan: first, to eliminate the guerrillas where they existed or were suspected to exist, and to place the rural population under army supervision through a variety of programs; second, on an international level, to obtain recognition of its human rights "advances," as well as international aid, through civic action in the highlands and the promise of elections.

Soldier in church belltower, Nebaj, Quiché. The 50-caliber machine gun is manufactured in the United States.

In Guatemala, while virtually every male registers for the army (failure to do so prevents one from obtaining a passport) almost no one from Guatemala City is ever conscripted. Although army recruitment is formally limited to males 18 to 45 years, some conscripts are as young as fifteen or sixteen. Recruits are traditionally rounded up by the army or local military commissioners on days when there will be a large gathering: following Mass, during local festivals, and at work sites. With rising unemployment figures, plus the ongoing civil patrol system, some men are voluntarily joining the army: patrollers enlist, deciding it is preferable to at least be a recruit with a gun and sixty *quetzales*—twenty-five dollars—monthly income, than to be a civil patroller and to incur the same risks, unpaid and unarmed. In some towns, half to two-thirds of a soldier's salary is automatically given to his family; each month there are lines of Indians standing outside army garrisons, waiting to collect their sons' paychecks.

**Dead suspected guerrillas,
army garrison, Nebaj, Quiché.**

"They dragged them out and knifed them. They stabbed and cut them as if they were animals and they were laughing as they killed them. They killed them with a machete that had no teeth. They put one old man on a table, and cut open his chest, the poor man, and he was still alive, and so they started to cut his throat. They cut his throat slowly. He was suffering a lot. They were cutting people under the ribs, and blood came rushing out and they were laughing. . . . How the blood ran! It ran all over me. Then they fired at the remaining people in the courthouse. Then they threw all the bodies in a heap. They dragged people by the feet, as if they were animals. They threw me on top of the dead bodies."

—Testimony received by Amnesty International of army massacre of 350 people in July 1982

Nebaj, Quiché.

A newspaper editor, speaking of past regimes, said, "Here, everybody did something positive, even Ríos Montt." "Do you mean the military too?" I asked. "Well, there are always the horrible exceptions," he answered.

—Editor at *Prensa Libre*, Guatemala City

In the countryside, the civic action program was implemented barely three months after the coup, initially through the civil patrol *patrullas de autodefensa civil* (PAC) program, which, although formally voluntary, obligated virtually every rural male to act as the army's eyes and ears and, at times, as its cannon fodder. Guatemala's civil patrol became the most extensive civil defense program in the world. While the idea for the PAC system was planted by Army Chief of Staff Benedicto Lucas García in September 1981, the patrol system was not formalized until after the Ríos Montt coup, in the April 1, 1982 security document, which called the PAC "central to this new model [of counterinsurgency]."

While the PAC was officially created to "arm civilians against subversive incursions," no one believed it. The PAC controlled a rural population the army did not trust. In addition to containing one-quarter million "former guerrilla collaborators," it also gave the military a defenseless scapegoat on whom to pass off its own atrocities, either by forcing patrollers to carry out their own dirty work, or by merely claiming that alleged killings were the work of overzealous PAC units.

Almost all condemned the patrol system as obligatory service incurred by those who could least afford the sacrifice, especially in rural areas, where PAC duty occurred as often as twice a week for twenty-four-hour periods. In addition to regular patrol duties, PAC members were also forced to accompany the army on sweeps into the mountains or to provide community labor. In mid-1982, there were 25,000 PAC members; by the end of the year, there were some 500,000.

Ríos Montt's civic action program provided less incentive for peasants to remain than it did for them to flee. By June 1982, the United Nations High Commissioner for Refugees (UNHCR) estimated that some 9,000 Guatemalans were living in southern Chiapas, Mexico; by October 1982 it announced revised estimates of 25,000 refugees.[18] One year later, the number had doubled. Unofficial estimates now cite some 120,000 political refugees in Mexico.

Some refugees had been in hiding since mid-1981. As Ríos Montt's troops were flushing some out, many others were still fleeing into the mountains. Under "Victory 82," the forced retrieval of internally displaced refugees began: throughout 1982 and 1983, army units, often accompanied by civil patrollers, combed the Guatemalan highlands in search of Indians. When Ríos Montt's troops went on these sweeps, the criterion for defining subversives was simple: "shoot those who run and capture those who remain behind."[19] Within months, highland towns were full of refugees, most of them women and children. Usually they were brought down on foot; sometimes, in larger operations, they were removed in army helicopters and trucks. Depending on the numbers, refugees were either put in holding centers—usually abandoned buildings—or transferred to army-controlled refugee camps.

Once caught, refugees also had the "option" of participating in a "Food-for-Work" program sponsored by the army-directed National Emergency Committee (CONE). (The Food-for-Work and the three-year National Reconstruction Committee [CRN] plans have their

18. Cynthia Brown, *Human Rights in Guatemala: No Neutrals Allowed*, p. 49.
19. Author interview, Sololá, October 1983.

antecedents in the 1979–82 "Integral Development of Rural Communities," part of the National Development Plan [PASO] of the Lucas García government.) Under Decree-Law 50–82, the Ríos Montt plan aimed to reach 125,000 people. The food was donated by the United Nations World Food Program (FAO); most of it came from the United States. In exchange for eight hours of work, participants received small amounts of food (for one day of labor, they were given 2 pounds 7.5 ounces corn; 1 pound 1.5 ounces flour; 5.5 ounces vegetables; 7.0 ounces milk; and 1.3 eighths of a quart dry milk). The majority of refugees were widows and children. In June 1983 the Tzacol camp in Cobán counted 198 women and 495 children among a total of 883 refugees: on rations barely enough to sustain one person, they were expected to feed their families. Sometimes Food-for-Work recipients worked to rebuild their own burned villages. Where corn and beans had once been grown, Indians now planted broccoli and snow peas for export, in exchange for canned vegetables.

The reality of rural civic action was self-evident. Army lieutenants standing on muddy expanses of land, pitched with sideless lean-tos three feet high, told foreigners that the Ac'Tzumbal, "New Life," camp was a blessing for the refugees huddled there, who had "fled" imprisonment among the guerrillas. Nearby, however, the same "grateful refugees," some still shell-shocked from the experience, would describe how army helicopters had descended on their cornfields, and how soldiers had ordered them to pack up their possessions, or be shot.

In early February 1983, the eight-month state of siege was extended; in March 1983, it was replaced by a "state of alarm." The Special Tribunal courts sentenced fifteen young men to death by firing squad. The first round of executions in September 1982 did not provoke internal criticism in a country still recovering from the Lucas years. The March 1983 pre-dawn execution of six men in the National Cemetery, however, seven hours before Pope John Paul II set foot on Central American soil, incited outrage from a Catholic population more incensed over this deliberate snubbing of the Pope (who had appealed for clemency) than from the arbitrary killing of six men. While the rest of the world now compared the Special Tribunals to the Spanish Inquisition, however, the U.S. Embassy defined the courts as "streamlined" in procedure.[20]

And, although U.S. aid was still officially suspended, in late 1982 the State Department approved a forty-million-dollar deal to the Guatemalan air force, a package that included the sale of two transport jets and eight T-37 trainers.[21] The deal was never consummated; the Guatemalan army said it could not afford the cost. Simultaneously, Green Beret army captain Jesse Garciá taught a counterinsurgency course at Guatemala's Politécnica Military Academy. He was at least the second U.S. Green Beret to occupy this position. The U.S. Embassy called him "an English instructor."[22]

At first, Ríos Montt's Protestantism had seemed a benign, if embarrassing combination of religion and theatrics, but certainly tolerable after years of heavy-handed government rhetoric. (Guatemalan housewives were particularly pleased with Ríos Montt's moralizing on the subject

20. U.S. Embassy, "Briefing Notes: Guatemala," Guatemala City, June 1983, p. 10.
21. Allan Nairn, "The Guatemala Connection," *The Progressive*, May 1986, p. 22.
22. Allan Nairn, *The Washington Post*, October 21, 1982, p. 1.

Commander of Ac'Tzumbal ("New Life") refugee camp, Nebaj, Quiché.

Lieutenant Gallardo, a graduate of the Politécnica Military Academy ("They do a great brainwashing job") had imprisoned half a dozen women for having resold corn to the army at a profit. When soldiers guarding the prison gave the women blankets for the cold, Gallardo imprisoned them as well, for insubordination. They were made to spend the night standing up in the jail, in subfreezing temperatures.

of marital fidelity.) Six of Ríos Montt's closest advisors and two government officials were Guatemalan and U.S. members of his Church of the Word, based in Eureka, California.

The government initially received some financial support from conservative U.S. evangelical sects; Ríos Montt boasted of having been promised one billion dollars. Although the aid never materialized, some $20 million, mostly in equipment and services, was actually received. Aid for the Protestants' programs in the Guatemalan highlands fell off even before Ríos Montt's removal from office in August 1983. A good deal of funds may have gone directly to army coffers, through the army-directed CRN program. Remnants of U.S. Bible-belt generosity, however, are still evident today. In the Quiché and Verapaces, hundreds of Indian boys wear tattered "Boy Scouts of America" shirts donated by well-meaning sects in the United States. There was less success where little girls were concerned: Indian mothers rejected this imposition of culture and sold the donated skirts and blouses in local markets.

By 1983, however, Ríos Montt's religious fervor was often indistinguishable from government politics, and senior army officials were irritated that young officers had garnered positions which, through seniority or leverage, should have been allotted to them. Ríos Montt's sermons exhausted the patience of Sunday viewers accustomed to sex and violence on television serials. One Sunday evening, however, ORPA guerrillas intercepted Ríos Montt's sermon, cut the sound, and delivered its own political message as Ríos Montt silently waved his arms across the screen.

By mid-1983, virtually all Guatemalan sectors were criticizing Ríos Montt, and not just for ongoing violence. In July, Ríos Montt had imposed a ten percent "Added Value [sales] Tax," (IVA), the first tax of this kind in Guatemala, which affected virtually everyone except the wealthy class. However, the oligarchy was incensed over Ríos Montt's repeated references to agrarian development, *desarrollo empresarial agrario*, possible land reform. The catalyst for the furor was a 1982 AID study, *Land and Labor in Guatemala*, called "communist" by Guatemalan landowners, since it stated that Guatemala had the most skewed land-distribution pattern in Latin America. Throughout late 1982 and early 1983 the government announced that it was considering an "agrarian program"; the last time it was mentioned was one week before the August 1983 coup. (One week after the coup, Minister of Agriculture Leopoldo Sandoval Villeda told Guatemalan landowners that "we have to do something, because if nothing is done to confront the problem of land distribution we are not going to have agrarian reform but a bloody agrarian revolution." By noon the next day, Sandoval Villeda was out of office.) Finally, although no one suffered more under Ríos Montt's beans-and-bullets ideology than Guatemala's highland Indians, his erratic admiration for their Mayan ancestry ("Guatemalidad," as he called it) did nothing to endear him to Guatemala's ladino middle and wealthy classes, especially after his appointment of ten Indians to the hand-picked 88-member Council of State in September

1982. Although the Council of State did not replace the abolished Congress, and served only in an advisory capacity, this was the first time that more than one or two Indians had actually been in government simultaneously.

In June 1983 retired army general and former defense minister José Guillermo Echeverría Vielman published an open letter to Ríos Montt, demanding the removal of the young officers and *Verbo* advisors from the Palace, and the promise of elections. Ríos Montt ignored Echeverría's demands, although they reflected those of most Guatemalans by that time. Instead of dismissals Ríos Montt insisted, two months before the August coup, that *Verbo* Palace officials Francisco Bianchi and Alvaro Contreras remain in office, saying, "If they go, I go."

In 1983 Representative Clarence Long (D-Maryland) visited Guatemala to investigate allegations of ongoing human rights violations. He left Guatemala several days later, saying, "We can see to it we don't give any military or economic aid to this crowd," after having confirmed the existence of massive, ongoing abuses.[23] Deputy head of state, General Mejía Víctores, responded by saying that Long "sound[s] like a member of the EGP"—not a surprising statement for General Mejía, who had previously served as a judge on the Special Tribunals, saying that "Guatemala doesn't need more prayers, it needs more executions," and criticizing Vatican condemnation of the Tribunals, calling it "interference in internal affairs." On August 8, 1983 General Mejía became Guatemala's next head-of-state.

23. Michael McClintock, *The American Connection*, p. 238; originally cited in *Latin America Regional Report*, August 19, 1983.

24. *Country Reports . . . for 1982*, p. 518.

The Code of Conduct

During 1982, as rural massacres peaked, the Ríos Montt government initiated a campaign of government house-cleaning: "This Government Has a Commitment to Change." The slogan, accompanied by three blue fingers against a white backdrop, promised, "I don't steal, lie or abuse [power]." The slogan and the fingers appeared on government press packets, matchbooks, posters, and bumper stickers, reaching even the most remote areas. The posters read: "Guatemala Does Not Need Cowards or Opportunists in its Path Toward Strength and Victory," "Patriotism is Not about Heroics, It is a Matter of Discipline," and "Selfishness as a Principle Results in Oppression." The campaign was not new. Under Lucas García, government decals adorned with dove and olive branch exhorted Guatemalans to *Mantener la Paz*: "Maintain Peace."

The State Department reported that "the Government of Guatemala has issued a new military code of conduct in August, stressing the importance of humane treatment of civilians, and reportedly provided each soldier with a pocket copy of it."[24]

**Wounded soldier being
evacuated in northern Quiché.**

An army doctor working in Nebaj said that between March and July 1983, there had been four major army offensives. "The bombings are the army's big 'secret,' " he said. "I've heard the bombs: they use two army A-37 planes. The bombings usually occur at midday, they last for about twenty minutes." The doctor said that the offensives were not successful: "A group of soldiers came in by helicopter from the mountains." The official statistics were fifteen to twenty soldiers dead and one hundred wounded.

Huipil, San Antonio Aguas Calientes, Sacatepéquez.

Some anthropologists say that Guatemalan _huipiles_, while widely thought to be Mayan in origin, originated following the Spanish Conquest, with the advent of the plantation system, as a means of identifying landowners' human property, thus explaining the diversification of different _huipil_ patterns—some two hundred in all today. In addition to importing new fabrics and colors, the Spaniards also mixed the coats-of-arms of Seville, Aragón, and Asturias among traditional Mayan designs, which had formerly read as graphic "messages." When army repression forced massive migration of Indians into Guatemala City, many Indian women abandoned traditional dress in order to hide their identities. Others still wore _huipiles_, but from distant areas, to avoid regional identification by urban government forces. "It's a form of life insurance," one husband explained.

Cadet at the Politécnica Military Academy, explaining different *huipil* patterns. San Juan Sacatepéquez, Sacatepéquez.

The Politécnica Military Academy, founded in 1873, is Guatemala's West Point. Until 1986 all of Guatemala's heads of state were graduates of the Politécnica; all have been ladinos.

Between 1931 and 1945, the Politécnica was headed by U.S. military officers whose pictures hang in the front hall of the main reception building. At least two U.S. Special Forces Green Berets have taught there as well, between 1980 and 1982. U.S. Army Captain Jesse García, a Green Beret who served in Vietnam, said that his instruction to cadets included reconnaissance, "direct action," and "destruction patrols." The U.S. Embassy called him an "English instructor."

The Code of Conduct for the Active Duty Guatemalan Soldier:

1. I will not take so much as a pin from the population.

2. I will not flirt with or take liberties with local women.

3. I will protect and not harm the crops where I walk.

4. I will pay the just price for whatever I buy. If there is a discrepancy, I will pay more.

5. I will return anything I borrow and I will pay for any property I may damage.

6. I will be courteous and show special affection for the elderly and children.

7. I will courteously welcome any person who desires to speak with me. I will greet everyone I meet on the roads and trails.

8. I will respect local customs and traditions, as well as their civilian and religious authorities.

9. I will yield the right of way of roads and highways provided it does not interfere with Troop security.

10. I will not accept gifts or favors from well-to-do or influential people.

11. I will not abuse peasant hospitality.

12. I will show respect for tombs, graves, Churches and other buildings of importance to the community.

In August 1982, while the Ríos Montt government was distributing the conduct code, a recruit stationed in the Mazatenango, Suchitepéquez army garrison on Guatemala's southern coast, witnessed the interrogation of alleged subversives:

"An officer said, 'Since the prisoners don't want to say anything, go get some gasoline.' They told the first prisoner that . . . if he didn't say anything, they were going to throw gasoline on him. The prisoner said he had nothing to say, he couldn't accuse innocent people. The officer said, 'Okay, if you aren't going to talk, then throw some gasoline on him.' A *kaibil* set fire to him, and it spread. The whole prisoner's body caught fire . . . but the prisoner didn't talk, he just shouted and sobbed. They locked him up again and told him they would return.

"With the next prisoner, they used a Gillette razor blade. They cut up his arm and then they threw salt and lemon on it. An army captain and three *kaibiles* did it. They said that this was the only way to get people to talk. The second one didn't talk either, so they locked him up and brought another prisoner. This time the torture was different. One of the civilians got a rope

Soldier dancing with girl, Independence Day, Nebaj, Quiché.

"Years ago, if someone left his sweetheart, if she was very traditional, she would have asked somebody to do some witchcraft against him. That was one thing you could do for unhappiness. The man, of course, would safely 'overcome' the witchcraft and the woman might feel better, since she thought that by doing something against him, she was getting even.

"Now, though, it is easier to denounce something to the army. All these things are on a different level: now you have immediate access to get somebody in trouble. Someone I know—I knew him since birth—was suspected of being a guerrilla and the army killed him in a horrible way. What I heard was that his [former] sweetheart had denounced him as a guerrilla."

—Former resident of Nebaj

and put it around his neck and pulled it to asphyxiate him, to get something out of him. And this one began to talk. The officer said, 'That's how we like it, you're our *cuate* [buddy] now.' He began to tell them how he had been deceived, how the guerrillas told him he wouldn't have to work someday, and how out of ambition, he had become involved with them. He said he would denounce all the *compañeros* he knew. The army loved this. They laughed and said, 'Today we really hooked one, and by tomorrow night, we'll have more.' They stopped torturing him.

"Three days later, the room where the three prisoners were being kept smelled so bad that the officer gave the order to take them out and kill them. I was there when he gave the order. The *kaibiles* killed them near the bathrooms in the barracks. When they did it, they turned out the lights. Five plainclothes soldiers strangled them to death. The police came in to pick up the bodies and throw them over a bridge near a river.

"I was there when they tortured them. When the *kaibiles* realized I was watching, they yelled and ordered me to get out."

Juan

Juan is a Quiché Indian in his early twenties. He belonged to Catholic Action, then to the Committee for Peasant Unity (CUC). In 1980 Juan joined the Guerrilla Army of the Poor (EGP). He described his initial involvement:

"In those days no one wanted to leave his land. We always had a thousand reasons for not leaving our homes, but after awhile there was no freedom, we were always in hiding, so we decided to see who would rise up once and for all. In the beginning, the army would come to your house, and if you weren't there, they would still respect your family. Later though, if you weren't there, they would grab whoever was around. By January 1981 all you had to do was complain about one little thing . . . so many people 'disappeared.' That period was a crash course in survival.

"I'll tell you how I got involved in the EGP. The heads of the guerrillas had their contacts in the CUC, and the first thing they did was to recruit leaders, and from there, the leaders began to move things along. But it was a slow process.

"It was August 12, 1980. I remember that they asked me, 'Are we just going to stay in CUC, more politics and more politics? Those *clientes* ["clients," colloquially, "enemies"] have guns—what are we going to do?' 'Shit,' I said. 'I'll join. I'll fight them with machetes if I have to.' 'Really?' they asked. 'If you're interested, we're going north of Chajul and Cotzal.'

"I remember getting my things together; I was just sixteen, I was still wet behind the ears When you are sixteen or eighteen you still feel like a beginner: you think of your family, your brothers and sisters, everything. But that idea of going up north sank in.

"There were 150 of us who went up, so many of us, not like in the army, where the military commissioner is running after kids in the market place. With us it was enthusiasm, pure and simple. Everybody was under twenty-five years old, men and women. Almost all of us had been in Catholic Action. There were a couple of atheists too.

"Up in the mountains, at the camp, they would wake us up at five-thirty in the morning. I'd still be dreaming. We had half an hour to tie up our boots and our backpacks, wash, brush our teeth, run a comb through our hair. They'd tell us there was no reason to get sloppy just because we were in the middle of nowhere. We'd do exercises until eight A.M.; we'd have breakfast until nine. When we ate, there was a cold tamale, a spoonful of beans, and a little coffee. It was so cold up there that it would kill the heat from the coffee in five minutes.

"From nine until noon, we'd have 'operations.' We would learn how to corner the army, how to fight, how to ambush. From twelve until two, we'd have lunch, and rest, and from two to four, political training. The idea was not just to be trained in a military sense, but to be trained as leaders as well. Morale and politics were very important. When we had political orientation, they talked to us about social and economic injustice, and how to be politically disciplined with people. They never talked about the Soviet Union being a nicer place, or Poland, or communism. Or the United States. They did talk about Marxism, but it was like something out of a textbook.

"At night, we'd listen to the news and eat. By nine P.M., we'd be telling each other stories. We'd ask each other if we were depressed, what we had done that day, and so on. When we weren't slapping mosquitoes, we were talking to each other. 'You know what?' one would say. 'I left my girlfriend behind.' There were a lot of couples up in the mountains. I remember one sergeant, Francisco, who married a *compañera* from the FACS [Augusto César Sandino front]. We had the ceremony right there at the camp. There was a marimba; even people from town came. But just the couple who got married were allowed to drink; the rest of us had to be alert.

"Everybody had guard duty, *posta*. You'd have it burned in your brain, the hour you had to do *posta*. Everybody wanted to forget *posta*; it was a big responsibility. I'd get up for guard duty from two to three in the morning; there was a rule that if you didn't get up on time, you had to do two hours the next day, instead of one. I remember that at five-thirty A.M., when we woke up, the girls would come along and tease us. 'Who was the guy who was snoring and hogging all the flies last night?' If you were snoring, the guy on *posta* would wake you up."

Dummies used for counterinsurgency training at the Politécnica Military Academy, San Juan Sacatepéquez, Sacatepéquez.

The army often chose its victims from computer lists of suspects: other times targeting was arbitrary. When the army did bother to collect names, there was little protection. According to a former resident of the Ixil triangle, the local military confused non-suspects with "suspects" who had the same name as real targets:

"Indians' names are often repetitive. For example, you'll find many called 'Ana López' or 'Miguel Sánchez.' Once, they killed three people with the same name before they found out that the fourth one was the person they were after. But he had already gone off with the guerrillas."

Occasionally, the confusion of names wasn't restricted solely to the Indian population. Guatemala's health minister, Dr. Carlos Armando Soto, fled the country during the Lucas years after the army had killed a second Dr. Soto by mistake, who was found hanging from a butcher hook.

Members of the EGP and civilians training, Quezaltenango.

In 1955, before a guerrilla movement existed in Guatemala, journalist Keith Monroe described the reasons behind the support for the local communist party, in the July issue of *Harper's* magazine: "When a poor man's shack burned down, the communists rustled up some boards and tin and built a new one. When an Indian child was sickly, communists rallied around with aspirins and hot water bottle. People who were hungry, or broke, or in trouble had virtually nowhere to turn . . . but they could always go to communist headquarters for tortillas, pennies, help and friendship."

Today, the growth of Guatemala's guerrilla movement and civilian support can be explained at least in part by the same reasons cited by Monroe twenty years ago. Guerrilla collaborators often give food and supplies voluntarily; many are paid, and collaboration can mean guerrilla protection as well. In addition, the guerrillas are the only outlet for local grievances against repression by the army, military commissioners, and finca overseers. For those who decide to join the guerrillas and become armed combatants, there is a measure of safety: despite the hardship and years of clandestinity, a gun in one's hand and and back-up support represent more safety than remaining behind in one's village, unarmed and unable to resist army repression.

131

Members of the EGP in maneuvers with sticks in northwestern highlands.

"Once, five soldiers were running after one of ours. The *compa* [friend, pal, buddy] thought, 'Ay! My time has come!' But he started throwing horse shit at them, fresh horse shit. And the five soldiers, when they saw the horse shit, they fell to the ground, and the *compa* kept running. He got away safely on a hill some distance away, he yelled, '*Maricones*! Fags!' You wouldn't believe how hard he was laughing. When the soldiers had seen the horse shit, they thought they were being attacked with grenades."

—Peasant, Guatemala City

Guerrilla Army of the Poor (EGP) and civilians training in the northwestern highlands.

"When the Indians go into the guerrillas, they have nothing to lose. Our job is to give them something they want to protect. If they have something to protect, they are not going to join the guerrillas. We [army] are going to survive only if the people are with us. We have to win—I don't want to end up in Miami washing dishes."

—Major Roberto Letona in an interview with Orville Schell, Chairman, Americas Watch, 1983

Acul

25. Ibid., p. 516.

The U.S. State Department praised the Ríos Montt government, saying that "[army] forces have begun to pay greater attention to the importance of proper treatment of the civilian population" and that the "overall conduct of the armed forces had improved by late in the year."[25]

In late 1982 the town of Nebaj, Quiché, celebrated Independence Day with marching schoolchildren, marching civil patrollers, marching soldiers, and a succession of floats, including the army's twelve-foot-wide camouflaged "helmet" suspended over a flatbed truck carrying the local beauty queens. In the soccer stadium where the march ended, Major Tito Arias, the local army commander, delivered a speech and was presented with the requisite Nebaj tapestry.

Halfway through the ceremony a young local government employee began talking to a foreign reporter, asking him questions: Was he with the U.S. Embassy? Was he a missionary? Was he in the Peace Corps? He then described a massacre he had witnessed in the village of Acul, near Nebaj, three weeks after the Ríos Montt coup. While Major Tito praised the people of Nebaj for their newfound faith in the Guatemalan army, the young man offered this account:

"It was early in the morning . . . there were two armed men . . . carrying Galils. . . . They came over and told me to accompany them to the church. Inside there were twelve other men, they looked very worried. They were praying and making the sign of the cross. The soldiers kept bringing people in, kicking them into the church. Just men and boys.

"A young boy was pointing out people. The army said those were the people they were going to kill because they were against the government. They took us outside the church patio and divided us up, saying, 'These go to heaven and these go to hell, these go to heaven and these go to hell.' Those who were going to 'hell' were going to be shot. They put me in the room called 'heaven' while others were taken to the next room to be killed. They tied them up and began to kick them, giving them karate chops. They kicked the others in the genitals so they would fall down. One of the soldiers brought a knife from the butcher shop and stuck it in a boy's back. My body went cold; I had never seen anything like it. Next, the army asked where they should shoot the people: there in the church or in the cemetery. The soldiers gave me the job of writing down people's names. Those of us who lived had to dig a grave fifteen feet deep and eleven feet wide.

"When they took people to the cemetery, their hands were tied in back of them. There, they kept hitting them and telling them that if they told where the 'arms caches' were, they would be pardoned. Four boys stepped forward and said they would talk, so they separated them. . . . The rest of the men were placed next to the grave and shot in the forehead. Their brains spilled out a few feet away; they were shooting so close that it looked like their clothes were burning.

"The army killed twenty-six people. We were standing there, watching this and the survivors cleaning it up. A soldier came up and said, 'So, why are you sad? Are you sad because we are killing these guerrillas? Wouldn't you like to take this gun and finish them off?'

"After they had finished, the army officer got on his radio and said there had been an armed confrontation, and that some 'fucking guerrillas' had died. When we were in the cemetery and they were about to machine-gun the people, the lieutenant had said, 'You who don't bring up your children in the right way are the cause of this. . . . Your sons get involved in shit that doesn't do them any good. But now we're not going to throw bodies on the sides of the roads; we're going to shoot, because this is the new law of Ríos Montt.' "

La Embajada

Just to mention *la embajada* in Guatemala assumes reference to the Embassy of the United States. A western diplomat who lived in Guatemala from 1980 to 1985, and an open critic of human rights abuses there, was also outspoken in his disdain over the U.S. Embassy's attempts to control events. What shocked the diplomat most was the Embassy's deliberate silence, when it was not actively disavowing the facts. In 1983, mid-way through the diplomat's stay in Guatemala, the U.S. Embassy claimed that massacres no longer took place, stating that "every known lead [regarding allegations of massacres] was checked, on site, and found to be false."[26] The diplomat recalled one such investigation. "The U.S. Embassy asked a colleague of mine if he wished to accompany them to La Libertad to check on an alleged massacre. He accepted. A U.S. chopper took them up to a remote village near the town. The village was entirely burned down but there was not one body. My colleague, who had gone off on his own, suddenly heard a noise. He saw the civil defense patrols talking to Willy McArdoe, the Embassy's MilGroup [U.S. Military Group] guy. McArdoe was questioning a patroller about the massacre. The patroller said, 'The army did it.' This guy was head of the patrol. My colleague heard this; he walked over to McArdoe and said, 'I see you've talked to the patrols.' McArdoe didn't say what he had heard. Finally, he told my colleague. 'I asked them how the people were killed and they said they didn't know.' My colleague had clearly heard the patroller say that the army had killed the people.

"For me, the U.S. Embassy's position is clear: if they hear the truth, they don't repeat it."

26. Unclassified document, No. 6253, approved by U.S. Ambassador Frederic Chapin and drafted by U.S. Embassy Human Rights Officer Val Martínez, July 29, 1983.

135

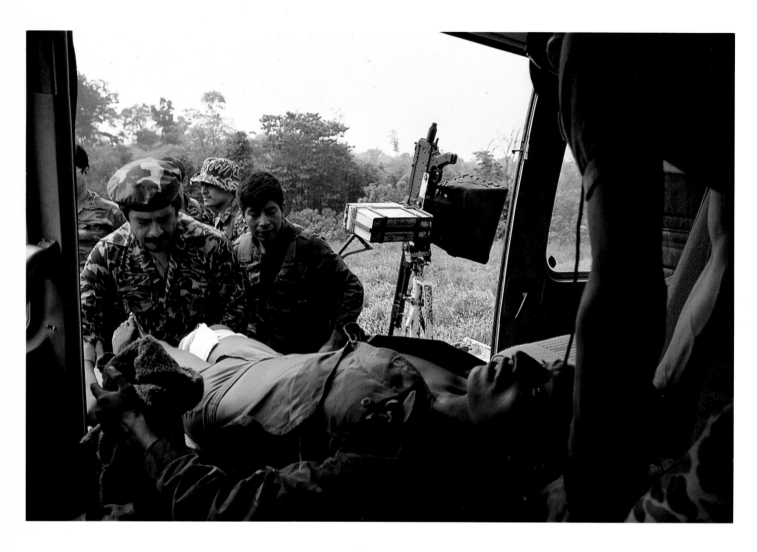

Wounded soldier, Quiché. The Ardón pension in Nebaj keeps a soiled notebook in the kitchen drawer to record the arrival of guests. Years ago, the proprietors did so in perfunctory lip service to dictums set by the Guatemalan Tourist Institute (INGUAT), and out of curiosity. By 1985, however, guests were required to register immediately—Nebaj's army commander had ordered the pension to turn over its guest list to the local garrison each evening.

According to the notebook, tourism peaked in 1979, with 344 signatures in the book; 1980 was next, with 260 guests. Tourism in Nebaj hit bottom in 1982, when 47 guests registered the entire year, and many of them were government workers supervising the construction of model villages. Between 1978 and 1984, the pension's notebook recorded the signatures of 338 U.S. citizens, 121 Guatemalans, and 43 Israelis.

In 1983 a few tourists began to return to northern Quiché, even as the army staged four major offensives there during the first half of the year. Nebaj's inhabitants accommodated as best they could to the evolution of foreigners' needs: women who had taught backstrap weaving now assaulted tourists with mass-produced *huipiles*, while a man well known for his local day tours offered visitors—mostly journalists—interviews with civil patrollers tortured by the army.

Organization of the People in Arms (ORPA) woman combatant.

In the 1960s the guerrillas were accessible to both local and international press for at least three years. Dozens of Guatemalan reporters went out with guerrilla cadres with the same facility that students would leave for weekend training in the mountains. Today, only a handful of foreign journalists have gone out with the guerrillas, and certainly no local reporter: the idea presumes either immediate self-exile or identification as a subversive. There are still reporters from the 1960s, now middle-aged functionaries, whose glass-topped coffee tables press blurry black-and-white photos in which they stand smiling next to the first guerrilla leaders, Luis Turcios Lima and César Montes.

EGP guerrillas at a party with
local villagers, northwestern
highlands.

EGP literacy manual, Nebaj, Quiché. *Agarrada* means "grabbed" or "kidnapped."

An ex-soldier visited a nun in Guatemala City. He told her that the first time he had to kill someone, "I cried and shouted." The commander told him that to "cure" himself, he would have to keep killing.

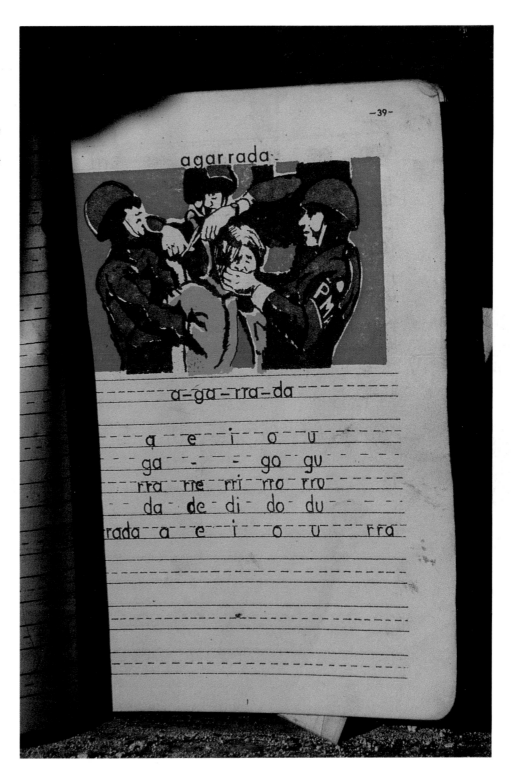

The Detectives

Since the creation of the *judiciales* in 1925, the plainclothes detective police force has changed its name at least six times, from the "Judicial Police" to the "Judicial Guard," to the "Judicial Department," back to the "Judicial Police," to the "Detective Corps," to the "Department of Technical Investigations," to the "Special Investigations and Narcotics Brigade" (BIEN) in 1986.

Today, to talk about the *judiciales* in Guatemala is not a simple reference to plainclothes detectives: *judiciales* can mean any section of the security forces who carry out "disappearances" and killings. While the National Police corps is officially under the jurisdiction of the Interior Ministry, this is not true in practice since, in Guatemala, every branch of the security forces is subordinate to the army. The U.S. government's own Area Handbook on Guatemala described the Guatemalan police as "heavily engaged in counterinsurgency for more than two decades."[27]

The following interview was conducted with a former detective of the now-defunct Department of Technical Investigations (DIT). He is a twenty-year veteran of the judicial police and served under the governments of Generals Laugerud García, Lucas García, Ríos Montt, and Mejía Víctores. The agent's description of DIT procedures throughout the 1980s contradicts that given by a State Department official in July 1982, who said that he could not "emphasize strongly enough the favorable contrast between the current human rights situation in Guatemala and the situation last December" (when security forces were "making significant progress" in human rights), adding that "National Police are now ordered to show badges and give names and numbers when stopping citizens for questioning."[28]

The following is the statement made by the DIT agent in April 1983:

"What are the DIT's methods? Very simple: they work everyone over with the famous *capucha*.

"The *capucha* is a hood made of rubber, which has a kind of tie at the end which goes behind it. You put the hood over the person, down to his neck, and you tighten the strings so no air can enter. Before, you blindfold the person and you tie his hands and ankles from behind, and you put him face down and then someone strong steps on his lungs while another holds his feet, and another his head. Then the strong guy starts 'rowing' the person's body while another is tightening the hood. What happens? He starts losing consciousness from lack of oxygen. And when he is just about to faint, they jump on him to bring him to or they throw cold water on his face, and slap him. They take off the hood and interrogate him. They say 'Are you going to tell the truth?' and 'Who is so and so?' If he doesn't know anything, they put the hood back on until he feels obligated to say something, or else he is very macho and doesn't speak, or to save his life, he invents just about anything. That's when it really gets started: torture. A lot of people

27. Richard F. Nyrop, *Guatemala: A Country Study*, p. xiv.
28. Letter from Stephen W. Bosworth, Deputy Assistant Secretary For Inter-American Affairs to Jerry Patterson, Chairman, Subcommittee on International Development Institutions and Finance, House of Representatives, July 15, 1982.

can't take it. They die, and that's when they throw them on the roadsides about ten kilometers from the city. That's why you often see people with their hands tied behind them, blindfolded; they were the ones who couldn't withstand the hood.

"There are sessions that last an afternoon, a day, a week, a month, depending on the seriousness of the alleged crime. Everything happens as easily as the way I am describing it."

The second interview was conducted in December 1985 with a former DIT agent, who described the DIT's function, his own participation, and the DIT's context within military rule:

"At first, there were *judiciales*, and then it became the 'DIT,' but it's the same thing. Only the name has changed. Lucas [García] always supported the *judiciales*; they inspired more fear. They would [kidnap] people, and even though the [victim] wasn't the right one, they would always take them anyway. A lot of mistakes were made.

"In the police, there is a little of everything. If we get someone, we're not going to coax him with lollipops. I was trained in the use of the hood; you have to do it. The older agents would train the new [agents]; they taught me. You would tie the hood around the person and treat him as if he were a horse; you sit on him, get up, then you cut off his air. If he doesn't collaborate, you keep torturing him. Two of us would begin the interrogation, then the other [would continue] when the first [agent] got tired.

"Our job is to be an *oreja*. When there's someone political, the army tells us that 'so-and-so' is 'suspicious.' We watch him: how he dresses, what he does. Then they say, 'Act on it,' and we act. We used to kidnap and kill suspects, but since the middle of 1985, we just kidnap them. The army does the 'disappearing.'

"When the person is finally abducted, it's not up to us anymore, it's the G-2. The army. We investigate and they carry the 'disappearance' out. Or the BROE, who are police and act just like the army. They take very drastic measures. Sometimes the orders go from boss to boss. The first and second in command give an order to the head of the [DIT] 'Section Six.' 'Look for so-and-so, do me a favor and capture him.' The boss does it. We're carrying out orders. We capture the person and then we hand him over. They [the army] call and say, 'Pick up so-and-so . . .' Afterwards, the *Estado Mayor* [Army high command] car comes and takes him who knows where. The car comes to the DIT [headquarters] at night and takes him away. We are responsible for the capture but the "disappearance" is not our domain anymore. It comes from the Palace; we just capture the person. Nothing is written out, the orders are over the phone. If you don't carry out orders, they kill you.

"If they want everything to be more civilized, they use the G-2. The G-2 does the same work [we do]. If they have to get a student, they say, 'Okay, you have to find out where he lives and follow him.' What do they do with someone who doesn't reappear? What do you think? They kill them.

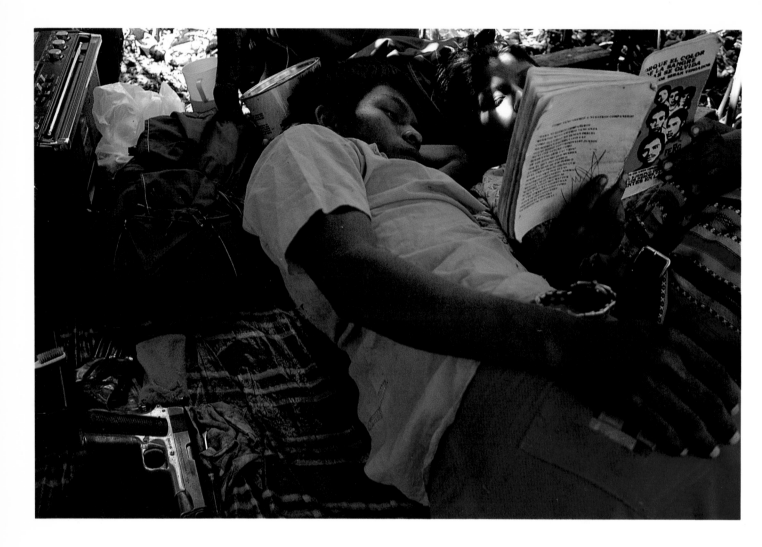

EGP combatants in the Luis Turcios Lima front reading a manual on the history of the armed opposition movement in Guatemala, Mazatenango, Suchitepéquez.

The two EGP members above were part of a group of seven combatants on one of the EGP's coastal units. Five were Indians. The woman on the right is six months pregnant. At the time, this unit was protecting a group of refugees who had fled into the mountains following repeated army incursions. Most of the combatants had joined the EGP following repression against their families: the youngest, a twelve-year-old courier, had witnessed his parents' death by the army. The leader of the unit had been a medical student in Guatemala City "until that seemed useless as well."

This unit was poorly equipped, with one submachine gun and five pistols. Although the refugees themselves had little to offer, they provided the unit with its meals: usually tortillas, a banana or two, and a hard-boiled egg, all to be shared among seven people, plus coffee diluted until it was brown sugar water. Some of these combatants had not been out of the mountains for three years; the one ladina woman in the group asked if it were true that every U.S. high school had an ice-skating rink.

EGP combatant and refugee, Suchitepéquez.

While the army has explained rural massacres as terrorist attacks by "subversive elements," President Cerezo himself has contradicted these allegations: "Leftist guerrillas attack the army and the security organizations, but up to now we have no knowledge of guerrilla attacks against the civilian population. However, the right-wing groups have attacked democratic opposition parties that are not participating in the armed struggle."

Guerrillas and supporters at rally, Quezaltenango.

For years, Guatemala's four guerrilla groups financed their movement through the sometimes spectacular kidnappings of wealthy Guatemalans, foreign businessmen, and the relatives of State leaders. In 1980 the Guerrilla Army of the Poor swept down onto a baseball diamond and kidnapped the team's shortstop, the son of businessman Jorge García Granados, obtaining a ransom of over seven million dollars. In September 1980 the Rebel Armed Forces, "FAR," procured a $4.7 million ransom for the release of Nestlé president José A. de Lima; the Cindal-Nestlé company also promised to distribute one million cans of powdered milk to rural children as part of the ransom bargain. In 1983 the FAR kidnapped the sisters of Generals Efraín Ríos Montt and then Head-of-State Mejía Víctores; although Mejía refused to negotiate with his sister's kidnappers, both women were released several months later. They were unharmed and the Guatemalan press also implied that months of captivity had proved beneficial to Ríos Montt's sister: two months pregnant at the time of her kidnapping, Elena Ríos received what she described as "excellent gynecological care" during her confinement with the FAR; she subsequently gave birth to a healthy baby, after three miscarriages in the past.

Graduation ceremony at the school for the army's elite *kaibil*, counterinsurgency unit formed in the mid-1970s.

This *kaibil* is receiving a machete for demonstrated excellence, presented to him by Deputy Head of State General Rodolfo Lobos Zamora, now Ambassador to Panama. At the close of the graduation ceremonies, the *kaibiles* sang: "A *kaibil* is a killing machine. . . . A *kaibil* is a man. . . . A *kaibil* . . . controls the situation." Not always. An hour earlier, Army Colonel Edgar D'Jalma Domínguez, then head of the Office for Army Public Relations, gave an abbreviated tour of the *kaibil* training grounds in La Pólvora, El Petén. He pointed across the river, where half a dozen marked graves were visible. "Those are the ones who didn't make it across during training," he said with a smile.

"We've had cases where there's a problem of a "disappeared" student: a *habeas corpus* writ is filed and we have to investigate. We go to the place, we figure out what happened. [We're told] that 'four plainclothes people with machine guns [kidnapped him].' License plates: numbers scratched off. We know it was the government, but *what do you do*? If we denounce it, what will happen? They'll kill us. The guerrillas? How can you think it was the guerrillas; the guerrillas take responsibility for what they do. It's the government.

"Why am I in the DIT? Financial need. If they get rid of the DIT, there's going to be a big problem. There are a lot of people who don't know any other kind of work."

Luckie

Ana Lucrecia Orellana Stormont, "Luckie," was a thirty-five-year-old psychology professor at the University of San Carlos (USAC). She belonged to an upper-class ladino family whose ancestors include three Guatemalan presidents. On June 6, 1983 Luckie was abducted along with several friends. News of her "disappearance" sent shock waves through her family's circle of friends and relatives. The family relied on a tenuous network of contacts in military and social circles both to obtain information, and, eventually, her release. Once, her mother received information from an old schoolmate, the wife of a high-ranking minister in the Ríos Montt cabinet; through her husband's information, the friend was able to tell Mrs. Orellana where Luckie was being held. In a formal conversation with the husband three weeks later at the National Palace, the minister denied any knowledge of Luckie's whereabouts. Later, two extortionists extracted thousands of *quetzales* from the family, promising her release.

Luckie was killed in late 1983; her body was buried in a cornfield near Guatemala City. The family was informed of her death seven months later by one of the extortionists. A family friend described the Orellanas' attempts to buy Luckie's release:

"The family would get many calls. The callers would say, 'Your package is dry,' or 'your package is wet,' or 'your package is this and that': they were always referring to Luckie's state of health with this 'package.' One time, they called and said, 'Look in the baseball stadium next to your house and you will find Luckie's body.' So they went out at 11 P.M. and looked for her there in the baseball field, but it was just a hoax.

"At first the family was also receiving information on Luckie from the wife of the government official: she would call up the family and tell them where Luckie was, and in what condition.

"Suddenly, however, a new person showed up. A woman would come to the house on Sundays; she would eat with the family. The woman said that she was the intermediary between the family and the government for Luckie's release, and there is no doubt that she knew something from the details she had. How else could she know that Luckie had a mole on a certain part of her back? In order to prove that she did have contact with Luckie, she said that Luckie had told her about a plant in her room, named *teléfono* and as long as that plant lived, it was a sign that she was alive too, because Luckie said that she transferred energy to that plant. She said that the plant was on the right-hand side of her room, and the family verified that indeed, the plant did exist, and that it was in exactly the spot the woman had described. She also talked about a piece of knitting that Luckie was working on, a weaving Luckie had told her was in such and such a part of her room, and it was there too. . . . Those details, so insignificant but so intimate, backed up her claim that she was indeed talking to Luckie.

"Another time, she said, 'Look, we're going to give her back to you on Sunday afternoon, and you must prepare to leave the country with her. I need you to give me some money to buy dollars and safe conduct papers.' The family gave the money and they spent the entire afternoon watching out the back door. The woman finally called back and said, 'I couldn't bring her today because they had to do a transplant on her fingers; the nails have been torn off.'

"Can you imagine? the nerve ends, the fingertips, she said.

"A second extortionist starting calling one of Luckie's aunts. This one said he was Luckie's torturer, he told this to the aunt. The aunt would pass medicine to Luckie continually; he would receive it and she would pay him to take it to her, then he would inform the aunt about her condition.

"Finally, this man told the aunt that Luckie had died around the fifth or sixth of November. Her last request was to be buried with her boots on so that her body could be identified. He said that she died in great pain. He told the aunt that he had stolen her corpse and bought a coffin, and he had buried her in Santa María Milpas Altas, so that when five years went by, he could exhume the body and get more money from her family."

Rock and Marimba

The ORPA guerrillas have existed since the mid-1970s. At the Luis Javier Tambrís Front, on the side of a volcano in the Sololá department, few combatants cited direct repression as their reason for joining, except for one individual who had been tortured under the Ríos Montt Special Tribunals.

ORPA guerrilla units included some one-hundred combatants. The ratio of Indians to ladinos was ten to one, and the ratio of men to women about the same. ORPA leaders joked that when new women combatants were about to arrive at the front, the men started shaving and washing their clothes days ahead of time.

Bus burned by guerrillas outside San Pedro Jocopilas, Quiché.

"To me, the lines were so clearly drawn: the rich people and their army, and the poor people and the poor people's army. It wasn't just political lines per se; it was basically that 'there's the people that have always had everything and they've got the official army,' and out of a hopeless situation, here's at least a way of striking back. After hundreds and hundreds of years of being put down, here was finally a chance to do something."

—U.S. citizen who grew up in Guatemala, 1984

Kaibil unit on Army Day, Campo de Marte field, Guatemala City.

A foreign priest living in Guatemala gave his assessment of the situation: "All these violations of human rights come from a coldly conceived and executed plan. There are no excesses; the soldiers do exactly what they are told—nothing more, nothing less." Pope John Paul II was even more succinct: he told a Guatemalan bishop, "All they do in Guatemala is give orders and kill."

ORPA members were less inclined to read Sandinista literature than Dickens, Shakespeare, and novels by Sidney Sheldon and Arthur Hailey. In their few rare moments of quiet, they preferred to forget about politics. They had a portable television as well, with a miniscule screen: Doris Day and Jimmy Stewart, somewhere in northern Africa.

In a gesture intended to please what they thought were the musical tastes of Indian combatants, one Christmas ORPA leaders provided marimba music. "We thought they missed it, but all they wanted to hear was Sting and Bruce Springsteen." One ORPA combatant, a young Indian, talked more passionately about rock-and-roll than about any battle or any victory. He had committed to memory the flip sides of Queen and Madonna 45s, reciting them the way other people do baseball batting averages. Sometimes, in fact, the Tambrís Front could be heard before it was seen: from inside the trees came "Born in the U.S.A." and "My Hometown."

Bomberos

In Guatemala there are few fires, but there is hardly a day when the *bomberos*, the firemen, are not mentioned in the local press. Guatemala's firemen are charged with picking up cadavers.

Unlike other places, where firemen can get satisfaction from saving human lives, Guatemalan *bomberos* have to be satisfied with removing the remains of daily terror before it can putrify. For honest firemen, it is a job. For others, however, being a *bombero* can produce a lucrative income. Some firemen double their salaries from newspapers anxious for news of shootouts and bodies, while others, first on the scene, pilfer watches and money before the arrival of the judge and the *judiciales*. There is fierce competition among funeral parlors, who pay the firemen, the police, and local hospitals in order to get to the body first. Even in death, Guatemalans are not immune from "disappearing"—at least once a year, local newspapers report the kidnapping of a cadaver from a funeral home hearse.

A fireman described his tasks:

"We find out about body dumps from three sources: anonymous phone calls, a tip-off from security forces, or someone who is passing by and smells the odor. When the National Police call, they don't identify themselves on the radio for their own security. There are five types of individuals who go to the site where a body is found: the firemen, the police, a judge, the *judiciales*, and funeral home employees.

"We pick up an average of three bodies per day. We don't get calls on all the bodies that are dumped, there are probably about six bodies a day—we see half of them. Ninety percent of the victims are men; ninety percent have been tortured, usually by strangulation. Over half of them are between twenty-five to thirty-five years old. Ten percent are children: the day before yesterday, we picked up a seventeen-year-old boy in a garbage dump. Under Lucas [García] we would find human bones and skeletons; usually they would be thrown in places not frequented daily, like ravines and garbage dumps.

"The crimes are attributed to crazy people or delinquents, as if they were the only ones who do anything. . . . It's paramilitary groups, though; a common criminal isn't going to kill and torture, he's interested in the money. The media limits what it says—for example, recently when [a young girl] was killed, she was beheaded, but the official account said, 'profound wound.' "

The Knees

Jerónimo, a ladino guerrilla leader in his mid-thirties, had been in the mountains with ORPA for seven years. He was married and had four children. He was also the front's electrician and the director of its weekly "culture night." He carried with him a letter, now tearing at the folds, protected in a wrinkled Baggie. It was the last letter he had received from his wife, three years before. He explained:

"We were in the same class at the university, and the first day, when I passed in front of her, I could only look at those beautiful knees. Incredible. I remember I saw the most beautiful legs I've ever seen. I followed those legs and we married two years later. I was twenty-two. She was a beautiful girl, very beautiful.

"My wife was always afraid that they were going to kill me. I would go to a meeting and get involved and start talking and talking, on and on. That was when I became involved in the guerrillas. I started to explain it to my wife, but she said, 'I knew that sooner or later you would end up in the guerrillas; at least in the mountains you'll be able to defend yourself, not like here, where one day you're going to end up dead.' My wife agreed that I should come up here. At the time, it was the only way out for me.

"I miss my wife very much; I haven't seen her in six years. I haven't been able to find out anything about her. I think she fled somewhere with the children. I have her last letter to me. She sent it three years ago and I save it because it's the only letter I have from her. When I wish for another letter, I take this one out and read it again. It says, 'I need you.'

"Sometimes I dream that I am returning home, and I go out and knock on the door of my house, and a little boy comes out. He says, 'Who's there?' and I ask him if his mother is around. He says 'yes' and he calls her. But then my dream takes a turn for the worse, because I see her married to someone else. I say to myself, 'Well, I understand, she was right to do it; it's better for her not to spend her life waiting for me to come home.' "

Civil patrollers burning army-made "guerrilla" flag at patrol rally, Nebaj, Quiché.

Although national symbols mean nothing to many Guatemalans, the national flag was of paramount symbolic importance during counterinsurgency campaigns. Peasants were required to buy, hoist, and carry the blue-and-white flag as demonstration of patriotic allegiance and submission, or burn guerrilla flags, as a rejection of subversion. This was particularly true for civil patrol units (PAC), to whom a plastic swatch of patriotism literally meant the difference between life and death. "When the army comes . . . if we aren't carrying the flag, they think we are subversives," a patroller said. Public ceremonies, such as this, were community rites of guerrilla exorcism; the army provided "guerrilla" flags to PAC members to be "spontaneously" burned by the rank and file.

According to church sources in rural areas peasants were required to post flags over their homes and municipal buildings as a symbol of repentance and rejection of communism. Plastic flags can be bought by the yard in any general dry goods store.

Chapter 4

Mejía Víctores

The August 8, 1983 military coup against President Ríos Montt came as no surprise. Rumors were so widespread that for days Guatemalans planned not to send their children to school the following Monday. A newspaper publisher found out about the coup two weeks before, when he had lunch with Ambassador Chapin.

Fifty-two-year-old defense minister, Brigadier General Oscar Humberto Mejía Víctores, had met with military officials aboard the U.S. aircraft carrier Ranger the day before the coup; two days before, Guatemala's military commanders had met at the Honor Guard barracks in Guatemala City, where they decided to oust Ríos Montt after months of mounting tension.

This time there were no promises of reform, and by now, no one expected them. The only difference between Mejía's rhetoric and that of his predecessors was the vague reference to presidential primaries the following year, and the abolition of the Special Tribunals and the state of emergency—concessions to a U.S. government that found secret courts and the absence of civil liberties increasingly hard to explain in a country "on its way to democracy." This also signified the end of official press censorship; now journalists could return to the ambiguities of self-censorship and double entendres. Although the Special Tribunals were suspended in 1983, remaining prisoners were not officially pardoned until almost one year later, in July 1984, and only one hundred of the alleged two hundred to four hundred prisoners were ever accounted for.

The Mejía government had three objectives: first, to keep Mejía in office by whatever means possible until 1985, since a third coup in as many years would send a clear signal that Guatemala was not on its way to political stability; second, to sweep up and eradicate what remnants of subversion still existed after four years of scorched earth, and to fortify the rural counterinsurgency program; and third, to garner international aid through a promised return to civilian rule.

During the Mejía Víctores regime, election talk was dulled by ongoing violence. The State Department initially praised the Mejía government, stating that "there was a dramatic decline in reports of violence and political deaths in the countryside, in sharp contrast to 1982 . . ."[1]

1. U.S. Department of State, *Country Reports on Human Rights Practices in 1983* (Washington, D.C., February 1984), p. 578.

(One year before, killings had been "really down," according to State Department officer, Dale Shaffer.)

While rural massacres did decline under Mejía, selective "disappearances" and killings soared. Four days after the coup, on August 12, 1983, agronomist Jorge Rosal Paz was abducted near the Monument to the Soldier, outside Teculután; although Rosal himself never reappeared, in December 1983 a G-2 army agent gave his wife Rosal's photo, torn from his identification card.

In October 1983 three bilingual teachers working for firms funded by the U.S. Agency for International Development (AID) "disappeared" on two separate days. Two bodies were later found, along with the daughter of one of the victims, next to a burned automobile. The Guatemalan government called it "a car accident." The third AID linguist, who had been dragged from his home by seven armed men, never reappeared. Newspapers carried constant news of rural abductions and killings. On September 29, 1983, *El Gráfico* reported that "more than twenty-five people were abducted from their homes by armed men" in Chiquirines Viejo, Ocós, San Marcos.

During 1983 and into 1984, the rate of mass urban "disappearances" and killings rose again. On September 3, 1983 the afternoon daily, *El Imparcial* reported the discovery of thirty-four bodies in one week, most of them tortured; two days later, the number rose to fifty. "The faces of the victims were disfigured to prevent identification," *Prensa Libre* stated. On October 3 another daily, *La Hora*, reported seventeen deaths in twenty-four hours, only two caused by accidents. On November 7, 1983, Franciscan priest Father Augusto Rafael Ramírez Monasterio, was shot and killed in Guatemala City; shortly before, three Christian Democrat leaders from El Semillero, Escuintla were assassinated. In late September 1983, in a series of urban sweeps dubbed "Operation Octopus," fifteen hundred police agents arrested over six thousand people on charges of alleged prostitution and lack of identification. In a second sweep, four thousand agents arrested five thousand people in eighteen hours.

In December 1983 Amnesty International reported the secret detention of more than twenty-six people inside Guatemala City's General Barracks and the old Politécnica Military Academy. Although the military denied these allegations, one of the survivors confirmed them. In an open letter published in local newspapers, María Cruz López Rodríguez, a Special Tribunal prisoner, charged that she had been held in the Politécnica. She was one of the few "disappeared" who was released alive.

Under the government of General Mejía Víctores, large-scale rural counterinsurgency peaked. "Firmness 83" and "Institutional Renewal 84" meant continuing army sweeps, the growth of the civil patrol system, and the construction of "model villages"—an extension of temporary refugee camps. Thousands of refugees were still being brought down throughout the

2. *Guatemala: A Nation of Prisoners*, (New York: Americas Watch, 1984), p. 110.

3. Ibid., p. 111.

4. Chris Krueger and Kjell Enge, *Security and Development Conditions in the Guatemalan Highlands* (Washington, D.C.: Washington Office on Latin America, August 1985), p. 30.

5. *Civil Patrols in Guatemala* (New York: Americas Watch, August 1986), pp. 26–27.

6. Michael McClintock, *The American Connection: Volume Two* (London: Zed Books, 1985), p. 256; originally cited in *The Observer*, London, December 4, 1983.

Mejía government; the more fortunate were able to salvage a rooster, or a sewing machine—the only remnants of a former life. Most refugees continued to be women and children—in one such sweep twenty-four of the twenty-eight people captured were children.[2] As under Ríos Montt, violence actually rose in some areas. Between August and November 1983, there were four documented massacres in the municipality of Rabinal, Baja Verapaz; the survivors were brought down to the Rabinal garrison by army troops, accompanied by civil patrol units. One young girl who was brought down spent one month in the Rabinal barracks, where she was raped over twenty times each night except for two when soldiers were too drunk, before being released by the local commander, who gave her a bag of corn and told her to "start a new life."[3]

Work began on model villages, clusters of crude settlements built under army supervision. Construction was labor intensive, drawing on a large pool of available refugee manpower, although, in most cases, that "manpower" meant widows and children tall enough to use a hoe. Most model village construction was carried out between mid-1983 and late 1984. In the Ixil triangle, in northern Quiché, where there were 60,000 displaced persons out of a total population of 82,000 inhabitants, nine model villages were built to replace 49 destroyed communities.[4] The first model village, Acul, was inaugurated in December 1983; one typical village had rustic playgrounds next to army garrisons, and a street named for the Taiwan Embassy, as thanks for introducing Chinese cabbage among the cornstalks.

The civil patrol system continued to grow until it included one million men by late 1983; fewer than ten percent were armed. In San Antonio Palopó, Sololá, the army ordered the PAC to arm itself with slingshots. Throughout the Mejía Víctores government, massive swearings-in took place, sometimes as many as ten thousand patrollers in a single day.[5] Their numbers became so great that a local newspaper featured a cartoon of a camouflaged soldier commenting, "With so many patrollers we can go on vacation."

The PAC system also created a means of carrying out repression without direct army involvement. In late 1983 reports of PAC killings began to surface in Chijtinimit, Chichicastenango, where fourteen patrollers were killed by fellow members for failing to arrive on time for duty, and in Sacpulup, Quiché, where patrollers killed twenty-eight peasants, including an eight-year-old girl. In November 1983 the Christian Democrat party charged that the PAC had "carried out systematic assassinations of the party's leaders . . ."[6]

In addition to direct containment of the population, the army consolidated its future power in rural areas through the Inter-Institutional Coordinating System (IICS), set up between October 1983 and December 1984, which gave each departmental military zone total jurisdiction over rural development projects of both governmental and outside organizations, and, more importantly, through the creation of the S-5, the department for army civilian affairs, and the expansion of the S-2 rural army intelligence network. (The army, on a national level, is

Civil patrol outpost, Panajxit, Quiché.

Civil Patrol Anthem

I am a victorious soldier
Of the Civil Defense
Always side by side like a brother
With the brave army.

For my country Guatemala
My blue and white flag
For my home, my ideals
I shall fight with fierceness. . . .

I swear to my country
To defend it to the death
To reject the subversives
And to help my neighbors.

At daybreak
With my hand I'll till
But my gun always ready
To fight for Guatemala.

**Civil patrol at army rally,
Nebaj, Quiché.**

Ten thousand men from Nebaj, Cotzal, and Chajul were ordered to attend this civil patrol rally. Those in the vanguard carried Winchester rifles and hand grenades, distributed just before the rally and collected again as soon as it ended. Most men carried only their machetes. While the patrollers shouted on command and flung themselves forward for the benefit of local military and visiting gringos, imaginary rifles in hand, a young soldier sitting at the back of the plaza talked with a journalist about the difficulty in quashing subversion. "There are so many of them," he explained, referring to the guerrillas. "They're more popular than we are."

divided into five sections: G-1: Personnel and Administration; G-2: Intelligence; G-3: Operations; G-4: Logistics; G-5: Civilian Affairs. S-1 through S-5 are their rural counterparts.) The strengthening of the rural G-2 counterpart, the S-2, proved pivotal in assuring continuation of army control under civilian government. While the new civilian government would be able legitimately to state that the army-controlled coordinators were now under civilian jurisdiction, and that in some places, the civil patrols had been abolished, these "diminutions" of army control would prove irrelevant so long as an S-2 army intelligence system existed in the highlands.

Throughout 1983 and 1984, guerrilla strength declined. All four groups had lost key leadership in government raids on urban safehouses. In addition, tens of thousands of collaborators had been killed, flushed out of the mountains, fled into exile, or withdrawn from guerrilla ranks. By late 1983, according to U.S. Embassy figures, there were some fifteen hundred armed guerrillas in Guatemala, a 75 percent drop from three years before. Despite this decline, "eliminating subversion," continued to be the rationale for justifying army repression, according to the U.S. government. In early January 1984, Elliott Abrams stated that "the price of stability in the middle of a guerrilla war is high, but I don't think you blame that on the government."[7]

Although guerrilla strength diminished, it continued to carry out military actions. In late 1983, a Western diplomat estimated that the army lost one officer per week.[8] A political analyst said that since 1977, two of the Politécnica Military Academy's graduating classes were so hard hit that out of fifty cadets, only three or four were still alive.[9]

On February 28, 1984 Ambassador Chapin, who by mid-1983 had said that he was "psychologically tired" of dealing with Ríos Montt ("you tell him to do one thing and he goes 180 degrees in the opposite direction") was recalled from Guatemala. Even Ambassador Chapin, who had "want[ed] to help Guatemala," abandoned his theme of Guatemala seeing the light and stated at a farewell dinner that he "would not speak of the violations to human rights because it is a reality that we all know . . ."[10]

This "reality" continued into 1984; even the State Department concluded that "disappearances" had risen. The U.S. Embassy estimated that 42 people were abducted each month. The OAS Inter-American Commission for Human Rights (IAHCR) reported that between August 8, 1983 and April 30, 1984 there had been 634 "disappearances"—almost 80 per month. The British Parliamentary Human Rights Group stated that in 1984, there was an average of 100 political assassinations and more than 40 "disappearances" per month.[11]

A "Peace Commission" formed in February 1984 was disbanded three months later when two key members, the USAC Rector and the Archbishop, resigned, announcing that the democratization process was "a mockery of the people." Six months earlier, USAC Rector Dr. Eduardo Meyer Maldonado had received a visit from army officials at his office, advising him to

7. "MacNeil-Lehrer Report," January 10, 1984.
8. Author interview, Guatemala City, October 1984.
9. Author interview, Guatemala City, April 1987.
10. *Central America Report*, Vol. XI, No. 12, March 23, 1984, p. 91.
11. "Bitter and Cruel . . .: Report of a Mission to Guatemala" (London: Parliamentary Human Rights Group, 1985), p. 1.

12. Elliott Abrams, U.S. Assistant Secretary of State for Human Rights, at hearing before the House Foreign Affairs Committee, Washington, D.C., May 16, 1984.

13. *Central America Report*, Vol. XI, No. 8, February 24, 1984, p. 61.

14. *Central America Report*, Vol. XI, No. 8, February 24, 1984, p. 61.

"quit meddling in politics"—the suggestion later was reiterated by an anonymous death note pasted in block letters and sent to his office. In mid-May 1984, Elliott Abrams told the House Foreign Affairs Committee that "the Mejía government has somewhat, I would say, to my surprise, continued a large number of [human rights] improvements that Ríos Montt began . . ."[12]

In February 1984 Under-Secretary for Press Relations Ramón Zelada Carrillo attributed the violence to barometric factors, saying that "the increase in violence being reported is directly related to the heat wave striking the country," adding that in March [1984] "most probably the violence will increase as the hot weather becomes more intense."[13] Head of State Mejía Víctores was more philosophical, saying that violence originated with "the problem . . . that nobody is content with anybody, and in Guatemala, where there are seven million inhabitants, it is a normal problem."[14] The "problem," however, was not always confined to Guatemala. On April 30, 1984 the Guatemalan army raided the "El Chupadero" refugee camp in Chiapas, Mexico, killing six refugees, including an eleven-year-old child and a nine month pregnant woman and wounding as many others.

While the U.S. Embassy could not "establish the identity of the perpetrators," Alvaro René Sosa Ramos, a trade union leader, had no such problem. On March 13, 1984 Sosa escaped army *kaibiles* after he had been abducted and tortured for fifty-two hours in a secret jail. While in captivity, he recognized two fellow "disappeared" trade union leaders; one of them was later found dead and the other has never reappeared. Sosa himself escaped after bolting from his captors' vehicle and jumping over the wall of the Belgian Embassy; he survived, despite a bullet wound in the leg, and was given political asylum in Canada.

On July 1, 1984 Guatemala held elections for a National Constituent Assembly (ANC), which was charged with writing a new Constitution, the fourth in five decades, and propelling Guatemala toward a presidential election date. The eighty-eight ANC deputy seats were almost evenly distributed among the four main political parties: the moderate Christian Democrats (DCG); the center-right Union of the National Center (UCN); the center-right Revolutionary Party (PR); and the right-wing National Liberation Movement (MLN). The winner, however, was the number of spoiled and unmarked ballots—17.3 percent of the total vote. After months of coup rumors—and at least six coup attempts—elections were set for late 1985. "They decided to set the election date," one U.S. Embassy official noted, "because people were getting pretty nervous."

The only human rights advance in Guatemala during this decade was the June 5, 1984 formation of the Mutual Support Group (GAM) for the families of the "disappeared," which was organized by a group of Guatemala City housewives following a series of abductions of labor and university professionals in early 1984. Although human rights commissions had existed in the past, they had been comprised of university intellectuals and well-known professionals

Civil patrollers marching into Nebaj from Cotzal and Chajul, Quiché.

Colonel Pablo Méndez, then second-in-command of the Quiché military zone, ordered our helicopter to circle over the lines of men below, who were marching into Nebaj under the watchful eyes of camouflaged soldiers. As the helicopter remained motionless over the men, Colonel Méndez held a bullhorn out the door and ordered the peasants to shout and wave. Indians do not traditionally yell, but on this day they dutifully waved the banners they had been given, which most of them couldn't read, denouncing subversion and the EGP. As the helicopter created a shadow over the men below, Colonel Méndez turned around and said, "See that river? That's where the local women bathe. They have great bodies; they don't wear bras."

who, despite their stature, were not immune from repression themselves; earlier commission leaders were assassinated and the commissions themselves were dissolved.

Twenty-five people attended the GAM's first meeting. All of them were urban residents; most of them had met while making the rounds of Guatemala City hospitals and morgues. In its early days, GAM leaders believed that by not blaming the government, they might obtain results—although every member believed that government forces were responsible. GAM ranks grew quickly—within a few months, there were over 200 members. Four-fifths were impoverished highland Indians who had learned of the GAM's existence over the radio.

On October 12, 1984, the GAM held an eighteen-mile march into downtown Guatemala City, the first of its kind since 1980. GAM leaders subsequently met with General Mejía four times in late 1984; Mejía told them, "I'm not going to say that the government doesn't [kill]; neither am I going to say . . . that it is common delinquency," and in November 1984 he announced the creation of a governmental "Tri-Partite Commission" to investigate "disappearances." GAM leaders were not satisfied ("If we wanted to know what the Commission was doing, we had to read about it in the papers") and shortly afterwards they publicly accused government security forces of having carried out their relatives' abductions.

GAM members peacefully occupied the Congress. Acting President of Congress Roberto Carpio Nicolle told them that "if we were the government there would be no more 'disappeared' people. . . . We are the voice of the people but it's something else again for [that] voice to be heard."[15] The GAM responded, "You can't write a Constitution thinking just of the future, asking people to forget the past. Don't try to suggest collective amnesia."

15. *El Gráfico*, November 15, 1984.

One positive development was that by late 1984 the GAM was attracting international attention. Had it not been for the GAM, in fact, Guatemala's ongoing human rights abuses would not have received much attention in the international press. The existence of the GAM meant that a long-awaited story on Guatemala finally had the necessary dramatic "peg" to get it into the papers back home. For visiting foreign legislators, the GAM meant a relief from the usual round of rote interviews with government officials well-versed in meaningless rhetoric. GAM's testimony also provided a pivotal counterpoint to assurances from the U.S. Embassy and State Department, anxious to prove to colleagues that Guatemala was on the road to democracy, in spite of its own figures for 1984.

The GAM's growing importance drew a predictable reaction from the Mejía Víctores government; as the GAM's denunciations against the government mounted, so did the government's response, from public declarations to private threats. An editor at *El Gráfico* who had accepted the GAM's paid announcements pleaded with them to stay away from his office— he was receiving death threats at home.

In late 1984 the *Miami Herald* published an article titled "U.S. Says Tourist Spots in Guatemala are Safe to Visit," announcing that the U.S. Embassy in Guatemala had "toned

Civil patroller, Nebaj, Quiché.

Throughout the counterinsurgency campaign, a small booklet titled, "Why I Am Against Communism" was distributed in Guatemala City as well as in the rural highlands. "Why I Am Against Communism" interspersed statistics on worldwide communist population figures with quotes from Pat Boone ("I have four darling daughters and I would rather see them blown to bits by atom bombs than blown to hell from communist teachings") and former YMCA director, George Fitch, who wrote about the inflexibility of Chinese communists.

Civil patrol rally, Nebaj, Quiché.

In its *Country Report* the U.S. State Department said that "in areas where service is required, exemptions [from patrol duty] may be obtained for medical reasons."

On February 20, 1986 twelve civil patrollers from a village near Santa Cruz del Quiché sent a telegram to President Cerezo requesting dismissal from patrol duty "for reasons of health and economy of time." Cerezo never received the telegram. The twelve patrollers were sent a response from the Quiché military base: "Take note: present yourselves to the civilian affairs [S-5] office of this military zone." The patrollers, who were afraid to go to the military zone, sent a note instead to the departmental governor. It never arrived. Instead, they received a second order from the army S-5 office. The commander reprimanded them for having refused to patrol, even though most of the men were elderly and, officially, exempt from duty. One patroller said he had tuberculosis; the officer in charge told him to be examined by the army's own doctor. The patroller was exempted from duty for two months. The eleven other men were ordered to resume patrolling.

16. *The Miami Herald*, September
    14, 1984.
17. "Bitter and Cruel . . . ," p. 10.

down" its travel advisory and that security had "improved considerably."[16] An enlargement of the article hung between the INGUAT desk and the immigration counter at the Aurora airport in Guatemala City. While U.S. travel advisories were being modified, however, other local news did not support the Embassy's renewed optimism. In an August 12, 1984 press statement, the Association of of University Students (AEU) denounced the "disappearance" and killing of sixty-four students that year.[17] On October 29, 1984 Guatemalan dailies reported six deaths in seventy-two hours: economics professor Carlos de León Gudiel; USAC economics dean Vitalino Girón Corado, machine-gunned at a gas station while en route to de León's funeral; and MLN congressman and Quiché personage Santos Hernández, shot in Guatemala City together with his two bodyguards.

One year before Guatemala's own presidential elections, local businessmen were more concerned with the outcome of the 1984 U.S. presidential elections than the future winner of their own. Movie screens were placed in luxury-class hotels so that foreigners—mostly Embassy political section chiefs and members of Republicans Abroad—could monitor the campaign. On election night, the Los Lagos salon of the Camino Real Hotel was expropriated by the Republican Club. An informal poll was taken; Reagan won hands down with 250 votes to Mondale's eighteen. Later, when official polls showed Reagan with a sweeping lead, Ambassador Martínez Piedra performed a jig for local television cameras. At the door, bilingual volunteers in straw hats distributed four-inch buttons: an outlined map of the Western Hemisphere, encircled by the slogan, "Two Hundred Years of Freedom is at Stake: Only Reagan–Bush Will Keep the Americas Safe."

Civil Patrols

Comments made on the civil patrol system (PAC):

Senior Military Officer, U.S. Embassy, Guatemala City: "Whether the PAC was created by accident or intentionally, it's a brilliant idea in the end. The army was very close to a major surprise [when the PAC was formed]. [The army] can't win without it; it's got to be there. If you're going to take an army that small—forty thousand men—and try to spread them out, then, for God sakes, you've got to have something else. With civilian leadership and elections, the PAC may become 'voluntary' and be reduced from 900,000 to 300,000 men—then everybody wins. It came right out of the Little Red Book; you have to separate the guerrillas from the civilian population. Civilians understand power."

Frederic Chapin, Former U.S. Ambassador to Guatemala: "[The PAC is like] the American frontier, with armed citizens defending themselves."

Men lined up for civil patrol assignment, Nebaj, Quiché.

"Years ago, men would go out with sticks and make sure that there were no drunks on the streets, and that no one was annoying people, but they were very quiet. At most, they would tell drunks, '*Hermano*, what are you doing here? Go home.' The sticks were to use only if one of the drunks got aggressive. Then they would say, 'I'm going to hit you if you don't get out of here on your own.' In 1976 they still had the *rondas* (patrols): four people in four groups and each one patrolled his part of town. In 1977 the *ronda* was banned because the army didn't trust anyone anymore."

—Guatemalan anthropologist, Guatemala City, August 1984

Patroller from Patzún: "This is what hell must be like."

Lynn Schiveley, Former Human Rights Officer, U.S. Embassy: "The patrollers like being out in the countryside, in the fresh air. It's a good life."

Guatemalan Nun: "To talk about the patrols is to talk about a new way of repressing the people."

Patroller from the Quiché: "The army would rape the women. . . . So the people . . . signed a statement to get rid of the garrison, but the army said, 'If you don't want a garrison, why don't you form a patrol?' We saw the choice: either choose to have your daughter raped, or choose the civil patrol."

Lord Colville, Former United Nations Special Rapporteur to Guatemala: "Where recruitment was needed and a man was reluctant, he was more likely to be shamed into joining by his community than compelled."

Archbishop Próspero Penados del Barrio: "The PAC is an obligatory, unremunerated system . . . which forces men to spy on their brothers."

U.S. State Department Country Reports: "Forced labor is not practiced."

U.S. Priest in El Petén: "In our region it's like a slave source. Our roads are falling apart and there is no one to fix it, so the civil patrol does it. . . . It's like Egypt and the Pharaoh . . ."

President Vinicio Cerezo: "Less than one-third of the civil patrollers serve voluntarily."

Patroller from Chimaltenango: "Five percent of the men actively support the PAC, twenty percent tolerate it, and the other seventy-five percent wish it would disappear."

U.S. State Department *Country Reports*: "It is . . . true that some villages that have organized local civil defense forces have been objects of guerrilla retaliation."

Religious worker from Sololá: "The army came and told the Indian patrollers that for every gun lost, a man would die."

U.S. State Department *Country Reports*: "Heads of the civil defense patrols in conflict zones express little doubt about the important role the patrols played in protecting their villages from attack."

Patroller from Sololá: "If the guerrillas come, I'm going to run under my bed and hide."

Patroller from Quiché: "Here nobody wants to patrol. So we're all in agreement; we all go out to our posts five minutes before the army comes through on their patrol of our patrol. When

Refugees being brought into town on trucks following army sweeps into mountainsides, Nebaj, Quiché.

Guatemala's displaced population began in mid-1981, in the departments of Chimaltenango and Alta Verapaz. Four years later Vinicio Cerezo explained: "There are one million displaced [people], but if one wanted to find them and locate them to kill them, they would find them and kill them, because the system of control and vigilance, and the army's information has become very widespread. So a lot of people would be found and assassinated, if one wanted to [do so]."

Army occupation of Río Azul model village, Nebaj, Quiché.

In September 1983 the National Reconstruction Committee (CRN) director, Army Colonel Eduardo Wohlers Rivas stated that four million *quetzales* were being spent on 250,000 internally displaced persons—about four dollars per person. According to Wohlers, the "Food-for-Work" program had three phases: "Beans and Bullets" (*Frijoles y Fusiles*), or survival; "Roof, Food, and Work," (*Techo, Tortilla y Trabajo*), or "return to one's place of origin"; and "Peace and Harmony," (*Paz y Tranquilidad*) or development. The Food-for-Work program was not formally obligatory but the point was gratuitous, since all its participants were starving refugees with no home, no food, and no options for survival. Given this situation, the army and the refugees both knew that anyone who did not participate would be viewed with suspicion by the local military garrison.

Interrogation of woman and child, suspected subversives, at army garrison, Chajul, Quiché.

The soldiers Haroldo López, Luis Antonio López, Alvaro Pérez, and Danilo Hernández Quiñones, described interrogation of captured Indians:

Q: "What methods do you use with subversives you capture?"

A: "Well, they're brought in and they give, little by little. We give them the hood with Gamezán (insecticide) and they let it all out, against their will. . . . It's effective. The hood makes your eyes burn, you feel asphyxiated. We put insecticide inside. It burns your nose, you can't take it, you feel almost dead. . . . We give them the hood and they let it all out, even against their will. They tell the truth in the middle of torture."

they leave, most of us go back to our house—one man stays on patrol—or else we all go off and listen to Radio Sandino. They play good music."

The Prayer

A civil patroller told a Guatemalan nun about an incident which occurred in southern Quiché two months after the 1983 coup:

"Around November 1983, a man I know very well came to see me. He was crying, he was very upset. He told me that the army had come to his village and presented five men from that same village to the people there. They were prisoners. The villagers knew the men, they were their neighbors. The army commander told the people that they were guerrillas, and the civil patrol must 'decide' what to do with them: they could kill them—that was their 'business'—or they could let them go free. The army said it would return to see what their decision had been.

"The civil patrol did not know what to do. 'How can we kill innocent people?' they anguished. They were very upset, they knew that their neighbors weren't guerrillas. And all this time, while they were deciding what to do, the five men were standing there, beside them, listening. Most of the patrollers were catechists and they decided to pray to God to tell them what to do. Everyone began to pray—the patrollers and the condemned men too. They came to a community decision to kill their neighbors, because, 'if we don't kill you, the army will come back and massacre the entire village, and then the women and children will die as well.' They already had experience with army killings.

"They told the prisoners that they were going to kill them not because they believed they were guerrillas, but simply to avoid a massacre. They asked the condemned men to forgive them for what they were about to do, and they asked God to forgive them too, for having to come to this terrible decision.

"Everyone in the village lined up and hugged the condemned men goodbye and they begged them for forgiveness. They asked the men to understand that they did it only for the good of the village, and that it was better for five to die than for the entire community to be massacred afterwards. One of the five, the next-door neighbor of the man who told me this, asked him to 'please take care of our widows and children, so they don't die from starvation, and please guard our crops and help our widows to harvest the corn.'

"The men shot the five. To their surprise, the army showed up moments after the killing; they had hidden nearby to see what the people would do. That day, there were five new widows and eighteen fatherless children in that community."

Cantel

Cantel is a Quiché Indian community of some thirty thousand people located in northwestern highlands, near the city of Quezaltenango. Cantel is best known for its textile factory, which used to be the largest in Central America. Its people are also known for their independent spirit; at no time was this better demonstrated than under Ríos Montt, when the army made three attempts to organize a civil patrol there.

The man who told this story was born in Cantel. He is a community organizer. The story is important not only for its content and detail, but also because it offers hope in what is usually a tragic landscape:

"I found out that the civil patrol was going to organize four days beforehand. I said, 'Look, go tell the people to say no.' As a result, we had forty thousand people in the square. The army had told the town crier to announce that all males between eighteen and sixty should show up on the colonel's orders. That was when the activity began. We prepared the exit by which people could get out in case something happened, and messengers who can run quickly—children in particular—to get the word out. We told people to simply say 'no,' not to say anything else that would compromise an individual or an organization in any way.

"The day itself was very interesting. The army asked the military commissioners to head up the preparations: loudspeakers, microphones, sound systems. They did this thinking they would distract the people who were arriving with music. But things didn't turn out this way, because we had already told the people not to go alone in small groups; we told everyone to wait until five minutes before the appointed hour. So there they were, waiting for the people with music to entertain them, but to their surprise, the first group of people to arrive included fifteen hundred men, and the second group had four hundred, and then another of eight hundred, and so it went. Men and women of all ages.

"The army was surprised to see so many people; they felt wonderful, until they heard a single shout of thousands of people saying, 'no.' The colonel said, 'So, you are in favor of the guerrillas' and the people responded, 'We are perfectly well organized to defend ourselves from the right *and* the left.' The colonel was furious with the military commissioner and the mayor.

"The first time there were so many people they didn't fit in the square; they were standing on church columns. It was a tremendous turnout. No one moved when the colonel started ordering individual villagers to present themselves. There were sixty soldiers that time, plus the press. When the colonel saw that everything was useless, he said, 'I am going to inform General Ríos Montt that you do not want the civil patrol.' And the people shouted back, 'Go tell him, and get out of here.' They said it in Spanish because the colonel didn't understand *lengua* [native tongue]. Before withdrawing, the colonel told the military commissioners to be at the

Guatemalan soldier and refugees at the New Life refugee camp near Nebaj, Quiché.

In Acul, near Nebaj, there is a "Taiwan Avenue" dedicated to the embassy that planted Chinese cabbage over razed homes, and delivered three-speed bicycles to refugees who had to solicit army permission in order to ride the bicycles out of the camp. In Tzalbal, near Acul, "Street of the Fallen" is perpendicular to "Avenue of Hope" and parallel to "National Army Avenue." Nearby is "Friendship Street." Outside the Acamal, Cobán model village, a sign says, "Terror! Crime! Deceit! Lies! How many days, hours, or minutes of terror would we suffer at the hands of subversives?"

Ixil refugee and children in the New Life refugee camp, partly financed by U.S. evangelical groups, near Nebaj, Quiché.

In October 1983 a Guatemalan refugee cited three products of violence in the Guatemalan highlands: children traumatized after witnessing their parents' deaths; unwanted pregnancies from rape by soldiers; and growing alcoholism among the survivors. The Spaniards introduced alcohol following the Conquest. In the 1800s, ladinos plied Indians with liquor, resulting in financial debt and forcing them to work on their fincas. Alcoholics Anonymous is ubiquitous: in Guatemala City alone there are at least 700 Alcoholics Anonymous (AA) chapters. In many slums there will be a cantina, an AA shingle, and no potable water.

army base the next day; when they showed up, he shouted and hit them and told them they were to blame for shaming the army this way. 'You screwed me over and humiliated me,' he told them. The military commissioners replied that they were not to blame.

"The second attempt went on for a month. The army went into Cantel: one hundred and fifty soldiers and twelve intelligence agents. At four in the afternoon, the soldiers would go into the streets and try to talk to the people, especially the children and women, but when we saw what was going on, we advised the people not to talk to them. The soldiers became angry and began to create a disturbance in the streets: they hit the drunks and raped the wife of the municipal policeman—seven men attacked her.

"Their other plan was to meet with people, but separately, so they met with the evangelicals, the Catholics, the union leaders, all of them separately. The intelligence branch of the army did this, but everyone defended himself. The evangelical pastors said that the Bible could not be interpreted in their terms; the unionists said that they weren't interested in Guatemala's social problems, just Cantel's. At those meetings, there were always obvious attempts by the army to organize the patrol. They would say, 'You aren't men, you don't defend your country against international communism.' They would also say that we were only good for having kids and nothing else. But we always had very specific responses to all that. 'Yes, our children give thirty months of service to the military,' we would say. 'Our sons are capable and we know all about guns.' We would also say, 'Our people have perfect organization: we have religious organizations, cooperatives, economic organization, and so on.' And with that, the second attempt—the thirty days—ended.

"Now, for the third attempt. The third time was more difficult for us, because there wasn't the same number of people. The army used the tactic of having meetings during harvest time, because they thought the less people who attended, the easier it would be. So this time the army didn't take 'technicians,' but preachers instead: people with a talent for speaking. They have a strong voice and they say a lot of words quickly. They began speaking of the experience in Cuba, in Chile, and in Russia, where 'communism enslaves people who have no right to anything, and where there is atheism and killings.' But the first preacher spoke for so long that everyone went home. When the second man came, he was worse than the first, and the people yelled, 'These guys are from the army!' 'We're not interested in how other countries live. Are we Cubans for you to be talking to us about Cuba?' 'Who has told you that we are communists, for you to be talking to us about communism?' The colonel replied, 'Well, we're talking to you about this because we want to see how to defend ourselves against bigger problems and the communists are going to kill you if you don't defend yourselves, if you don't organize.' Then, one young man got up and said, 'I know that the assassins here are the military. I was in the army under Lucas. . . . Lucas sent us out to kill peasants and to burn their houses.'

Widows on their way to work near the model village of Acul, Nebaj, Quiché.

Many women knew that their husbands were dead and that the army had killed them. Although the men were officially "disappeared," they treated the women as widows, a Guatemalan anthropologist explained: "Women were trying to plant, and this caused another kind of anguish among the families, because, traditionally, there is a very marked division of labor. The woman does all the housework: the weaving, sewing, and cooking, but all inside the house. The man's role was in the field: hunting, planting corn and beans, harvesting. Now, you would even find children trying to plant crops in order to keep the family alive—little boys, ten or twelve years old, who had to assume the role of a man."

Young child captured by army after being hit by aerial bombardment, Nebaj, Quiché.

Major Saúl Figueroa Veliz, officer in charge of the Army's S-5 Office for Civilian Affairs, in Cobán, Alta Verapaz, explained why captured refugees were given ideological talks by the army:

"People come down from the mountains out of necessity. It is definitely not ideology that brings them here . . . that is our obligation, to make them see the situation. . . . We make them see the difference between being with the authorities and being with [guerrillas] . . . Indians are very susceptible; they are easy to ply, just like clay. The enemy succeeded in finding that soft part of the Indians and the Indians began to believe them. But what happens? So much fighting in the mountains, so much suffering. The children get sick and die and there they are, in the mountains, going hungry and thirsty. Up there in the mountains, they don't even have salt, and the enemy leaves them because they have no means to subsist either."

Deputy Head-of-State Rodolfo Lobos Zamora and fellow officers at the *kaibil* training camp, La Pólvora, El Petén.

In 1977 Guatemala refused U.S. military aid before it was given or denied. As Head-of-State General Mejía Víctores explained six years later to a British television crew, "It was the United States who used to help all countries fight communism. But they abandoned us. They justified it with their big and famous theory of human rights which applies to small countries while big countries do what they like. We [Guatemala] were alone. [We won] without anyone's aid." Nine years later, on the evening before President Cerezo's inauguration, outgoing Head-of-State Mejía embraced his ideological adversary, Nicaraguan President Daniel Ortega, and said, "Keep screwing over the gringos."

Everyone present supported the young man, saying that this was true, that 'the assassins are you, the army.' There were about 150 soldiers present. When the colonel heard this, he looked like he was going to cry. He smelled of liquor and the people realized he was practically drunk. He said, 'Let's go,' to his men, and they retreated."

Ideological Talks

Major Saul Figueroa Veliz, the head of the S-2, army civilian affairs, in Cobán, Alta Verapaz, explained the reasons for ideological talks at the Tzacol refugee camp:

"People come down from the mountains out of necessity. It is definitely not ideology that brings them here . . . that is our obligation, to make them see the situation . . . We make them see the difference between being with the authorities and being with the guerrillas . . . Indians are very susceptible; they are easy to ply, just like clay."

The refugees' daily schedule was as follows:

wake-up at 5 A.M.

civic talk

continuation of talk

breakfast

ideological talk

civil defense

recreation

health lecture

prepare food

ideological talk

lunch

ideological talk

agriculture

recreation

group dynamics

recreation

patriotic symbols lecture

flag lowering

dinner

film

The Film

Refugee camps were little more than flat, muddy expanses abutting army garrisons, on which lean-to shelters were built. For those who had been forced out of the mountains by the army, or who had come down voluntarily, life in an army-controlled refugee camp had one basic advantage: food. To receive food, refugees had to work eight hours a day. Some camps required indoctrination as well. When a delegation from Americas Watch visited the Tzacol, Cobán, camp in November 1983, several dozen rifles were laid out in the schoolroom; children who were trooped in to sing for the visitors had to jump over the guns to get to their desks. Next to the schoolroom blackboard was a slap-dash poster with graphic photos of a dead guerrilla combatant, "Commander Camilo." The message was obvious, and it was reinforced when an attorney in the delegation, Robert Goldman, responded to an army officer's statement that all the camp's inhabitants had been subversives. Goldman pointed to a four-year-old girl dragging a doll and asked whether she too was a subversive. "Yes," the officer replied.

In August 1983 Army Sergeant Julio Corsantes, director of re-education at the Tzacol refugee camp, described his duties:

"The first group [of refugees] came here on June 6, 1983; the last group came on August 11, 1983. People cannot come and go freely here because in all this there is always an infiltrator, and it could be someone who leaves, who gets some information out of us, to the enemy. Here refugees are not under strict measures, but we have them in the camp, and there is only one way to get in, and they know that they are not going to leave here because, in the first place, they don't have money to go into town to buy anything—they came without anything.

"We have one example from last year, during Ríos Montt, when a group turned itself in near Panzós, in San José Tinajas. They were helped with food and medicine and we tried to help them ideologically and they demonstrated their total deliverance to the authorities, and so we gave them amnesty and turned them loose. We believed in them; they left, and we told them we would keep helping them in their communities. But when we went to look for them we found out that they had gone back to the guerrillas—they just came to get food and medicine and then they went back. This was late 1982. Now we don't turn them loose until we think they have totally changed their ideology.

"Our desire is to have one hundred percent success, but you can't because there are people who have been so brainwashed in the mountains—they themselves admit it to us. Those we have to work hardest on, I take them myself, and I talk to them, or we teach them through movies—how people work in the U.S., with freedom, without pressure, and then a movie from Russia, where you see soldiers. Then I ask them, 'Do you want to have to work like this?' 'No,' they say. 'Look at the difference,' I say to them. It's like rewinding a cassette, because this is a tape recording and you have to keep taping it over and over again. In the movie from Russia,

Army-appointed doctor checking internally displaced for worms, Nebaj, Quiché.

Although forty percent of all children die before the age of five, the American Chamber of Commerce had glowing words for the Colgate-Palmolive Guatemala branch: "GUATEMALA CITY, Oct. 12 (1981) (AmCham)—The 'Oral Hygiene' program of the Colgate Palmolive Company for the Guatemalan public school children is one of the best among the many and largely unpublicized, beneficial activities of the international and local companies, many of them members of the American Chamber of Commerce in Guatemala. . . .

"The Colgate 'Mouth Cleanliness and Teeth Care' program started in 1969. It has been carried out, on schedule, and without any interruption month after month. It eventually reaches every public school house in the country, however remote the place. . . . The dental teams go out in rainy season and dry—east, west, north and south. The trucks usually are jeep type, four-wheel drive for even the most difficult access roads. In the visits, each small child receives an attractive envelope. The colored posters and pamphlets say, 'Avoid sweet foods and drink and visit the dentist at least twice yearly.' Of course, in some places no dentist is available . . ."

—American Chamber of Commerce bulletin, No. 178, October 19, 1981, Guatemala City

Colonel Roberto Mata Gálvez, commander of Military Zone No. 20, Quiché, distributing candy to children during civic action counterinsurgency program, San Sebastián Lemoa, Quiché.

Colonel Roberto Mata Gálvez, ("Bobby" to U.S. Embassy political officers) was commander of the Quiché military zone from 1982 until 1985, and was subsequently director of the Politécnica Military Academy. Between 1982 and 1983, no other area of Guatemala suffered more from repression than the Quiché department. As military zone commander, it was difficult if not impossible for Colonel Mata not to have been completely aware of what was occurring even in the most remote garrisons, since he had daily, sometimes hourly radio contact with his field commanders. One of them, Lieutenant Romeo Sierra, who headed the La Perla garrison in the northern Ixcán commented, "We're on a very short leash."

Colonel Mata did not even have to step outside his own military headquarters in Santa Cruz del Quiché in order to assess army efficacy: in 1983 on the second floor of the building housing his office, some dozen prisoners were held at any given time in a room above his beans-and-bullets map, where they were interrogated and tortured repeatedly. This was described by two prisoners who survived: one was released after he was identified as the owner of the store that sold underwear to Mata's soldiers, and the second was a Christian Democrat activist, released through the intervention of Cerezo's Christian Democrat party.

In 1986, President Cerezo appointed Colonel Mata as his Presidential Chief of Staff.

181

you see soldiers in the fields, where they are hitting the people, and the leaders, the 'premiers,' are in their big cars, where they are doling out food, rationing it. And then I say to them, 'Look at the United States: he who works, eats.' In the U.S. movie you see freedom and tractors and people working freely; you see them relaxing. We get these movies through institutions: one movie from Russia, where Fidel Castro is talking, and then we get another movie where they are looking at a country that is not under socialism. 'Look,' we say, 'no pressure.' My slogan is not to badmouth them. We sit down here and we talk to them. When they say that soldiers just kill, I say, 'But here the soldiers are helping; they are working with us. You have to become good people, you really are good people; what happened was that you were deceived.'

"We have classes with the children from 8 A.M. until noon. The adults get up at 5 A.M.; at 6 A.M. we raise the flag and we have a civic talk; at 6:15 there is breakfast; from seven to eight we have an ideological talk. An ideological talk means talking to them about how they felt up in the mountains, how their life was up there, how they feel now, what changes there have been with us, if we treat them well or not, if they trust us. Then we have talks on the civil defense patrols, we say that they have to organize security groups themselves; if there are four houses, they have to defend themselves among the four houses. If someone suspicious comes, like those who deceived them, they have to denounce it immediately. Then we have directed recreation, and a health talk: how to use toilets, how to boil water. Then we have a snack and food preparation. Then we have ideological talks from 11 A.M. until noon, and lunch. Look, we have ideological talks about ten times a day, because that is our job. At night we have social events. Sometimes I play the marimba with them."

Lord Colville

In 1946 the United Nations created the Human Rights Commission; in 1967 the Commission passed resolution 1235, authorizing the Commission to undertake studies of countries where there had been consistent patterns of human rights violations. As a result, the position of Special Rapporteur was created and recommended for some half dozen countries, including Afghanistan, Chile, El Salvador, Guatemala, Iran, and Poland.[18] In large part, the guidelines which determine a Rapporteur's area of investigation in the appointed country are defined by the Rapporteur himself. In early 1983 the United Nations appointed Viscount Colville of Culross of Great Britain as Special Rapporteur to Guatemala, after its first nomination had been rejected by the Guatemalan government. He was charged with undertaking an in-depth study of Guatemala's human rights situation; in 1985, the Human Rights Commission extended the mandate and called for Colville to "assess in particular allegations of politically motivated killings, disappearances, extrajudicial executions, and confinements in clandestine prisons."

18. "Colville for the Defense: A Critique of the Reports of the U.N. Special Rapporteur for Guatemala" (New York: Americas Watch, February 1986), p. 3.

19. Ibid.
20. *La Hora*, August 30, 1986.
21. David Asman, "Guatemala in Clearer Focus," *The Wall Street Journal*, April 30, 1984.
22. United Nations, Introduction of the "Report on the Situation of Human Rights in Guatemala," A/38/485 by the Special Rapporteur, Viscount Colville of Culross, at the United Nations, November 30, 1983.
23. Author interview, Guatemala City, May 1985.

According to Americas Watch, "Lord Colville not only deviated from this mandate, he unilaterally redefined it."[19] Lord Colville chose to investigate only accusations that directly blamed the government; "groups of armed men"—by far the most frequent description given by relatives of the "disappeared" for abductors—were not investigated. Lord Colville's decision to ignore one of the most basic facts surrounding "disappearances" in Guatemala—the fact that "heavily armed men" is almost always a password for army or paramilitary forces—did not reflect any naïveté·but, instead, Colville's own political agenda for Guatemala: to aid the Guatemalan military in convincing the outside world that Guatemala deserved aid. Colville himself was blunt regarding his preconceived pronouncements. In November 1983, while at lunch with several lawyers, he said he had a "plan" for Guatemala. When the lawyers asked him what it was he said, "I shan't tell you." Three years later, Colville told the Guatemalan press that his "plan" had been to "support the democratic opening that the army began."[20] Colville had been even more specific two years earlier, when he told the *Wall Street Journal* that "unless you're in favor of a communist victory how do you persuade a military government to give up its power and go back to the barracks? You don't do that by writing a 100-page report of pure condemnation."[21]

The Mejía Víctores government did not have to fear that Colville would produce such a report. His was the only human rights reporting undertaken during this period that received praise from the Guatemalan government.

Between 1983 and 1986 Colville made at least eight trips to Guatemala, even after his mandate as Special Rapporteur ended. Nowhere was Colville's jaundiced reporting more evident than in his trips to Guatemala's model villages, which he toured on his first, second, and subsequent trips. He called the Acamal and Saraxoch model villages "transit centers" and the refugees' daily presence at flag-raising and lowering ceremonies "their own idea," and reported that informants had spoken to him with "incredible candor." What was most incredible was Colville's description of the model villages. In November 1983 he reported his findings on Acul, which had been burned three times by the Guatemalan army between 1982 and 1983: "The people working there with such enthusiasm to build the new community included the same group of Ixil people . . . I had met, wretched and hopeless last June."[22]

According to one of the architects of the model village plan, however, Lord Colville's descriptions did not reflect reality: "We really pulled one over on Colville. He said that he wanted to see Pulay [a village burned down by the army and reconstructed as a model village]—he had been told about 'scorched earth.' But we had already cleaned up Pulay. So, he came in a helicopter to Pulay, and he got off and asked the people what had happened. And those people really know how to lie. They were really great for answering questions; they said that nothing had happened."[23]

183

Widows building homes in San Felipe Chenlá model village, Quiché.

Although President Cerezo has stated that model villages are now under civilian control, many systems have not been demilitarized. The only substantive change has been the amount of foreign aid the development poles now receive.

In April 1986, the government daily, *Diario de Centro América* reported the delivery of seventy bicycles to the Chacaj, Huehuetenango development pole, by the Embassy of Taiwan, "so that Chacaj's inhabitants can enjoy a cheap and easy mode of transportation." The bicycles, however, were not a donation: the Taiwanese government sold them to Chacaj's inhabitants on a five-year low-interest repayment plan. Taiwanese embassy officials explained the reasons for the aid: "This idea relies upon the [assumption] that Indians are capable of responding to gestures of international assistance . . . [the Indians] need an opportunity and sufficient support to be able to continue, on their own, on the path toward civilization."

184

Model village, Acul, near Nebaj, Quiché.

"The Government of Guatemala continued its model village rural resettlement program, a joint civilian/military effort to reconstruct and settle 49 villages on or near their original sites. Each town has a potable water supply and electricity, at least one school, a church, postal and telegraph service, private bus service, and a health clinic. Some of the model villages have a military detachment nearby to provide security."

—"Economic, Social and Cultural Situation," *Country Reports on Human Rights Practices for 1985* Department of State, February 1986

Colville's lack of enthusiasm for thorough inquiry also extended to the GAM, the only human rights presence inside Guatemala throughout his entire mandate. GAM leaders, who eventually called for Colville to be *persona non grata* in Guatemala, recalled their attempts to meet with him in early 1985: "Clicking his fingers, he said, 'Get to the point because I'm in a hurry.' . . . 'How do you want me to listen to so many people?' We told him it would take three hours. With a sarcastic smile he said, 'Me? Three hours with you? Impossible. I am very limited I can only give you one hour.' "

Archbishop Penados had his own interpretation of his visit with the Special Rapporteur: "What did he expect me to tell him when he had the number two in the G-2 standing behind him the entire time?"

The Wife

Nineth de García has spent the past four years seeking information on her husband's whereabouts. Fernando García was a union leader at the CAVISA glass factory. "I was always scared about my husband's union activities," García said. "You worry that something might happen, but when you see your husband come home, when you hear the tires squeak in the driveway, you feel so relieved that he has returned, and you think, 'how wonderful, how beautiful.' "

Fernando García was abducted by the BROE (*Brigada de Operaciones Especiales*, the National Police Special Operations Brigade) on February 18, 1984, at 10 A.M. in front of an open market near their home in Guatemala City. There were hundreds of witnesses, Saturday shoppers, who saw García grabbed, shot, beaten, and dragged away in a van. The day after García's kidnapping, BROE agents returned to the García home:

"At three A.M., the day after they took Fernando, ten armed men came to my house in cars with polarized windows. Five stayed on the roof and five were downstairs. They whistled just like my husband; at first, I thought he had been released. They told me, 'We just wounded your husband in the leg; you'll get him back in a few days.' They sat on my chairs, they ate here, they never identified themselves. I even accompanied them to the gate when they finally left. There I was in the street, with my daughter holding on to me.

"When I began to denounce this, government officials said to me, 'But maybe your husband went off with the guerrillas, or another woman.' When I would go to the police, they would say that maybe the army did it, and when I went to the army, they would say, maybe it was the police."

Several weeks after García's abduction, Nineth received a telegram signed by the G-2, summoning her to an obscure, fourth-floor office in the National Palace. A hooded man surrounded by plainclothesmen carrying machine guns interrogated her and told García that if her husband was not a communist, "then we don't have him." Three weeks later, a televised army press conference displayed Fernando García's books among arms and bombs allegedly gathered in a raid on a guerrilla safehouse.

In July 1985, Nineth wrote an open letter to her husband:

"I have many letters to you, and I hope that, someday, we can read them together, and toast each other the way we did that last night. Do you remember—when, amidst laughter and jokes and happiness we toasted life and thanked it for having brought us together. . . ."[24]

24. *Prensa Libre*, July 18, 1985.

The Father

Irma Marilú Hicho Ramos, a twenty-three-year-old economics student at the University of San Carlos and a leader in the Association of University Students (AEU), was one of the seven members of the AEU leadership abducted in early 1984. Hicho herself was kidnapped near the university, on her way to classes, May 21, 1984.

Before joining the Mutual Support Group (GAM) for the families of the "disappeared," her father, Herlindo Hicho, visited local morgues. Mr. Hicho said that he saw some one hundred bodies in one month, seventy-five percent of them bearing signs of torture:

"At first I would go to the morgue almost daily. If I couldn't go, my wife or my daughter would go in my place, or we would go to the identification office where they have a record of the people who come in unidentified, as 'XX'.

"The most startling thing was the kind of torture—you have to see it to say, 'So what they do to people is true.'

"The worst experience I ever had was one Saturday: I don't remember the date, but my wife had heard on the radio that in El Progreso they had found the body of a woman. I called the hospital there and they confirmed it. I asked for the person's characteristics and they matched my daughter's. I asked the nurse if the body had a gold crown, since my daughter has a gold crown on one of her upper teeth. The nurse told me she couldn't tell, because the body had a lot of dirt in its mouth. I had no choice but to go to El Progreso.

"When I got there, the nurse looked at me in such a strange way, and that made me nervous. It seemed as though she was trying to tell me that it was my daughter. I even asked, 'Is it her?' The nurse told me to calm down and she went to look for a tranquilizer for me. At that moment, the man with the keys to the morgue came and opened the door to a refrigerated room. And then I saw—it wasn't my daughter. The poor girl, though—she was very young and

Soldiers on weekend leave and sunbathers at beach in Panajachel, Sololá.

In April 1984 *This Week Central America* described an army search of foreign tourists at Panajachel's "Gringo Beach" in Sololá: "Guatemala's tourism promoters and hotel owners not only have to contend with a negative image abroad and an official U.S. travel advisory, but also with their own government, particularly the state Tourism Bureau. . . . Last week . . . Bureau chief Yolanda Ordóñez de Monzón sent 150 armed members of the feared Treasury Police to the resort of Panajachel on Lake Atitlán to arrest 'foreign delinquents.' The armed men, many of them in plainclothes, burst into hotels, ordering tourists to stay in their rooms while their belongings and documents were inspected. Other visitors were forced to stay on the beach or wherever they happened to be when the raid started. . . . Despite the universal condemnation of the police offensive in Panajachel, there is little danger Mrs. Monzón will lose her job. Her husband is a former military academy classmate of the chief of state."

**Soldier resting in barracks,
Playa Grande, Ixcán, Quiché.**

Conservative Guatemalans compare violence in their own country to violence in the United States to diminish the enormity of statistics, and their significance.

In 1981 the assistant director of the Guatemalan Tourist Institute, INGUAT, cushioned her advice to avoid the Quiché department, saying, "Well, you wouldn't think of walking down 42nd Street in New York City, would you? It's the same thing here."

United States citizens living in Guatemala were no different. In 1981 the coordinator of an AID bilingual education program criticized a cover piece on Guatemala in a major U.S. magazine. "I just can't believe that the Guatemalan army could be as cruel as this reporter describes," he complained. "I mean, everyone knows that whether it's here or in the U.S., the army can be kind of rough at times."

there were bullet wounds on her breasts and there was still dirt in her mouth. According to the judge, she had been raped as well. Thank God it wasn't Marilú."

The Letter

25. *Country Reports*, February 1985, p. 544.

In 1984 the State Department, in its annual report, stated that "while various cases of [the 'disappeared'] have been attributed to government forces of political extremists of the far left or far right, the bulk of "disappearances" are in fact never definitely linked to any faction."[25]

The following letter was written by a "disappeared" husband to his wife. It was smuggled out of an army secret prison by a sympathetic soldier:

June 21, 1984

*Although the real names appeared on the actual letter, they have been changed to protect the man's family and the soldier.

To Lidia del Cid:*

I am on the brink between life and death because they accuse me of being a guerrilla. Lidia, please don't cry. I am not the first or the last such case in this world; after awhile, you come to realize that anything can happen. I am very sad because I think only of death, and of you and my children, and the mother I will never hug again. A kiss for them all. Treat them well. Put David to work and take good care of María, as well as Marta, Juanita, and José Armandito. Give them all your love, because they will not have a father any longer. Only God's will can save me now.

In my savings account in the factory, I have 901.25 *quetzales*; take it out. I also owe Joaquín Méndez 126 *quetzales*. Use our savings and ask the union people to help you with all this.

I was able to write this thanks to a good friend. Please don't tell anyone about this letter so I can avoid problems for the person who did me the favor of giving me a good soldier to help me.

There are no more words from your husband who has loved you so much with all his heart and soul. Please face life like a real woman. Take care of my children. Leave behind your quarrelsome temperament and try to be loving instead.

You are not the first woman in the world to become a widow.

Goodbye forever.

Cristóbal Armando Barrientos Mendoza

The Press

Guatemala has four newspapers, dozens of radio stations, and five television news programs, including Channel Five, the government station. News varies little among competitors, except for nightly army news programs featuring a young woman in uniform who delivers army pronouncements in Tokyo Rose tones.

Radio news is usually more direct, since the announcer's tone often says more about the news than what is reported in the newspapers. "Most people tend to think of radio news as ephemeral," says Ramiro MacDonald Blanco, Jr., of the Guatemala Flash radio program, which broadcasts three times a day to over one million listeners. "Since nothing appears in printed form, it seems less dangerous." Radio is, in fact, so ubiquitous that batteries are price controlled by the government as "essential items," along with food.

The four daily newspapers have a combined circulation of from 100,000 to 120,000 readers. *Prensa Libre*, with a circulation of sixty thousand, is the largest; *El Gráfico* is owned by former presidential candidate, Jorge Carpio Nicolle. The only widely read newspaper is *Extra*, a weekly compilation of photos of cadavers and macabre discoveries. When there are no bodies, *Extra* prints stories of children born with two heads or the head of a frog.

A radio producer and an editorialist assess journalism in Guatemala:

Radio producer: "What is freedom of the press? Supposedly, it's the freedom I have to express myself, but here the government hides information from us. In Guatemala, there are two news phenomena: the army always wins—the losses are always 'on the other side'—and anyone against the army is always a delinquent, a subversive, or a criminal. Once I said to Colonel Nuila Hub [Army Chief of Staff under Mejía], 'Is there freedom of the press in a country where I can only give your version and not the guerrillas'?'

"Forty percent of the news is censored—there is self-censorship among ourselves and from our sources. We get news from friends in morgues, hospitals—they call us directly. They often use pseudonyms. I'll give you one small example of people's reluctance to speak. Recently, a woman came to me, trembling, begging me not to reveal her name. She explained to me that there had been some scholarship competition at her school, and the candidates were given a test, but afterwards, the scholarships were given out not on the basis of need, but through local leverage. She wanted to denounce this but she was very frightened. It wasn't even a political problem, but people panic."

Newspaper editor: "Here, with every goddamn headline you're risking your neck. If I had written an article two weeks ago denouncing the death squads I'd be dead. I can't put the guerrillas in a headline, it would mean closing down the newspaper.

"Every year I get this anonymous phone call from somebody who says, 'Merry Christmas, you bastard, enjoy it, because this is going to be your last.' I'm not saying the left or the right is going to get me, but somebody is going to get me. Of course, there is no middle here. You join the side you dislike the least, not the one you like the most—and that's not to say that it's 51–49. How can you tell if a journalist is 'objective' in Guatemala? If he's still alive."

Isabel Choxom and Nineth Montenegro de García, of the "GAM" (Grupo de Apoyo Mutuo), the Mutual Support Group for the families of the "disappeared," one week after the deaths of fellow GAM leaders Héctor Gómez Calito and Rosario Godoy de Cuevas, Guatemala City.

The GAM was formed in June 1984 by the wives and mothers of unionists and student leaders, after a wave of mass urban abductions earlier that year. The GAM's initial members were from Guatemala City—they had met each other during trips to city morgues and government offices, in search of news of their relatives. Nineth de García described her feelings after the abduction of her husband: "The day comes when they capture him—there are no words to explain it, it's so terrible. You feel that you have lost life itself. To be alone and helpless and with that uncertainty of what can be happening to the person you love so much—if you are eating, you wonder, 'Is my husband eating too?' If you are trying to fall asleep, you wonder, 'Can they be torturing him?' 'What can they be doing to him?' "

GAM leader Isabel Choxom continued to hope. In an open letter to her companion, Gustavo Castañón, she wrote: "Keep fighting! Fight to survive in that secret corner, and here we will continue fighting for your freedom, because they will never ever be able to make honorable men vanish into thin air, as if they were nothing."

Chapter 5

Presidential Elections

A middle-aged political analyst, married with four children, described chance street encounters with acquaintances whom he hadn't seen in years. "Instead of saying 'hi,' " he said, "they just remark, 'You're still alive?' "

By early 1985, when political campaigning should have created some general interest and a sense of optimism, many Guatemalans were too exhausted or skeptical to care; voting was hardly uppermost in people's minds. The survivors—those who weren't dead, "disappeared," in exile abroad, in refugee camps in Mexico, or in model villages—began tallying the effects of violence. In early 1985, based on earlier numbers from the Juvenile Division of the Guatemalan Supreme Court, officials estimated between 150,000 to 200,000 highland orphans; based on these figures, they concluded that between 45,000 to 60,000 parents had been killed in Guatemala since 1978.[1] Monsignor Juan Pablo Urízar, former Church administrator for the Quiché department, stated that 20,000 Indians had been killed in the Quiché alone in the 1980s.[2] Former Bishop Angélico Melotto of Sololá said that in his diocese of 1.5 million people, he had lost 500 catechists between 1979 and 1983.[3] The conservative relief agency, PAVA (*Programa de Ayuda Para Los Vecinos del Altiplano*—Assistance Program for Altiplano Communities), estimated that 53.6 percent of the 1980 Quiché population was displaced and/or needy.[4] PAVA also counted at least 2,090 widows in just ten highland communities. Even into 1985, the Guatemalan army estimated that there were still more than 6,000 refugees hiding in the mountains of northern Quiché.[5] In Guatemala City the Guatemalan Education Workers' Union (STEG) reported that of the total number of schoolteachers who were "disappeared" or kidnapped since 1982, the whereabouts of 74 remained unknown.[6]

There were three major issues during 1985: a vapid presidential campaign dulled by ongoing repression, the growth of the Mutual Support Group (GAM), and the worst economic crisis in Guatemala's history.

Throughout 1985 selective killings and "disappearances" continued. On January 22, 1985, in the village of Xeatsán Bajo near Patzún, Chimaltenango, eight men were killed by army forces after being tortured in the local schoolhouse, their bodies buried in a ditch nearby. In Patzún

1. Chris Krueger and Kjell Enge, *Security and Development Conditions in the Guatemalan Highlands* (Washington, D.C.: Washington Office on Latin America, August 1985), p. 2.

2. *The Wall Street Journal*, September 20, 1985.

3. Author Interview, Guatemala City, December 1985.

4. Krueger and Enge, *Security and Development Conditions in the Guatemala Highlands*, p. 5.

5. George Black, "The Power of the Guatemalan Army," North American Congress on Latin America (NACLA), Vol. XIX, No. 6, November/December 1985, p. 17.

6. *La Hora*, November 4 and 6, 1986.

**Mercedes Gómez at coffin of
her husband, GAM leader
Héctor Gómez Calito,
Amatitlán.**

The Gómez family are bakers who have lived on the same plot for four generations. Héctor, his father, and his brothers were well known for their community service, building schools, organizing parades, and helping out the neighbors. In return for its civic spirit, the Gómez family has suffered from government repression since 1981, when Héctor's nephew, Iván, was killed in a suspicious motorcycle accident, followed by Héctor's brother, René, who "disappeared" in July 1983. Héctor's niece, Yolanda, was kidnapped twice by security forces, raped, and tortured with electric shocks.

The official coroner's report stated that Gómez had died from "internal hemorrhage from a ruptured liver." Two weeks after Gómez's funeral, the coroner himself was shot to death.

Members of the GAM for the families of the "disappeared" at press conference, Guatemala City.

"Who in your family has 'disappeared?'"

"My father, Rigoberto Morales.
My brother, Máynor Morales.
My brother, Otto Raúl Morales.
My brother, Armando Roberto Morales.
My uncle, Moisés Morales.
My uncle, Salomón Morales.
My aunt, Lilián Aída Morales.
My aunt, Elizabeth Morales.
My aunt, Sipriana Ramírez de Morales.
My cousin, Damaris Marleni Morales.
My cousin, María Victoria Morales.
My cousin, Héctor Manolo Morales.
My cousin, Noé Salomón Morales.
My cousin, Byron Moisés Morales.
My cousin, Abygail Morales.
My cousin, Claudia Roxana Morales."

itself, one resident estimated that at least 200 people were "disappeared" or killed there in 1985; he attributed two of the killings to the guerrillas. On February 9, 1985 Brother Felipe Balán Tomás was kidnapped from his church in the village of Las Escobas, Choatalum, Chimaltenango, less than two hours from Guatemala City. On April 12 Celia Floridalma Lucero, union leader at the Chiclets-Adams factory, was abducted with a friend after leaving her home. The friend was released, Lucero did not reappear.

By January 1985 the GAM had 355 members. The following month it began hour-long weekly vigils outside the office of the attorney general to protest the intransigence of the Tri-Partite Commission in delivering the results of its findings. Now, with its pot-and-pan banging demonstrations, the GAM was drawing local attention. As a result, the GAM began to receive direct threats. "At GAM meetings we noticed people who weren't coming because of a 'disappeared' relative, but to get information on us and the GAM's activities. We received phone calls at home, where anonymous callers would turn on a tape: 'Tell her to go and get the body.' They they would call again and I would hear terrible peals of laughter." Members coming in from the countryside were particularly vulnerable. In January 1985 the civil patrol in San Martín Jilotepeque, Chimaltenango, began threatening local members of the GAM. In February the government began a public press campaign of subtle, and then outright, threats against the GAM.

Headlines read, "Mutual Support Used by Subversives," and "Government Warns GAM," while Interior Minister Gustavo López Sandoval told GAM leaders that he would feel "very badly" if he had to "take action" against them.[7] In mid-March when a local reporter asked General Mejía his opinion of the latest GAM protests, the head of state replied, "You'll know it when you see it."[8]

On March 30, 1985 GAM leader Héctor Gómez Calito attended the weekly GAM meeting in Guatemala City. When it was over, he walked five blocks to a shopping center near his bus stop for take-out chicken for his family's dinner. He never made it onto the bus. Gómez was kidnapped at 3 P.M. on a heavily-traveled highway; his body was found the following morning. At his funeral, GAM secretary Rosario Godoy de Cuevas gave the eulogy on behalf of the GAM. Three days later she, her two-year-old son, and her 21-year-old brother were found dead at the bottom of a ditch two miles outside Guatemala City. The government called the deaths "accidents" and labeled worldwide condemnation of the killings the product of "dis-information."

Archbishop Penados called that Easter "a week of blood and terror." The Christian Democrat party issued a press statement denouncing the killings. In private, however, leaders of the Christian Democrat and Social Democrat parties said that the GAM continued to be "manipulated by subversion."

7. *La Palabra*, March 15 and March 22, 1985, and excerpt from GAM conversation with Interior Minister López Sandoval on March 13, 1985.

8. "Guatemala: The Group for Mutual Support," (New York: Americas Watch, 1985), p. 34.

9. Ibid., p. 55.
10. *The Boston Globe*, November 24, 1986.
11. Author interview, Guatemala City, May 1985.

Two months later, on June 6, 1985, the Tri-Partite Commission produced its findings: three double-spaced pieces of paper with no information on any of the "disappeared" and only the recommendation that future commissions "exclude government institutions or officials." The GAM denounced the Commission's findings and met with General Mejía on June 21, 1985. General Mejía smoked, picked at his nails, and criticized the GAM, telling them that they "hadn't let the Commission work well."[9] By November, the GAM had over 760 members.

It was not human rights, however, that sparked the largest mass demonstration in Guatemala during the pre-electoral period—it was the Guatemalan economy. By 1985 inflation had reached an unofficial rate of over fifty percent, and combined under- and unemployment was estimated at forty-five percent. Guatemala's inflation was, in part, the result of rampant corruption in the military and tax evasion by the wealthy over the past decade. In 1986 Interior Minister Juan José Rodil Peralta stated that $600,000,000 had been stolen under the Lucas regime alone.[10] Other estimates are much higher, placing it as high as two billion dollars during the same period. One political analyst stated that corruption placed such a burden on the local economy during those years that if it hadn't existed, the *quetzal* under the Cerezo government would be pegged at 1.50 against the U.S. dollar. Archbishop Penados commented that "whenever aid comes into Guatemala, half of it goes right back out again on a Pan Am flight to Miami or Switzerland."[11]

Following the legalization of the *casas de cambio* (exchange houses) in 1984, the black market became an open venture. High-ranking military officers, including Deputy Head-of-State Rodolfo Lobos Zamora and Head-of-State Mejía Víctores, had big stakes in it. Although legalization was intended as a stop-gap measure against continuing *quetzal* devaluation, it had just the opposite effect. By 1985 the *quetzal* had dropped to a 4:1 ratio with the U.S. dollar. At the same time, consumer prices shot up, sometimes as much 300 to 400 percent in a matter of months. In September 1985 a UPI wire report stated that wages had increased by only five to ten percent that year, signifying a thirty percent drop in real earnings.

Growing anger and frustration over mounting prices surfaced in late August 1985; the catalyst was a proposed fifty percent bus fare increase from ten to fifteen cents. Although the amount seems negligible to foreigners, this meant real sacrifice for many Guatemalans. Families with four children would now spend 1.20 *quetzales* for round-trip bus fares which, to some, represented a third of a day's wages.

For two weeks, Guatemala City resembled a war movie set, as armadillo tanks and camouflaged soldiers in gas masks repelled angry citizens. On the first day, half a dozen buses were burned, eventually two dozen. Lightning demonstrations continued, and downtown shop owners prudently boarded up store fronts as angry crowds ran up and down the streets, followed by riot squads and helicopters overhead, machine guns pointed directly at them. For

Demonstration by the GAM on April 13, 1985 following the deaths of GAM leaders, Héctor Gómez Calito and Rosario Godoy de Cuevas, as well as her two-year-old son and her twenty-one-year-old brother, Guatemala City.

A protest march planned months before the killings of Héctor Gómez and Rosario de Cuevas metamorphosed into an angry tribute to its two slain leaders. Some thought that the march would be, as one human rights leader called it, the GAM's "swan song." Just an hour before the march, GAM leaders wondered "if one dozen people would turn out." Despite obvious intimidation in the wake of these murders, dozens of highland Indians had traveled to Guatemala City the day before, after hearing of Rosario's death on the radio, spending the night before the march sleeping in bushes and on benches.

One thousand people attended the march, at least two-thirds of them Indian women, some walking barefoot with their children on their back. They were accompanied by law students and unionists, their faces covered with handkerchieves, who stopped in front of National Police headquarters, one fist clenched, the other holding a carnation.

**GAM members outside
Metropolitan Cathedral,
Guatemala City.**

Into the twilight months of the Mejía Víctores government, "disappearances" were still so
common that they warranted a form letter sent from then Interior Minister Carlos Guzmán
Estrada. Over the letterhead, "1885–1985: Centennial of the Heroic Death of General Justo
Rufino Barrios," and stamped with three reference numbers, the government issued its
xeroxed reply: "With regard to your inquiry of [date], I am taking this opportunity to inform
you that on this date [your petition] was sent to the National Police headquarters with
instructions to continue the investigation of the disappearance of [name]. As soon as results
become available, you will be notified. . . ."

Form letters are not the only bureaucratic indignity suffered by the families of Guatemala's
"disappeared." Families could not collect pension or social security benefits until the victim
had been declared "disappeared" for five years. In early 1987, the Congress approved a four-
million-dollar budget, allowing family members to declare their "disappeared" as dead. Most
families have rejected this offer. "Show me my husband's grave first," one GAM member said.

four days, army trucks sped up and down zone one: soldiers would jump off and round up at random anyone seen running down a street. Some 1,000 people were arrested, many of them high school students; urban markets closed down in protest at the height of the tension. At night, downtown Guatemala City was an occupied zone: roving army vehicles mounted with machine guns and blinding lights stopped citizens at will, while in poorer neighborhoods boys burned tires on major streets, sometimes aided by their parents.

A manager at a downtown take-out restaurant said, "We're sorry that the people are destroying our property when they know who is responsible for all this—the army." Later, the mother of one of the arrested students said, "What our sons are doing, we should do as well."

On September 3, 1985, following several mass demonstrations at the University of San Carlos (USAC) and at least two student-led marches, five hundred government troops stormed the USAC grounds. Army tanks rolled over the campus lawn and troops broke into the classrooms. Fifteen hundred student files were ransacked, and computer codes were broken. G-2 intelligence units were reportedly accompanied by members of the U.S. Embassy's own intelligence unit.[12] While tanks occupied USAC parking lots and troops split desks with the butts of their guns, the Office for Army Public Relations called up foreign reporters and offered them a tour of the USAC's "subversive roots." The troops left the USAC campus four days later, after causing over half a million dollars in damage.

At the same time, word leaked out that a "soft coup" was being set in motion, and that Congress would select three officials—civilian and military—to rule Guatemala until the election date. Although the coup never materialized, these events provided a dramatic barometer of Guatemala's level of political instability just two months before the elections.

Throughout the lackluster campaign, major issues—human rights violations, military power, agrarian and economic reform—were not even campaign platforms. Three presidential debates sponsored by the Chamber for Free Enterprise resulted in little more than monotonous bandying of personal accusations among the eight primary candidates. The Camino Real Hotel's Los Lagos salon, where the debates were held, resembled a riotous traffic intersection: a large traffic light positioned in the back of the room signaled each candidate's remaining speaking time: yellow and red lights blinked warning and stop signals. Newspaper publisher Jorge Carpio Nicolle of the Union of the National Center (UCN), who had sustained *El Gráfico* through loans from the Army Bank, insisted that his campaign was not being financed by Lucas García's former interior minister, Donaldo Alvarez Ruíz. Mario Sandoval Alarcón, his voice destroyed by throat cancer, struggled to replace the MLN's "party of organized violence" slogan with Milton Friedman economics. Candidate Jorge Serrano Elías of the Protestant-affiliated Democratic Party for National Cooperation (PDCN) assured his listeners of his ecumenical spirit; Serrano, who had headed Ríos Montt's Council of State (*Consejo de Estado*), cited President Reagan as his hero,

12. Author interview, Guatemala City, September 1985.

calling him "a man of great vision." Mario Solórzano Martínez, a Social Democrat, was the only candidate to advocate agrarian reform. "He knows he doesn't have a chance, so why not be a hero?" one observer remarked. Vinicio Cerezo advertised his future government program with oversized, easy-to-read flashcards.

Despite the room's carnival atmosphere, however, there were few illusions that day about any possibility for real "democracy" in Guatemala one year down the road. Just before the debate the managing editor of *Prensa Libre* told a photographer to "take a lot of pictures because in five years half the people in this room will be dead."

Electoral propaganda blitzed the urban and rural landscape. Television programming metamorphosed into a deluge of campaign ads: candidate Carpio ran at least five television spots per hour on one channel, featuring a suburban family singing his praises to celestial muzak; a young Indian child appeared at the end, throwing a dove into the air. Candidate Cerezo opted for the personal touch—"Vinicio" on everything. An athlete, an artist, Archbishop Penados, and Miss Guatemala 1984 went on television, urging Guatemalans to vote for democracy. The UCN later accused the Catholic Church of influencing voters in favor of the Christian Democrat party, after Bishop Gerardo Flores of the Verapaces, in his pre-electoral Sunday sermons, urged his congregation to vote "as Christians . . . and democratically."

In the countryside, political flyers carried candidates' pictures. Party calendars were used as wall hangings and dustcovers. An emaciated refugee at the Las Violetas camp outside Nebaj had saved a Christian Democrat flyer; when asked to point to the presidential candidate, he turned over the paper and fingered the local mayoral candidate.

The U.S. Embassy and USIS (U.S. Information Service) commandeered a floor of the Camino Real to monitor Guatemala's progress toward democracy, paternalism so blatant that it prompted a local newspaper columnist to ask whether the U.S. government would allow the Guatemalan Embassy to set up a similar press office when U.S. citizens went to the polls in their next elections.

Three hundred foreign journalists traveled to Guatemala for the elections, and the U.S. Embassy distributed three-pound press packets, titled "Democracy: Elections 1985," which included candidate profiles, GNP statistics, and the names of local translators. The Guatemalan government press office was more direct. Their own press packet, titled "Elections 85: The Military Carries Out Its Promise," provided journalists with the phone numbers of the National Police radio patrol squad, the Guatemalan Red Cross, and the local firemen.

Over 1,900,000 Guatemalans voted on November 3, 1985. Half as many did not, despite legal penalties. In the first round of elections, the Christian Democrat party captured 39 percent of the valid vote, with the Union of the National Center finishing second, with 20 percent. The remaining six parties were eliminated from the run-off. Fifty-two percent of the voting

Coca-Cola workers eating lunch in plant's cafeteria; on the wall behind them are eight photos of Coca-Cola union leaders slain by government forces between 1978 and 1980. Guatemala City.

The Coca-Cola bottling plant, EMCESA (*Embotelladora Central Sociedad Anónima*), has operated in Guatemala for 45 years. The Coca-Cola union, organized in 1974, became known internationally when the IUF (International Union of Food and Allied Workers' Association, an international trade union coalition with 186 affiliates in 63 countries), organized a 1980 boycott of Coca-Cola's Guatemala City bottling plant, following targeted repression against its leaders. In 1975 the fledgling STEGAC union became embroiled in a series of clashes with local company president, Houston lawyer John Clinton Trotter. Trotter, a close personal friend of security chiefs in the Lucas García government (1978–82), kept a permanent presence of *kaibil* soldiers, attack dogs, and Mobile Military Police (PMA) at the Coca-Cola plant. Following the publication of three death-squad lists in 1978–79, eight Coca-Cola union leaders were killed or "disappeared": Pedro Quevedo y Quevedo, shot in the face; Manuel López Balam, throat slit; Marlon Mendizábal, machine-gunned; Edgar Aldana, shot "by mistake" on the plant grounds when he was mistaken for a fellow unionist, himself a government target, after borrowing the man's jacket and cap. On June 21, 1980, 27 unionists meeting at CNT (National Confederation of Workers) headquarters were abducted in broad daylight, including Coca-Cola unionists, Ismael Vásquez and Florentino Gómez. By this time, union membership dropped from 500 to 63.

202

Coca-Cola worker at Mass in warehouse during 1984 occupation of Coca-Cola plant, Guatemala City.

On February 17, 1984 Coca-Cola's new owners, Anthony Zash and Roberto Méndez y Méndez said that they were going to close the Coke plant on grounds of imminent bankruptcy, offering four union leaders sixty thousand dollars to quietly acquiesce. The new leadership, which had steadily rebuilt union strength since 1983, refused the offer and decided to occupy the plant instead. By 4 A.M. the following morning, some fifty workers were "taking care of the plant"; within days, a round-the-clock vigil had been organized which, at its peak, included some 600 workers. "How can Coca-Cola possibly go broke in a place like Guatemala?" one unionist laughed. Babies are weaned on bottles of Coke since it is cheaper than milk, and the only non-lethal reference ever made to Cuba is the requests for *Cuba libres*—rum and Cokes—mixed daily in hotel bars. The unionists discovered that owners Zash and Méndez had kept two sets of books, the original and another presented to the Ministry of Labor. Instead of going broke, they were clearing over one million dollars in profits per year. While Coke unionists never anticipated that their lightning takeover of the plant would last more than a few weeks, they refused to give in and accept severance pay. The occupation lasted one year. During the takeover, Coke unionists received support from U.S. and European unions, Guatemalan unions, and fellow citizens. A drugstore gave medicines, and two doctors donated thousands of dollars of services. On March 1, 1985, the plant reopened under new management and workers were able to go home to their families at night, instead of maintaining rooftop vigils.

population had either abstained or deposited invalid or blank ballots. Two U.S. congressional observer delegations traveled to Guatemala to witness the elections, believing or pretending that a turn-out of 2.7 million voters was testimony to incipient democracy, and as if democracy happened overnight, with $234,000 of AID water-marked ballot paper and lines of voters as proof. Republican Senator Richard Lugar (R-Indiana), headed the first observer delegation, together with *contra* supporters Boston University President John Silber and Rep. Mickey Edwards (R-Oklahoma), and, as the one "human rights observer," *contra* lobbyist Bruce Cameron. The delegation announced its "satisfaction," adding that "these elections are enormously significant for Guatemala and for the other nations of the Western Hemisphere

13. Remarks made on November 3, 1985, Guatemala City.

. . ."[13] Others, however, were more skeptical. An independent delegation co-sponsored by the International Human Rights Law Group (IHRLG) and the Washington Office on Latin America (WOLA), in its December 1985 report, called the elections "far from perfect" and said, "For the elections to mark a first step in Guatemala's progress toward democracy, the results must be respected. . . . This advance [toward democracy] will be possible only if the new civilian government has the full cooperation and respect of the entrenched military, economic, and religious sectors. . . ." What was not mentioned on election night was that voting is an obligation; failure to register and to vote is officially punishable by fines equal to two days of wages. Non-voters can also be refused employment or a passport for failure to have the voting stamp in their I.D. card. Finally, non-voters can be killed for having failed to vote, since the army has been known to interpret this as "proof" that the person was in the mountains with the guerrillas before the elections.

The December 8, 1985 run-off election was a formality. Vinicio Cerezo beat Jorge Carpio Nicolle by a landslide, receiving 1.1 million votes—68 percent of all ballots cast. In the second round, almost 40 percent of the registered voters did not turn out, despite the penalties. The second delegation, headed by Senator Mark Hatfield (R-Oregon), gave a short press conference; for the second time, the only human rights observer was Bruce Cameron. Senator Hatfield, who had intended to remark on Guatemala's onerous past, and the need for caution in praising its future, was voted down by fellow delegation members.

On December 8, election night, Jorge Carpio acknowledged defeat before the Supreme Electoral Tribunal could announce Cerezo's victory the following day. Minutes later, President-elect Marco Vinicio Cerezo Arévalo stepped from his Mercedes-Benz and entered the Camino Real lobby, engulfed by a throng of party supporters, diplomats, journalists, and bodyguards. The U.S. Embassy was relieved that Guatemala had made it through the election period. Weeks before, an embassy official had remarked, "We don't care who wins—even the Social Democrats would be okay"—meaning that even Mario Sandoval's "organized violence" victory would have been "okay" too as long as there were elections, since that meant "democracy." The aim was not change, but merely to make it through the delicate pre-electoral months and the elections, without fraud or another coup. Even before elections had taken place, the Reagan administration's real aims were clear. Two months before, a confidential State Department memorandum had appeared in U.S. congressional offices, recommending that five million dollars in police and military aid be appropriated to support Guatemala's "process of democratization."[14]

During election week, in the town of Escuintla, twenty miles from the capital, 14 bodies appeared in the morgue, most of them found with severed limbs. Two days after Cerezo's victory, Eugenia Beatriz Barrios Marroquín, a 26-year-old mother and law student, was wheeled into Escuintla's morgue, hacked to death one day before. President-elect Cerezo promised an investigation. None was ever reported. In Santa Rosa five days later, a 64-year-old evangelical pastor was found beheaded. A week before Cerezo's inauguration, Senator Hatfield recommended that the United States withhold all military aid and all but the most essential economic aid until Guatemala demonstrated real improvement in human rights. "To do otherwise," he said, "is to succumb to the unforgivable naïveté that the military network that has perpetuated systematic torture . . . has somehow magically 'disappeared'—like so many thousands of Guatemalan citizens."[15]

On January 14, 1986, Cerezo was installed as President of Guatemala, with a satin sash and the key to the Constitutional urn, by outgoing Head-of-State General Mejía Víctores, who yawned throughout the ceremonies. Guatemala's National Theater was filled with current Latin American leaders and Guatemalan VIPs, who must have experienced a familiar sense of history as Guatemala took its place on the map of nine Latin American nations "democratized" since 1979.

Dignitaries who attended Cerezo's inauguration included a Guatemalan Who's Who roster of former political leaders: General Carlos Arana Osorio, the godfather of scorched-earth counterinsurgency; Dr. Francisco Villagrán Kramer, Guatemala's only vice president to flee for his life while still in office, and Julio César Méndez Montenegro, the last civilian president before Cerezo. For Méndez Montenegro, the moment must have been particularly evocative—twenty years before, he accepted the same presidential sash after relinquishing all real powers of office, tacitly acquiescing to the onset of systematic repression under his civilian government. In his inaugural speech, President Cerezo spoke of "returning to our homes." Apparently, he was alluding to the 100,000 dead or "disappeared"; 1,000,000 internally displaced; some 120,000 refugees in Mexico; another 70,000 in model villages; and thousands of others living in cardboard boxes in Guatemala City slums.

14. *The Los Angeles Times*, September 22, 1985.
15. "Aid Guatemala Doesn't Need," *The New York Times*, January 6, 1986.

Peasants resting during 150-kilometer march into Guatemala City, Escuintla.

In its 1986 *Country Report* the U.S. State Department described Guatemala as "characterized by a badly skewed distribution of land and capital." The mere mention of land reform in Guatemala is taboo, provoking the same reaction as the mention of Marxism as a university course offering. In late April 1986 Father Andrés Girón, a Guatemalan priest, led 14,000 peasants from Guatemala's highlands and southern coast in a four-day march into Guatemala City. Shortly afterward, Father Girón received anonymous death threats and found his walls spray-painted with the phrase, "Priest Son of a Bitch, We're Going to Kill You." He now travels with armed G-2 bodyguards provided by President Cerezo.

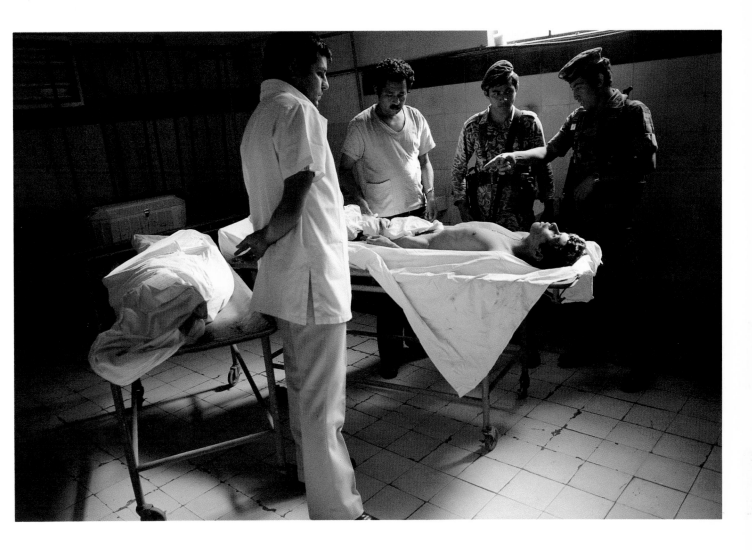

**The Verbena cemetery
morgue, Guatemala City.**

According to the Verbena forensic pathologist the victims in this morgue represent the three major killers of Guatemalans: a woman run over in a traffic accident (a driver's license can be bought for fifteen dollars); a baby who died from malnutrition; and a man killed by gunshot wounds. According to Guatemalan law, corpses must be buried within twenty-four hours after death or retrieval, whichever comes first. Bodies that remain unidentified for over a day are buried as "XX": "anonymous" in local cemeteries. Sometimes, when families later determine where their relative may have been recovered, they pay the local morgue to dig up a corpse.

The relatives of the "disappeared" make regular rounds of local morgues; for many, after months of search, identification of a corpse produces as much relief as sadness; photos of Guatemala's "disappeared" hang from the walls of local morgues, with instructions on how to contact the family in the event of positive identification.

The Confession

Archbishop Próspero Penados del Barrio is privy to much information on human rights violations. Although he does not denounce specific acts, Archbishop Penados is vocal in condemning general abuses—a change from his predecessor, Cardinal Mario Casariego, who once remarked, "If I hadn't been a priest, I would have been a soldier." While the U.S. Embassy claims to investigate human rights abuses, they have never made an effort to check their information with the Archbishop. "They only came to me twice," Penados said in 1987, "when a U.S. priest and a U.S. nun were in trouble."

In April 1985 a civil patroller from southern Quiché asked Archbishop Penados to hear his confession. The Archbishop said:

"I was in Santa Cruz del Quiché one month ago, to ordain an Indian priest. A patroller called out to me, he wanted to speak with me in private. He was very sad, very depressed, because he had been forced to kill. He told me that when someone is being hunted and the soldiers and army officers don't want to go, they send the patrollers and tell them, 'Go and kill so-and-so; he is a subversive.' The patroller said to me, 'How am I supposed to do that, if I don't have anything against anyone?' He was very anguished and remorseful. He then told me that the army made him drink the blood of a dead man. He was made to drink from the dead man's aorta. I think that this is a kind of psychology the army uses, so people become more brutal, more fierce. . . ."

The State Department described Archbishop Penados as having cautioned "against blaming any one sector of society for the violence which has beset Guatemala, claiming many groups were responsible."[16] On the other hand, the Archbishop told me, "Indians come here and tell me, 'It is the army who is killing us.' But it is nothing new to hear that the army is the one doing the killing. Everybody knows it."[17] The State Department did not mention a blood-stained handkerchief the Archbishop received as a "Christmas present" in 1984.[18]

In 1985 Archbishop Penados commented on the Guatemalan army:

"The military refuses to compromise. They don't even ask me to hear their confessions. I have spoken many times with General Mejía. I've eaten dinner with him, when he invites me. And he never says anything, ever. I have taken lists of 'disappeared' people and the names of the locations from where they were taken. Mejía says, '*Bueno*, I'm going to take this to the police, the army, and so-and-so.' But everything stops there. They protect each other, they cover their interests. Sometimes, they do let something out, it escapes. But they always try to maintain a certain veneer.

"There is hope for elections, and that a civilian takes office, but he will do very little. He will have very little power to command and make decisions. To this day, they have never brought a

16. *Country Reports . . . for 1985*, (February 1986), p. 552.
17. Author interview, Guatemala City, June 1986.
18. James LeMoyne, "New Army Slayings in Guatemala Reported by Villagers and Church," *The New York Times*, July 28, 1985, p. 12.

military man to trial, even after two coups d'état. They will never tell the truth, it's not to their advantage.

"Here, whoever becomes president is going to have to be very diplomatic with the military—he is going to have to do business with a bottle of Johnny Walker Black in his hand. In the eyes of public opinion, they are going to hand over the apparent power, but I am sure that they are going to put conditions on the new President, and he is going to have to accept this. There are secret pacts—a civilian president isn't convenient for the army, because he doesn't think the way they do. Maybe things can change in ten years."

Holy Week

Héctor Gómez Calito, a thirty-four-year-old baker from Amatitlán, near Guatemala City, was abducted shortly after leaving the weekly GAM meeting in the city. Although several GAM members witnessed his abduction, they were afraid to denounce it. Gómez's body was dumped the following morning on the exit to Amatitlán, less than a mile from his home. Gómez's niece, Yolanda, who had herself been kidnapped and raped, was the first to identify him:

"Héctor had been tortured with a blow torch. His stomach was burned and his pants too. They had tied him up with a rope—his wrists and feet had marks on them. His mouth was what affected me the most . . . he didn't even have his tongue. All he had were a few hairs around his mouth and coagulated blood. He had a clump of hair in his fist too, as if he had tried to struggle with his torturers. Héctor would always say to me, 'Leave the country, they're going to kill you.' I never thought it would be his turn first."

Isabel Choxom, Nineth de García, and Rosario de Cuevas arrived next, while Héctor's body still lay on the highway. From Rosario's car, they noticed several men—*judiciales*—standing less than a block away. They believe that Héctor's killers stayed to see who would claim the body. That night, his body was laid out in an open casket. The Gómez home was filled with mourners. Héctor's face was a contortion of bruises and broken teeth; where his tongue had been, a wad of cotton had been placed. The autopsy report said that he died from "internal liver damage." The forensic pathologist who carried out the autopsy was shot to death several weeks later.

At Héctor's funeral the next day, GAM leader Rosario de Cuevas grabbed the megaphone and promised Héctor that his "terrible death would not be in vain." On the way home from the funeral, Rosario joked that she and the other GAM members were probably safe, at least during Holy Week, since "even killers have to take time off for Easter." Three days later, Rosario was found dead at the bottom of a shallow ditch outside Guatemala City, along with her two-year-

**Army occupation of
downtown Guatemala City
during September 1985
protest over bus fare increase.**

According to one economic analyst, each year there are 150,000 new young people in the work force. Yet in 1982, the CAVISA, Chiclets-Adams and Ginsa factories each fired 100 to 200 people. In February 1982 a local business fired 14 out of 30 employees. Just two weeks earlier they had advertised for two new positions: a secretary and messenger, for which 150 applicants showed up, many of them students and professionals. Two years later, a man showed up at their front door, offering his youngest child to anyone who would take her. He did it out of love; he couldn't afford to care for her anymore.

Students fleeing after bus burning, zone one, Guatemala City.

According to the Latin American Economic Planning Council, 79 percent of all Guatemalans live in poverty, 61 percent in extreme poverty. The minimum cost of living for a family of seven is 16.50 *quetzales* per day, although annual per capita income is 211 *quetzales*.

One Guatemala City chambermaid earns less than three *quetzales* per day. In September 1985, when bus riots broke out, the owner of the hotel where that maid worked sided with the bus burners, placing a sign outside the lobby, saying, "No to Bus Fare Hikes." He was not worried about the future of Guatemala's citizenry; he only feared that a bus fare hike would force him to raise hotel salaries.

211

old son and her twenty-one-year-old brother. Like Héctor, Rosario's kidnapping had taken place at midday in a shopping mall in a residential zone. Witnesses to the abduction later told Rosario's mother what they had seen; Mrs. Godoy did not make any public comment "because I still have one son left." Nineth de García and Isabel Choxom were called to identify Rosario's body at the Verbena morgue. Nineth described their arrival:

"By the time we arrived at the morgue, the DIT agents we had seen a few minutes before had beaten us there. They didn't let us see the bodies first. 'We're very busy right now,' they said. They were in there, with their cameras and guns, taking pictures of Rosario, the baby, and her brother. . . . Who knows what the DIT was doing to the bodies in there. When they finally let us in, it was hard to look. Rosario had bite marks on her breasts; her pants were covered with dirt, as if she had been dragged on the ground; her underpants were covered with blood. I think she was raped. We asked a DIT agent if it was an accident or murder. He replied, 'Look, this was all very strange.' They said it like that, so brazenly, there in the morgue. 'Who knows what happened,' he said, 'but this wasn't an accident.' When Rosario's mother had called the DIT earlier in the day for information, DIT agents had told her, 'Don't worry, you will have news later—and you watch it too.' "

Mourners at the funeral home recalled something odd that they had seen:

"Those of us at the wake commented on something very strange. Usually, when people are laid out, the palms of their hands face upward; we noticed that little baby Augusto's hands faced down. Some of us went closer to look; we saw that his fingernails were missing. We later commented on this."

The Candidate

Years before taking office, Vinicio Cerezo had a following of paid bodyguards, childhood friends-turned-advisors, and second-string politicos and military men hoping to ingratiate themselves early on.

Cerezo's life was most striking for its complete absence of privacy. He was attentive with advisors, charming with the secretaries, and affectionate with friends' children, treating them as his own, perhaps because his own had been living in Washington, D.C., since 1980 following an army raid on his house in Guatemala City and a subsequent assassination attempt against him just one year after the murders of two presidential aspirants. The family's quarters in Guatemala looked like a subterranean Holiday Inn: bullet-proof sheet-metal covered every window and nondescript furniture was relieved only by Goya posters from the Spanish Tourist Office. Then there were the presents. The Christian Democrat logo, a white star, was everywhere: stamped on the tea set, set in the flower arrangements, and embroidered into Indian weavings. Out in the driveway sat Cerezo's white, bullet-proof Mercedes-Benz ("My supporters decided to protect their investment"). In the bedroom, a VCR was kept well-stocked by a local video store.

The difference between Cerezo and every other candidate was his complete ease in every social situation, whether on the road, on the podium, cajoling his aides, or quaffing beer before lunch ("It's eleven in Guatemala but it's five in Paris"). En route to rallies, Cerezo had a small arsenal of tape music: Latino pop, sixties rock, and Sandinista music with lyrics on the ABCs of weapons handling. Cerezo's sincerity was only hard to gauge where politics was concerned. Cerezo himself acknowledged this, explaining that his mother had taught him a Latino maxim: "Two things have to be done with great care: one is eating fish and the other is the art of sinning"—a play on the words, *pescado* and *pecado*.

Prior to his election, Cerezo said that, while he would not bring the military to trial, he would encourage other reforms:

Q: In your opinion, who has been responsible for the majority of human rights violations over the past five years?

A: Look, we can't talk about the last five years. Human rights violations have definitely come from the government security forces, in general. Next, from sectors of the organized right, some of whom are protected by the MLN [National Liberation Movement]. And last, from leftist sectors.

Q: In your opinion, who has been more truthful regarding human rights in Guatemala: Amnesty International or General Lobos Zamora [Deputy Head of State under the Mejía government]?

A: I won't even answer that one.

Q: What do you think of the low percentage of people—seven percent—who, in a recent survey, said they were politically aligned with the left?

A: To be a leftist in this country is to sign your death sentence. And that makes it very hard for anyone, in a political survey, to state that he is a leftist.

Q: As President, are you going to bring the military to trial?

A: We are not considering bringing anyone to trial, because Guatemala is not Argentina. In Guatemala we are going to try to get along with an army which considers itself successful and victorious, and not with an army that came out of a war with its tail between its legs.

Students from University of San Carlos (USAC) in front of National Police headquarters during march by the Mutual Support Group (GAM), through downtown Guatemala City.

"For the last thirty years, people haven't had any escape from repression in Guatemala. If you try to treat the problem, you are a subversive. Most human rights are censured. I've never seen a country with problems of this magnitude; there is no community organization, it is national castration, inverted values."

—Child psychologist in Guatemala City

Police carrying away protesters outside University of San Carlos (USAC), Guatemala City, September 1985.

Student and popular protests culminated in the army's occupation of the USAC in early September 1985, an act which outraged USAC rector, Dr. Eduardo Meyer Maldonado and the international academic community as well, since the USAC has officially been autonomous from the government since 1944.

Troops urinated on classroom walls, wrote "Long Live the Army" on blackboards, and stole whatever they could, including stands belonging to candy vendors. In October 1986 a military tribunal announced that the army had not occupied the university illegally, since the USAC constituted "a favored area for violence, drug consumption and the publication of subversive propaganda . . ." adding that damages had already been paid for.

Some damage was of a different ilk: in the days surrounding the USAC occupation, student leaders left the country, while hundreds of others were wondering whether to return for final exams, since the G-2 had also broken the university's computer code.

215

Q: If you do find proof of army human rights violations, are you going to proceed against those responsible?

A: We are going to create conditions so that if someone confronts me with proof, the courts will have to act. That is, if we find sufficient proof, which I doubt, because we'll see who dares to give declarations against those responsible for repression in Guatemala.

Q: If the military is so strong, what are you going to do to change this?

A: The military is going to have to decide: if they decide to take power again by force, everyone is going to know it. Or they can let me give the orders. Because they have one option: either they let me govern or there is a coup. It's not complicated, it's simple. They're going to have to decide. If there is another coup, the whole world will be watching. I've written my role. People ask me: "Why has the Christian Democrat party stopped proposing structural reforms?" Because I realize that, historically, my role is to open the door for the democratic process. I'm not even going to think about reforms but simply put the military behind me. . . . And then open up the doors for everybody else. That does not mean that we don't have . . . improvements. But this is not fundamental. There are other, more important things.

Q: If the army massacres or if people "disappear" under your government, who is responsible, you or the army?

A: I will be responsible but I am going to try to hold responsible those who carry out this [repression] because this is going to be against presidential orders, and here we are going to be very heavy-handed. With respect to past crimes, the people will have to demand justice.

Q: Would you bring army officers to trial if you find proof?

A: If we find evidence, it's possible. But the problem is that no one can categorically respond . . .

Q: In the countryside, exactly how will you transfer power from the military to a civilian government?

A: Through a demilitarization process. I think we could achieve it during our five years in office, on the condition that the country is led by civilians and that the military has a defined role.

Q: What is that role?

A: National defense. And of course, there are many who are not going to be happy with that.

Q: Are the civil patrols going to continue under army orders?

A: There is going to be a presidential control with regard to the civil self-defense; they are going to be eliminated in most departments because they will vote against it. . . . I think that in general, people have rejected the patrol because it is a means of control for the majority.

Q: If the army had to choose between eliminating the guerrillas or continuing the civil patrol system, which would they opt for?

A: I think that the civil patrol is more important to them. Elimination of the guerrillas is not necessarily the most important item. The guerrillas, in some ways, justify all the army's actions. They are not sufficiently strong to destroy the army: what the army does is to justify its presence in all those villages where they suspect the guerrillas have some kind of presence. So every time the guerrillas carry out some small act of sabotage or something, it just reinforces the theory for the need for civil patrols and the Inter-Institutional Coordinators. The way I see it, at this point the guerrillas are a thorn in the army's side, but not the biggest thorn. Instead, they provide the justification for the control the army exercises over the civilian population. The guerrillas are like a vaccine: they provoke a reaction that strengthens the body instead of weakening it.

Q: What do you think of President Reagan's human rights policy in Guatemala?

A: Does President Reagan have any policy on human rights in Guatemala?

Cerezo decided to run for President while he was still in grade school:

"I have spent my entire life preparing myself for the worst. My political career began when I was twelve years old. I was sitting in a tree in front of our house on the Bolívar Avenue, crying and watching U.S. planes flying overhead. At the time, I didn't know exactly what it meant, but I knew it had to be something very bad.

"My father worked under the Arbenz government; he was a Supreme Court judge. When Arbenz fell with the 1954 coup, they imprisoned my father on charges of communism, saying they were going to shoot him. They took him from our house, beating him and pushing him. They put him in prison. They said they were going to kill him. Our family knew who was behind this, and my cousin and I made a pact that if anything ever happened to my father, we would get even. We spent three months standing watch in front of the guy's house. Finally, they let my father go.

Widows in Chupol receiving propaganda from the Union of the National Center (UCN) political party, on the Pan American Highway, Chichicastenango, Quiché.

In 1987 the Roosevelt Center for American Policy Studies in Washington, D.C., invited Guatemalan scholars to preview a "new educational tool on Central America"—a role-playing policy game designed to introduce Americans to Guatemala. The game was called "Bullets and Ballots":

"Set in Guatemala, the game revolves around negotiations among members of five teams facing an upcoming presidential election: the army/private sector, guerrillas, peasants/workers, the Guatemalan government, and the United States. The outcome depends entirely on the interactions among the groups and might include an army coup, a guerrilla takeover, or democratic elections. Hundreds of participants in the game play-tests across the country over the last few months have praised BULLETS AND BALLOTS as an exceptional tool for gaining a deeper understanding of the region's conflicts. . . ."

Mauricio Quixtán, Indian congressman, during signing of 1985 Constitution, Guatemala's fourth since 1945, Guatemala City.

Former U.S. Embassy human rights officer, Lynn Schiveley, gave visiting congressional aides his assessment of the 1985 presidential elections in May 1985: "Indians are just like Italians; they vote for whoever is ahead."

"During those years, from 1954 to 1958, people in the Castillo Armas government didn't dare say 'hi' to us. Our neighbors would leave their sidewalk bench if my father was walking by. My mother suffered deeply. Once, when I was about fourteen, a friend of my father, a colonel, threw a party at his *finca*. I went, and they sent me to the kitchen to eat. I left and walked back out on to the highway and hitched a ride back to Guatemala City.

"My grandmother, my father's mother, was key to my upbringing. She was the first woman to work in the courts, her name was Elena Sierra. They called her 'La Elenita.' She had a group of admirers, six or seven lawyers. They would take her to fancy restaurants and go crazy over her. There was some kind of fascination with her. She was very liberal. 'The woman who is afraid of losing her dignity for having spent the night with a man has no dignity to begin with,' she would say.

"She taught me to fight, telling me never to let myself get beaten. 'Show who you are,' she would say, 'even if you're in the worst possible situation.' 'What are you sobbing for?' 'Go back and hit the brat.' Once, I came in third in my class at school and she stormed off, saying 'You're first, not third.' She blamed the teacher. She drank pure whiskey until the day she died.

"My wife, Raquel, is like the reincarnation of my grandmother. We started going out during our third year in law school. The first time I met her, she was in front of Congress, burning a government decree legalizing electoral fraud. My grandmother was very critical of my girlfriends, but when she met Raquel, she said, 'I like this one.' Raquel picked up all my grandmother's habits. Before, she couldn't drink. Once, we left the kids with someone, got a bottle of tequila and spent the afternoon finishing it off. Raquel got sick. Now, she says, 'Give me a whiskey,' and she drinks it straight, just like my grandmother.

"Little by little, I've become accustomed to things I didn't like or feared. That is how I've done everything in my life that used to frighten me or make me shy away. I didn't used to swim, for example, so I'd spend half an hour, then an hour, in the pool, until one day I could swim the length. I've learned karate the same way. The only thing I haven't learned to do is to ride a motorcycle; it scares me.

"A politician in Guatemala has to be the same way. I've been carrying a gun for eighteen years; first I had a Colt .45, then I traded it for a Luger pistol. The idea of being killed becomes part of your normal feelings. If you don't accept the possibility of being killed, you can't be a politician. I never go anywhere unless it is to my home or my office. I never go to the movies, or restaurants—nothing, if it isn't related to politics. I have twenty bodyguards protecting me, but the day they decide to bomb this house, they aren't going to keep me from getting blown up. And I have always told my security people that I would never ask them to do something that I wouldn't do first.

"My old man taught me two things: not to hate, but to do what is just, and to recognize the 1944 Revolution's errors and to believe that we would once again have a democracy in Guatemala. My father always thought that the Christian Democrats were conservatives."

The Officer

There is no single structure in Guatemala as powerful as the army intelligence network, the G-2. All branches of the government, including the police, the *judiciales*, the judiciary, and the president, are subordinate to it, if not its potential target. The G-2 keeps extensive files, including photographs on anyone it considers a potential threat to the state. While all governments have military intelligence and similar files, in Guatemala the G-2 is also responsible for deciding who will live and die. In July 1986 the army denied that the G-2 operates out of the National Palace, saying instead that "it is everywhere." This is true. In the countryside, the G-2's rural component, the S-2, oversees similar surveillance and elimination operations.

The G-2 continues to operate under the Cerezo government. The following interview was conducted with a senior Guatemalan army office who served for over twenty years. He is strongly anti-guerrilla, and is one of the few ranking officers willing to discuss the G-2:

"Here, the G-2 is God on earth. There are two thousand agents, about fifty full-time officers. Employees can be nurses, cooks, chauffeurs, personal friends of army commanders, who are spying on him. The G-2 headquarters is in the National Palace, but if you go there, all you see is a pretty little office.

"The G-2 controls the head of the Armed Forces. They watch the mail, cables, telephones, and the communications system, including the airports, hotels, and GUATEL as well. [GUATEL, the national telephone company, was placed under the supervision of the Defense Ministry by Ríos Montt. It has the ability to tape five hundred calls simultaneously. During the 1982 elections, foreign journalists observed four tape recorders working openly and simultaneously in the basement switchboard of the Camino Real Hotel, taping guests' calls.]

"The process of eliminating someone begins with the three G-2 commanders. There are files—on the ones still alive. There are no duplicate sets of files; they are all in one place. The computer has people's sheets with photos and their political parties. A file might read: 'In 1957 he participated in such-and-such a workers movement; in 1960 he went into exile for the following reason; in 1972, he returned to Guatemala; 1975, he participated in a demonstration at the university. And finally, on such-and-such a date, he died.' It never says who was responsible.

Candidate Vinicio Cerezo speaking before the Guatemalan Businessmen's Association (AGA), Guatemala City.

Although Vinicio Cerezo had been too young to participate in the 1982 presidential elections, he was clearly the favored candidate from 1980 on. In early 1985 he explained his attitude toward the army:

"The first thing that has to be done is to diminish the army's power. They'll either have to accept the country's demilitarization, or they will have to create another coup, and then things will become very clear. . . . It is not our job to determine if [the army is permitting elections] willingly or unwillingly, for strategic reasons or out of democratic conviction. This is not important. The facts are that less people are dying and that is good, whatever the reason. It is not our job to judge attitudes: the good or bad attitude of the army [is not important], only the attitude with which we have to work. [The army will] hand over a part of the power, or else they're going to have to make things very clear, and show the world who is ruling in this country. The coup will not be the tragedy; it is simply a clarification of things."

Mario Sandoval Alarcón, leader of the right-wing National Liberation Movement (MLN), at home during the 1985 Presidential campaign, Guatemala City.

The MLN was founded in the late 1950s by supporters of the 1954, CIA-backed coup; its leader is Mario Sandoval Alarcón, called *El Mico*, "the Monkey." Politician Manuel Colom Argueta called Sandoval "a buffoon straight out of the middle ages." In 1980 the MLN deputy director, Leonel Sisniega Otero, defined the MLN: ". . . I admit that the MLN is the party of organized violence. Organized violence is vigor, just like organized color is scenery and organized sound is harmony. There is nothing wrong with organized violence; it is vigor, and the MLN is a vigorous movement."

Sandoval, who was vice president under Laugerud García (1974–78), has attacked everything from the Catholic Church ("infiltrated by Marxists") to the United Nations ("controlled by communists"), something of a contradiction to his claim that Pope John Paul II is his "spiritual leader." Sandoval claims to have a private standing army of 6,000 men, and the capacity to arm 100,000 on 24-hours notice; in the mid-1960s the MLN publicly acknowledged that they had organized the *Mano Blanca*, "White Hand," death squad, which claimed to have killed hundreds of citizens.

Sandoval told me, "If I have to get rid of half of Guatemala so the other half can live in peace, I'll do it." Since cancer has destroyed his vocal cords, I later asked an aide if I had heard him correctly: the aide hesitated and said, "Well, you have to put it in context . . ."

223

"At first, the G-2's information is crude; it can be true or false. When they have three or four sources, however, they start to watch the suspect until they confirm that their information is not a simple rumor anymore. Then Mejía gives the order for a political kidnapping. Nuila [presidential chief of staff under Mejía Víctores, then commander of the Poptún, El Petén military base, before being recalled in 1987], says to Mejía, 'So-and-so is against us.' He makes a suggestion: Nuila says, 'We have to get rid of this one.' Mejía says, 'Okay.' His actual knowledge of someone's 'subversive activities' is not important. Nuila has a coded phone, the red phone. He is patient, though—they wait three or four months to do it well, without witnesses, to let the hatchet fall. There are a thousand passwords, they use terms that would never stand up in an investigation.[19]

"They take kidnapped people to private rented houses. The G-2 does not have fixed, stationary jails. It uses the DIT and military bases outside the capital where, even if a North American journalist put on his best boots from Vietnam, he would not be able to find them, because this not like El Salvador, where everything is concentrated. Guatemala is different.

"They can be in these houses anywhere from one to two hours, a week, even a year, before being eliminated although there is a thirty percent chance that someone is alive three months after they kidnap him.

"The army is a machine: it can build a town or destroy a village. And the soldiers are kids, they cannot analyze anything. If the commander says, 'Objective: this hamlet is infested with communists who have destroyed and killed soldiers and we have to raze it,' then, they have to finish off the hamlet. This is the environment we live in—because of our terrible economic situation, you either become an *oreja* or a guerrilla.

"Democracy isn't born with elections, it is a process. These elections will be one of the few honest elections in Guatemalan history. They are an international show to convince the United States and Europe of the 'heroic handing over of power,' and the scenario will be played out according to foreign guidelines. Vinicio is going to let the G-2 surround him so he doesn't get killed; he is going to try to gain their trust. They will put on a great show, but afterwards if they want to make him look bad, they will make violence go up again. If I were the president right now, I would have to continue the 'show' too, because who can erase the reasons for our tears?"

Secret Prisons

Throughout the Lucas García, Ríos Montt, and Mejía Víctores governments, secret torture houses continued to exist, many of them in downtown Guatemala City. Some of them were private houses owned by army officials; others were residences rented out by private citizens.

19. Guatemala has its own lexicon for the business of repression. *Orejear* means to spy on someone; an *oreja*, literally, "ear," is a government informer. *Desaparecer*, formally an intransitive or reflexive verb, has another meaning in Guatemala: *lo desaparecieron* means "they 'disappeared' him." To kill someone is *darle pasaporte*, literally to "give someone a passport." The terms *volar al pájaro*, "to make the bird fly away," *darle agua*, literally to "give someone water," *mandarle para el otro lado*, literally, "to send someone to the other side," *irse con Pancho*, literally, "to go with Pancho," and *mandarle a uno a ver las margaritas desde abajo*, literally, "send someone off to look at the daisies from below," all mean "to kill."

224

The common torture sites included the army barracks, the DIT headquarters, the Mobile Military Police (PMA) headquarters, and the old Politécnica Military Academy. In late 1983 María Cruz López Rodríguez, a Special Tribunal prisoner, stated in an open letter published in the local press that while still in prison she had been held in the Politécnica barracks, where she had seen other "disappeared" individuals, including university student Ileana Solares de Castillo.

In 1986 a government security agent told a civilian official that one year before, while assigned to guard army buildings in Guatemala City, he had once witnessed the removal of "disappeared" persons just prior to the arrival of journalists, following an invitation from the Office of Army Public Relations, to prove that secret prisons did not exist. Meanwhile, the State Department said that with regard to the existence of secret prisons, "these allegations and their accuracy has never been confirmed."[20] Two months before the presidential elections, Julio Celso de León Flores, the fifty-six-year-old director of the conservative CGTG (*Coordinación General de Trabajadores de Guatemala*) union federation, was abducted in downtown Guatemala City on September 11, 1985 and taken to a one such prison. De León was fortunate; through international pressure, he was released two days later, drugged but alive.

"There was nothing spontaneous about my kidnapping. Once I was in the car, the driver communicated with *la base* [the base] saying, 'We have the package.' . . . The place they took me to was in Guatemala City.

"They tied me to a desk; that night they interrogated me for five hours. They asked me all about the unions I advise. They said, 'What a coincidence that those unions are the very ones which create the most problems.' They said the unions were Marxist.

"The next day, they took me from a room out into a patio. I was still blindfolded. It seemed like a very big room—it smelled badly. As we went into the next room, the man who took me yelled, 'Bend over!' into the room as we went by. I believe there were other prisoners whose eyes were not blindfolded and my kidnappers didn't want them to see me. All day, I heard shouts, all afternoon. They had the music turned up loud the entire time, but I heard earth-shaking screams. They would untie my right hand so I could eat tortillas. Although I was blindfolded, I managed to look down—I saw that the mattress they had sat me on was soaked with blood; I think they had tortured people on it. There were strong bars over the doors.

"That morning they threatened me. They said they were going to bring in my wife and daughter so I would 'soften.' They asked me if I had life insurance. . . . They said that they couldn't keep people very long because it was 'a lot of time and bother and money.' They told me I was going to 'rest' soon."

20. *Country Reports . . . for 1985*, (February 1986), p. 546.

Presidential candidate Vinicio Cerezo and supporter at a Christian Democrat rally, Mazatenango, Suchitepéquez.

Under the government of President Juan José Arévalo (1945–51), Guatemala's first democratic leader, there were some thirty coup attempts. In 1949 President Arévalo himself said, "In Guatemala, there are two Presidents and one of them has a machine gun with which he is always threatening the other." Eighteen years later, one year into the Cerezo government, *Prensa Libre* reported a rush on local supermarkets on December 30, 1986, after "unusual troop movement" throughout Guatemala City provoked coup rumors, and food stockpiling.

Christian Democrat presidential candidate, Vinicio Cerezo, bodyguards and supporter, at rally in El Progreso, Chiquimula.

At public meetings with local Christian Democrat leaders, Cerezo was confronted with petitions for paved roads, water systems, and full-time teachers. In private, supporters pleaded for an end to army repression: during the campaign, one aide received five dozen letters each day, many giving details of repression carried out by rural commanders, the location of secret prisons, and names of "disappeared" relatives.

Throughout, however, Cerezo made no promise of retribution for past government repression. On November 4, 1985 the *International Herald Tribune* quoted him as saying, "We are not going to be able to investigate the past. We would have to put the entire army in jail."

**Voter lines, Nebaj, Quiché,
November 1985.**

A wealthy Quezaltenango businessman described his disillusionment with the sanguine 1985 electoral campaigning:

"Guatemala is so sick that even its national symbols are negative. The national flower, the *monja blanca*, is pretty, but it is parasitic; the national tree, the *ceiba*, doesn't produce anything; the *quetzal*, the national bird, cannot sing; the national anthem was written by a Cuban; and now, we're going to have a *maricón*, (colloquially, 'a coward') for President."

Ixil schoolgirls on Independence Day, Nebaj, Quiché.

"You lift your head and they break it. You open your mouth and they shut it. You take a step forward and you're dead."

—Rafael Yos Muxtay, kidnapped in 1985

Vinicio Cerezo and his wife, Raquel, in their bathroom after his November 1985 victory, Guatemala City.

President Cerezo has worn a pistol for seventeen years. His wife, Raquel, carries a small pistol in her handbag, and tells foreign journalists that all her children know how to shoot. President Cerezo said, "Where else but in Guatemala do you have three people at your house in one day, with presents of a machine gun, a pistol, and a grenade in a bag?" Even—or especially—before taking office, arms were everywhere in Cerezo's campaign: on the bodyguards, on the back seat, by the pool. Sometimes they were also part of the entertainment. On one excursion, party members practiced shooting rusty cans on a deserted beach, while bodyguards split open coconuts at forty feet.

Appropriately, Nicaraguan President Daniel Ortega, presented President Cerezo with an inscribed machine gun at a private breakfast the morning after his inauguration.

Colonel Roberto Mata and President Cerezo on inauguration night, National Palace, Guatemala City.

"Here the game is played by three groups: the rich, the military, and the U.S. Embassy. For Guatemalans, democracy means elections and nothing more. Political parties are part of the game. That's the only 'human rights' in Guatemala right now: respecting political parties."

—Guatemalan political analyst, January 1986

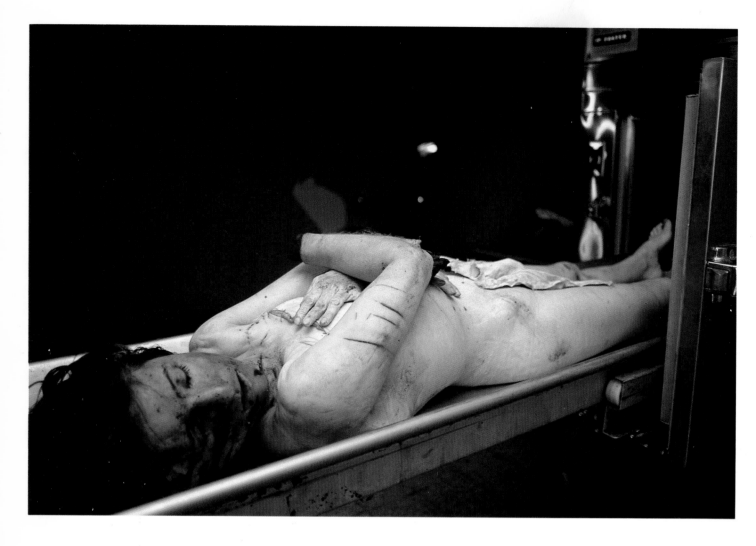

Eugenia Beatriz Barrios Marroquín, 26-year-old mother, in morgue, Escuintla, Escuintla.

On December 10, 1985, two days after Cerezo's presidential victory, 26-year-old Eugenia Beatriz Barrios Marroquín, a schoolteacher and mother of two small children, called for a taxi to go to a friend's home.

Minutes after she left in the taxi, she and the driver were stopped by a car carrying three armed men who forced her out of the taxi and into their vehicle. Barrios had either been under heavy surveillance or the call that she made to the taxi dispatcher had been monitored by government intelligence. Although the taxi driver returned to tell her friend about the abduction, it was too late.

Her body was found the following day, near Palín, Escuintla, by the painted *quetzal* bird rock: it had been hacked, her face carved out, her hands severed at the wrists. A piece of cardboard found near the body carried her name and the words "more to come." When security agents arrived to take fingerprints from her severed hands, Captain Armando Villegas, head of the Honor Guard G-2 intelligence office was already there. When they asked him, *"Muchá*, what happened?" Villegas responded by taking out a card on which he had written Barrios's name, and told them that it was she. The writing on Villegas's card matched that on the cardboard message.

President-elect Vinicio Cerezo condemned the Barrios killing and "expressed his desire to see those guilty caught as soon as possible."

No one has been arrested. Captain Villegas is now a director in Cerezo's presidential guard.

Chapter 6

1986–1987

During Holy Week 1987 Guatemalan hotels were filled to capacity for the first time in seven years. Tour buses resumed excursions to highland towns deemed off-limits by the State Department three years before, and restaurants were packed with tour groups.

On April 9, 1987 Debora Carolina Vásquez Velásquez, a twenty-seven-year-old architecture student, returned to Guatemala to spend Easter with her family. It was her first trip back since 1980. Six days later, at noon on Holy Wednesday, seven men armed with machine guns surrounded Vásquez at a neighborhood gas station and forced her into a waiting vehicle. When her father protested, the abductors struck him semi-unconscious. Over fifty people witnessed the midday abduction; two policemen, who chased the kidnappers after they ran a barricade, saw them drive Debora Carolina into the *Cuartel General* military barracks nearby. Her own car was left abandoned by the kidnappers one hundred yards from the *Cuartel* entrance. The next day, a highly placed official in the Guatemalan security forces told Mr. Vásquez that the G-2 had taken his daughter and warned him not to intervene. On April 21, the Guatemalan Interior Ministry denied government involvement in the kidnapping. The Reagan administration was no more honest: U.S. State Department Guatemala Desk Officer Jim Cason dismissed evidence of government complicity, saying, "Robbery at gas stations is very common these days." Nothing was stolen.

At a private meeting, President Cerezo told Mr. Vásquez that he knew the details of the kidnapping, and promised that Carolina would be released soon afterwards.

Carolina Vásquez was lucky. Thanks to her family's leverage and international pressure, she was one of Guatemala's few "disappeared" who was released. She fled the country. On April 24, the day Vásquez was released, the Guatemalan press reported the discovery of eight bodies, including five strangled peasants and twenty-six-year-old architecture student Edgar Salvador Ascensio, kidnapped one day before Carolina Vásquez. While the Guatemalan government says there are no political killings, in April 1987 Archbishop Penados said, "The G-2 continues to kill many people."[1] In April 1986 Archbishop Penados had stated that President Cerezo held "twenty-five percent of the power" mandated by his office. One year later, in April 1987, the Archbishop said that Cerezo held "even less—perhaps twenty percent."

1. Author interview, Guatemala City, April 1987.

233

2. *Central America Report*, Vol. XIV, No. 18, May 15, 1987, p. 139 and "Human Rights in Guatemala During President Cerezo's First Year," (New York: America Watch, February 1987), p. 34.

3. Amnesty International, Urgent Action, 124/86, May 22, 1986, regarding six "disappeared" peasants.

4. *Country Reports . . . for 1986*, (February 1987), p. 509.

5. James LeMoyne, "Central America's Arms Buildup: The Risks of Guns Without Butter," *The New York Times*, April 19, 1987, p. 1.

6. *Central America Report*, Vol. XIV, No. 14, April 10, 1987, p. 106.

7. *La Hora*, November 4 and 6, 1986.

In May 1987 the English-language weekly, *Central America Report* (*CAR*), reported 321 acts of political violence between February and April 1987, figures higher than those for the same period during 1985, under a military dictatorship.[2] Amnesty International has documented dozens of abductions, all allegedly carried out by security forces. It has also stated that the Cerezo government explains violence in much the same manner as previous governments, attributing those acts to "armed groups operating clandestinely, right-wing groups and guerrillas. . . ."[3] Yet the Cerezo administration denies government complicity in its country's ongoing atrocities.

The Guatemalan government blames current violence on the same intangibles cited by previous administrations, including common crime and phantom "death squads." The U.S. State Department attributed these killings to the guerrillas and "extreme right-wing groups of self-appointed vigilantes," making the unrelenting violence sound more like a scene from the Wild West than organized government killing. In its 1986 *Country Report*, the State Department acknowledged only 131 killings with "possible political implications," attributing 72 to "the guerrillas," 3 to "right-wing groups," and 56 to "unknown assailants"[4]—in short, not a single killing attributed to security forces, according to Embassy statistics. Even statistics from the conservative Guatemalan press do not coincide with those of the State Department: of 1,039 killings reported between February 1986 and January 1987, 18 of them—less than two percent—held the guerrillas responsible. At present there are some 2,000 armed guerrillas and 43,600 security forces.[5]

In April 1987 *CAR* reported that "cruelly tortured and mutilated bodies . . . appear to have increased in number to such a degree that the local press concludes that death squads are operating in the country."[6] Well into Cerezo's second year of government, selective "disappearances" and killings have risen, the victims thrown into well-known body dumping sites after having been brutally tortured. The government either denies knowledge of the abduction or claims to be investigating it. The victims today are the same kinds of people eliminated under previous governments: unionists, doctors, students, and lawyers. On February 27, 1987, 24-year-old law student José Derick Calderón Figueroa was abducted from his home; the following day, Manuel de Jesús López Morales, a unionist with the state electric company "disappeared." Both bodies appeared at the same site on March 7, their arms amputated and Morales' head crushed. On March 19, 1987, 34-year-old medical doctor Edgar Arana Castillo, who had returned from exile the year before, was kidnapped near his home; his tortured body was found under the Los Esclavos bridge outside Guatemala City. And according to the national teachers' union, STEG, by late 1986 at least twenty schoolteachers had "disappeared" under the Cerezo government.[7]

In rural areas, the situation is no better. In early 1986 a group of 37 refugees under Church protection came down from the mountains; weeks later, two were kidnapped by armed men as they stood outside the Cobán convent. They have not reappeared. On December 18, 1986 Basilio Tuiz Ramírez, brother of a GAM leader, was abducted from an ambulance carrying him to Sololá—he had been shot the day before. Six armed men took him away. The government denied complicity in the killing, stating that Tuiz could have died "in a guerrilla/army confrontation." The same week, near Cobán, radio announcer Francisco Torres Vides was found three days after his "disappearance," in an isolated ditch with six bullets in his head, surrounded by the toys he had bought for his children as Christmas presents.

News of repression in highland towns is harder to come by because they are isolated and local reporters seldom travel there, and even if they did, villagers are reluctant to talk. The only vehicles for their denunciations are the GAM or the Church. In June 1986 two letters signed by fourteen religious and the Bishop of Izabal denounced eight "disappearances," two abductions, and the massacre of women and children in the Sepur-Zarco region of Alta Verapaz. Again, President Cerezo denied the allegation, saying that the peasants had been killed in army/ guerrilla battles. Following the return of 108 Kekchí Indians from the mountains, where they had been hiding since 1980, the army bombed the village of Las Pacayas in late February, where the refugees had been met by the Church and the departmental governor. According to church sources, the army attacked Las Pacayas to punish local inhabitants, who, they believed, knew of the refugees' planned return. In April 1987, the Acting Bishop of Izabal sent a letter to President Cerezo, denouncing the attempted assassination of a local priest, Father Luis María Carenzi, on April 15, by government security forces near Los Amates, Izabal.

In addition to outright repression, there has been no attempt to bring civilian rule to those institutions controlled by the army. The civil patrol system, while still formally "voluntary," and renamed *Comités Voluntarios de Autodefensa Civil* (Voluntary Committees for Civilian Self-Defense) continues to function as an adjunct to army surveillance over the rural population. There are currently some 700,000 patrollers combing the countryside for the subversives who the State Department, in its 1986 *Country Report*, says "are no longer a threat to national stability." In some areas, such as the Ixil triangle, Quiché, men continue to patrol once a week for twenty-four hours in addition to accompanying the army on one- to two-week *rastreos* (sweeps). In some highland villages, patrollers did vote to continue patrolling, but for survival's sake rather than from enthusiasm: they concluded that the army would stay out of their communities if they voted to maintain the patrol.[8]

8. Author interview, Guatemala City, April 1987.

9. *Central America Report*, Vol. XIV, No. 10, March 13, 1987, p. 74.

Guatemala's 24 model villages have not been dismantled; today, they contain some 70,000 people. While the State Department calls them "half-way houses" and "rural settlements," they have been called "concentration camps" by everyone from rural religious workers to Nobel laureate Adolfo Pérez Esquivel.[9] And they are models of nothing except confinement and misery. Where barbed wire and overt army presence are no longer necessary, fear and mistrust of one's neighbors provide sufficient control over villagers' movements. Nowhere is the true nature of the model villages better demonstrated than in Saraxoch, near Cobán, Alta Verapaz, inhabited by some 570 people. On the hilltop overlooking the tin roofs there is a sign saying "Welcome to Saraxoch: An Ideologically New, Anti-Subversive Community." A few yards further down, another sign reads simply: "Halt: Identify Yourself." A civil patrol shelter next to the sign is manned by armed men and boys; those who can read record license plate and passport numbers on dirty scraps of paper.

With regard to Guatemala's external refugees, the Cerezo government can claim little if any success. Of 100,000 refugees, 343 returned in 1986.[10] The rest sent a collective letter to President Cerezo during his trip to Mexico in June 1986, refusing to return to Guatemala until civil patrols were disbanded and guarantees given that they would not be forced to live in model villages. Statements on repatriation from government sources have been no more encouraging. In February 1987 Defense Minister Gramajo said that "guerrillas have infiltrated the refugees' ranks, preparing them with Marxist doctrines." Gramajo added that the Defense Ministry expected to repatriate 17,000 refugees during 1987. Revolutionary Party (PR) Congressman Víctor Hugo Godoy recommended a halt to the refugee program since potential returnees "run the risk of dying," while the teachers' union, STEG, advised refugees to stay in Mexico, since "paramilitary groups" intended to maintain repression.

Internal refugees continue to be subject to army control. Hundreds come down from the mountains each month. According to religious sources, virtually all of them are brought down by the army and submitted to several days of interrogation in army garrisons. The only instance where the army has not imposed its will over internal refugees is in Cobán, Alta Verapaz. Some 250 peasants came down from the mountains between early 1986 and February 1987: the last two groups of over 100 refugees each turned themselves in only after receiving assurances from Bishop Gerardo Flores that they would not be turned over to the army. Throughout, the army's displeasure with Church protection of the refugees has been apparent. In March 1987, following the arrival of the 108 refugees, then-head of the Cobán military base, Colonel Raúl Dehesa Oliva, pressured Bishop Flores to turn them over to the Army and ordered plainclothes G-2 agents to infiltrate the refugee groups. The Church has refused to abandon its role of protection. Other refugees have not been so lucky. In April 1987, ninety-six refugees from Sepur-Zarco, Izabal, were being held at the Cobán military base, "until we can get them land titles," an S-5 civilian affairs officer explained. A church official stated that the refugees were prisoners there.

Even where there is no army presence, no civil patrol or model village, such forces are no longer necessary to maintain army control. While the Inter-Institutional Coordinators Systems (IICS) are now formally under civilian jurisdiction, the army "still supplies the expertise, the machinery, and the manpower," according to former Quiché commander, Colonel Byron Disrael

10. "Guatemalan Refugees in Chiapas," *Refugees*, No. 34, October 1986.

11. Cliff Krauss, "Guatemala Will Elect a Civilian, But Will He Control the Military?" *The Wall Street Journal*, October 30, 1986, p. 1.

12. Author interview, New York City, January 1987.

13. Richard Meislin, "Guatemala Aided Contras, Despite Denials, Panel Says," *The New York Times*, February 28, 1987, p. 10.

14. "Human Rights in Guatemala during President Cerezo's First Year in Office," (New York: Americas Watch, 1987), p. 13.

15. "Urgent Action," 124/86, May 22, 1986.

Lima Estrada.[11] A Guatemalan journalist was more succinct: "Who needs the IICS when you've got S-2 army intelligence in every corner of this country?"[12]

To understand the extent of its continuing power, one only has to view the roster of commanders active under this government, almost all of whom occupied key positions under previous governments. In Guatemala there is no punishment of the military for past crimes. Instead, they are rewarded.

General Héctor Alejandro Gramajo Morales, now Cerezo's defense minister, was head of the *Cuartel General* military barracks from 1983 through 1985. The *Cuartel* served as a torture and interrogation center for people "disappeared" and later executed by the G-2. The *Cuartel's* new commander, Colonel Otto Erick Ponce, was commander of the Cobán military base during the early 1980s, at the height of army scorched-earth offensives against the civilian population. General César Augusto Cáceres Rojas was named army chief of staff in February 1987, one week before *The New York Times* stated that in 1985 General Cáceres had approved the use of Guatemala by the U.S. government for laundering illegal arms shipments to Nicaraguan *contras*.[13] Colonel Roberto Mata Gálvez, presidential chief of staff, was commander of the Quiché military base at a time when army repression in the Quiché claimed tens of thousands of victims. Colonel Pablo Nuila Hub, presidential chief of staff under Mejía, and former head of the G-2, was transferred from his position as head of the strategic Poptún military base to head the *Centro de Estudios Militares*, (CEM, Center for Military Studies), the training center for counterinsurgent technocrats. Colonel Byron Lima Estrada, former top G-2 officer and Colonel Mata's successor as commander of the Quiché military base, whose heroes according to the *Wall Street Journal* are Napoleon and Hitler—"I respect conquerors"—has been reassigned to Colonel Nuila's post in Poptún. And G-2 Army Captain Armando Villegas, responsible for the killing of Beatriz Barrios Marroquín, was appointed to Cerezo's presidential guard. In 1986 President Cerezo conceded that only 9 of 26 former military commanders had been replaced.[14]

Cerezo's dissolution of the DIT plainclothes detective corps three weeks after taking office received international kudos, yet little applause at home, since the detective corps has been renamed and relocated three times in the past decade and is still widely associated with repression. As Amnesty International stated, "Only the names of security agencies were changed while the personnel employed by them and their working methods remained essentially the same."[15]

In mid-1986, the DIT was replaced by the *Brigada de Investigaciones Especiales y Narcóticos* (BIEN, Special Investigations and Narcotics Brigade); the BIEN operates from National Police headquarters. The National Police itself is now headed by Army Colonel Julio Enrique Caballeros Seigné, who began his career under Colonel Arana during the scorched-earth counterinsurgency of the 1960s, and, until his appointment, was head of the *Archivo* army

Religious procession, San Antonio Aguas Calientes, Sacatepéquez.

"Alma América Garrido de Girón, a (nursery school) teacher, was abducted in Guatemala City on 14 January 1987 by unidentified men who forced her, in front of her 10-year-old daughter, into a car with darkened windows and no license plates. Her body was found three days later on the road between Escuintla and Antigua Guatemala, bearing signs of torture. According to local news reports, her father said at her funeral that he had not asked for justice from the authorities, as he suspected that those responsible were members of a government security agency. . . ."

—*Guatemala: Human-Rights Violations Reported Under the Administration of President Vinicio Cerezo Arévalo (January 1986–present)*, Amnesty International/London, April 1987

238

intelligence section, according to U.S. Embassy sources. Colonel Caballeros has announced that the army and the police will coordinate future "anti-delinquent" actions. He also ordered that the police would assume the volunteer firemen's duties of retrieving cadavers; local journalists claim that this has resulted in a partial blackout of reported killings. The National Police has also created "PN-2" divisions within each city precinct station and rural substation, which serve much the same function as their army counterpart, the G-2. Other police units are still held responsible for abductions and killings. This was well-evidenced in early 1987: following the January 25 kidnapping of peasant farmer Camilo García Luis, his wife, Marta Odilia Raxjal Sisimit, denounced the kidnapping to the Fifth Police Precinct, the BROE. The next day BROE officials demanded that she appear at their headquarters or pay a fifty *quetzal* fine. Raxjal "disappeared" on her way to BROE headquarters on January 27; her mother, María Esteban, was kidnapped hours later. Their two bodies showed up on January 30, fifty miles from Guatemala City.

There has been an almost complete absence of human rights efforts by other sectors. The GAM continues to be Guatemala's only internal human rights group, and President Cerezo has called its members "masochistic," telling them to "forget the past." In January 1987 the Guatemalan Congress approved a four million dollar budget to be dispensed among the families of the "disappeared," on the condition that they formally concede that their missing are "presumed dead." So far, eight of the GAM's 1,500 members have accepted Cerezo's offer, although 95 percent of them are impoverished peasants. In addition, the government's appointment of a special Supreme Court investigator to investigate some 2,377 *habeas corpus* writs has been a useless exercise in *pro forma* court procedure. As of April 1987 Special Prosecutor Olegario Labbé Morales had produced results on 93 writs, the findings super- ficial and slipshod. If President Cerezo were truly intent on eliciting information on the "dis- appeared," he would not have relied on one judge to investigate over two thousand writs; if Judge Labbé were serious in his own efforts, he would have protested from the start his lack of access to military intelligence information.

The Congressional Human Rights Commission has been called ineffectual by its own members. In January 1987 its chairman, Jorge Luis Archila Amézquita announced that "on an international level we received innumerable denunciations . . . but in truth we could not do anything more than give *pro forma* responses."[16] The Human Rights Procurator, to be appointed by Congress in 1986, had not even been nominated as of July 1987. "Nobody wants the job," one lawyer explained, "either out of fear or because they know they're not going to have any power anyway."

The GAM, which has demanded its own independent human rights commission since 1986, has been continually disappointed by President Cerezo's vacillations. After promising the GAM

16. *Prensa Libre*, January 31, 1987.

an independent commission shortly after taking office, President Cerezo abruptly reneged on his decision in June 1986; most recently, in a four-minute speech on April 7, 1987, Cerezo announced the formation of a four-member governmental commission. The GAM said it would accept the Commission on the condition that Adolfo Pérez Esquivel and Bishop Gerardi be included and that the International Committee of the Red Cross (ICRC) be allowed to enter Guatemala—conditions rejected by Cerezo in the past. The ICRC has been banned from Guatemala since 1980—one of the few countries in the world that prohibits it. The Church's own *Vicaría de Solidaridad* human rights office, scheduled to be functioning by December 1986, announced its opening in May 1987. Church spokesperson Monsignor Juan Gerardi said that the office would procure I.D. cards for peasants and deal with land problems. The reasons for this limited role were explained by Archbishop Penados. "People are afraid to be associated with the office," he said. "This isn't Chile or Salvador."

It is not surprising that there have been few efforts at organizing on a popular level. According to *CAR*, "The grass roots enthusiasm one would expect to find in a youthful democracy is missing in Guatemala. Neighborhood organizers, union activists, rural development workers, and virtually all those with a history of involvement in popular organizations express serious doubts regarding the permanence of the present 'democratic' opening." [17]

17. *Central America Report*, Vol. XIII, No. 45, November 21, 1986, p. 353.
18. U.S. Embassy, "Labor Trends in Guatemala," Guatemala City, August 1986, p. 14.

One attempt at organizing has been Guatemala's unions, one of the hardest hit sectors in the past. The two main coalitions, CUSG (Guatemalan Confederation of Labor Unity) and UNSITRAGUA (Syndicate of Guatemalan Labor Unions), announced their formal alliance on February 2, 1987. CUSG, which was formed by Ríos Montt in 1983 and is funded by the AFL-CIO, claims to have some 200,000 members, although real estimates place the number at less than 100,000. UNSITRAGUA, formed in February 1985, includes some 33 unions with over 18,000 members. Although UNSITRAGUA was formed from the remnants of the decimated CNT and FASGUA labor coalitions, it has succeeded in forming eight new unions since its inception. "Given our history, that's a big victory," one UNSITRAGUA leader said. The U.S. Embassy has redefined what it had called, back in 1980, "ineffectual union leadership." In August 1986, an Embassy publication signed by U.S. Ambassador Martínez Piedra called the unionists belonging to UNSITRAGUA "shock troops of radical unionism in the past." [18] Given past repression against Guatemalan unionists, the Embassy's definition sanctions possible future government repression against Guatemala's unions. Since Cerezo took office, at least four unionists have been killed and some two dozen others have received death threats. "It's not a question of *if* the guillotine will fall again," stated one UNSITRAGUA leader, "but *when.*"

For the most part, Guatemala is a country stripped of its leaders. According to Congressman Víctor Hugo Godoy, "Here in Guatemala the leaders have been decapitated. Those of us who are politicians today have been thrust into this role by process of elimination—

Army directing the annual Indian festival in Nebaj, Quiché.

Between 1982 and 1984 rural massacres increased under Ríos Montt, and urban "disappearances" soared under the government of Mejía Víctores. Yet the U.S. Embassy and the State Department were determined to prove that Guatemala was on its way to democracy, beginning with the 1984 National Constituent Assembly (ANC) elections. Even the U.S. Embassy, admitted that "disappearances" had increased in 1984, yet Congressman Mickey Edwards (R-Oklahoma) had favorable remarks on Guatemala's democratic process: "[T]here's no question that by all objective observations the human rights record in [Guatemala] has improved tremendously over the last two or three years. . . . I think the process deserves to be rewarded by the United States."

241

the army got rid of everyone else who could have ruled—Meme Colom Argueta, for one, and those of us who are left are just taking our first 'steps.' "

Today, even those who have not suffered from government repression are no better off than they were ten or even thirty years ago. Minimum wage is still between three and five *quetzales*—$1.10 to $1.80 per day. Of the five demands presented to the Cerezo government by the CUSG/UNSITRAGUA alliance in February 1987, three were directly related to wage and price controls. The five demands included salary increases for workers and peasants, price reduction on basic goods through profit controls, a freeze on electrical rates, broad agrarian reform, and support for the GAM's demand of an independent investigatory commission. Cerezo rejected all five demands. At the same time, the Guatemalan Congress voted itself a two thousand *quetzal* per month salary increase.

Almost half the Guatemalan workforce is under- or unemployed, which leads to common delinquency. Interior Minister Rodil and National Police Director Caballeros insist, however, that the solution to common delinquency is to increase the number of uniformed agents and to professionalize their ranks through training abroad and the introduction of modern detective equipment. Yet despite the obvious rise in uniformed police, delinquency continues. This is not surprising: in Guatemala City, the population has grown from 600,000 in 1975 to 2.3 million in 1987. Over half a million people inhabit *asentamientos*, or slums, which have been called "the belt of misery."[19] In March 1987 a member of the Church hierarchy was assaulted by youths who demanded, "Give us money. We're sorry, but we are hungry."

The perennial question of land distribution continues to be an issue in the Cerezo government. Although land reform was one of five proposed reforms on the Christian Democrat ticket back in 1974, when its candidate was General Ríos Montt, Cerezo made no such promises for his administration. "These are different times," he says. The only attempt to address this question—Guatemala's most basic problem—has been through the organization of 200,000 peasants, one third of them led by Guatemalan priest Father Andrés Girón, who, in April 1986, led 14,000 peasants on a 150-kilometer march into Guatemala City, demanding that *compañero Vinicio* help them get land. Girón's efforts have produced the purchase of three small farms. Even this small purchase of land provoked deep criticism from Guatemala's powerful business associations. At the November 1986 Association of Guatemalan Cattlebreeders' annual fair, its president, Edgar Sandoval, demanded that the government ignore petitions for land redistribution, including Father Girón's, saying that "the agrarian reform that has hit other Latin American nations brings only misery."[20]

The United States is now eager to resume economic and military aid. Interior Minister Rodil has contracted the Washington, D.C., law firm of Reichler & Appelbaum to act as its paid lobbyist for five million dollars in "non-lethal" police aid, including mobile detective units

19. Julio Godoy, "Displaced Peasants Flock to Capital's Slums," *Latinamerica Press*, April 9, 1987, p. 3.
20. *Prensa Libre*, November 20, 1986.

equipped with fingerprinting and identification equipment. A former *judicial*, who was himself sent to the Washington, D.C., International Police Academy back in the 1960s, is amused by the parallels between the aid received then and the aid solicited now: "It's the same thing. We got those mobile police units then, they had everything—fingerprinting, blood-sampling equipment. . . . You know what we called those vans? 'The Never-Never Land Ships,' *Las Naves del Olvido*. They were used to 'disappear' people. Once they loaded a dozen people into one, put silencers on their guns, and shot them inside."[21] He explained that the agents stripped the vans of their equipment before converting them into "death-mobiles."

The Cerezo government has also received considerable police aid from Taiwan, West Germany, France, Venezuela, and Mexico. In February 1987 West German Ambassador Peter Bensch and the director of the West German police formally presented the Cerezo government with over one hundred Mercedes Benz and BMW vehicles, plus radio communications sets. Although Police Director Caballeros said that the cars would not be given to police agents who were "car killers," two vehicles crashed and suffered heavy damage within the first month. In addition, Guatemalan police agents are being sent to Taiwan, the United States, France, and West Germany for two-week to two-year courses.[22] Additional police aid from the United States is likely to pass in Congress, since it seems potentially less lethal than outright military aid, despite lessons from the past, which the U.S. government seems reluctant to absorb. The U.S. State Department and the Guatemalan Interior Ministry, which oversees the police, have even succeeded in co-opting Harvard Law School. Harvard professors have received a substantial U.S. government grant to train the Guatemalan judiciary in Cambridge, as though common law professors, even from Harvard, could usefully advise civil law judges, and as though the resolution of common crime in Guatemala could alter the army's apparatus of State terrorism.

When asked why his civilian government does not prosecute perpetrators of human rights abuses, President Cerezo says that Guatemala is not Argentina, that Guatemala's army is "victorious." But for whom? Certainly not for the families of 100,000 dead Guatemalans. The Cerezo government has simply agreed to ignore past crimes. It accepted a series of Decree-Laws passed by the Mejía government four days before Cerezo's inauguration, which cemented army immunity from unexpected future indictment. The most famous is Decree-Law 08–86, an "Amnesty Law" that provides a general pardon to security forces for all crimes committed between March 23, 1982 and January 14, 1986. No one accuses President Cerezo of personally approving assassinations but his quiet acquiescence to the demands of the military and Guatemala's ruling elite has produced no tangible improvements during his term in office, nor has he succeeded in gradually consolidating a power base, which was the rationale for Cerezo's nonconfrontational approach.

21. Author interview, Guatemala City, April 1987.
22. *Prensa Libre*, October 1, 1986 and *La Hora*, October 2, 1986.

Soccer stadium, Nebaj, Quiché.

"Here in Guatemala, many times you see something, but you don't say anything because you don't want to die yet."

—Archbishop Próspero Penados del Barrio, Guatemala City

Indian family, Nebaj, Quiché.

In 1984 a journalist asked Colonel Edgar D'Jalma Domínguez, head of the Office for Army Public Relations, how the military would react once a civilian government was installed, and human rights organizations began to talk of military trials and retribution for past "disappearances." "We'll just give the civilian leaders a little pat on the ass and they'll shut up," D'Jalma retorted. Then he added, "Do you think that we've left proof? In Argentina, there are witnesses, there are books, there are films, there is proof. Here in Guatemala, there is none of that. There are no survivors."

President Cerezo has underestimated the potential support of tens of thousands of Guatemalans whose memories of the past are graphic and indelible. A Guatemalan Army officer, one of a handful of reformists in the 2,000-man officer corps, addressed the problem succinctly: "On his first day in office, Vinicio Cerezo should put on the presidential sash, go out on the Palace balcony, and tell the Guatemalan people that he was forced to make a pact with the military. Then he should ask the people, 'Should I break the pact? Should I fire so-and-so?' He would get 50,000 people in that square, shouting 'yes' in response. If he doesn't do this during his first two weeks in office, then he has lost."[23]

President Cerezo chose to ignore the most powerful bargaining chip in his possession: the support of the people he governs and the army's need to maintain a civilian in the presidency in order to win renewed foreign aid.

Back in 1966, when President Méndez Montenegro took office, he publicly named the secret prisons that had existed until then, promising that torture under the *judiciales* would end and that the "Tiger Cage" secret prison would be "eradicated."[24] President Cerezo has instead told the relatives of the "disappeared" to forget their dead. Twenty years ago, President Méndez offered a friend on a death squad list the only protection he could—his home in the National Palace.[25] Today, the Christian Democrat government offers even less, making no genuine attempt to do justice to the past or to the present. President Cerezo has given his personal assurances to the families of at least half a dozen people "disappeared" under his government that their abductions would be investigated. So far, not one investigation has produced results. For its part, the U.S. government is eager to support Guatemala's incipient "democracy," and to whitewash the horrors of recent years. But the U.S. government is unequivocally complicit in the Guatemalan government's "program of political murder"—past and present. The same repression abetted, if not instigated, by the U.S. government in Guatemala would be called murder at home, and those responsible for these crimes would be called criminals. In an essay on the military governments of Latin America, Mexican writer Carlos Fuentes addressed U.S. responsibility in these countries' horrors: "They [the army] know that up till now they have been able to torture at home and be rewarded abroad. Haven't American ambassadors dined with these good authoritarians the very same night they launched their wild adventures? . . . The United States owes an apology to . . . the people of Guatemala . . ."[26]

In late 1985 then-candidate Vinicio Cerezo visited a local orphanage: he hugged the widows, embraced the children, and left. One of the orphans, a boy who had lost both parents, had earlier told a friend that he would try to put the past behind him for the moment, while "the army still has the guns." But someday, he added, when he was grown-up, and his friends were too, then it would be "time for us to remember."

23. Author interview, Guatemala City, September 1985.
24. Michael McClintock, *The American Connection: Volume Two* (London: Zed Books, 1985, pp. 53–54.
25. Eduardo Galeano, *Guatemala: Occupied Country*, (New York: Monthly Review Press, 1969) p. 59.
26. "Power Against the People," *Newsweek*, April 21, 1986, p. 25.

Survival

In Guatemala the word "survival" has many interpretations. First, the physical survival of a people besieged by centuries of subjugation, whether from Spanish conquerors or army colonels. Then there is the cultural survival of Guatemala's Mayan population. Survival was also a theme of the 1985 presidential campaign. Virtually every foreign journalist reported that President Cerezo "survived at least three assassination attempts" between 1980 and 1981, one of which put three dozen bullet holes in his bullet-proof van. Supporters of Cerezo's leading opponent, newspaper publisher Jorge Carpio Nicolle, referred ruefully to survival as well. "It's a matter of survival to be in the UCN party here at the newspaper," one editor stated back in mid-1985. "You have to be 150 percent in agreement with Carpio here at the paper or you're out."

The following statement was made by a young anthropologist who lived in the Ixil triangle in northern Quiché during the late 1970s:

"There is a mythical person who represents the traditional Indian, mixing the savage, wild individual with the modern one. His name is 'Gaspar,' or 'Xan,' and he is the identity of the Chajul people. That is why the town is called San Gaspar Chajul; he is its spirit. The people began talking about him as if he were trapped by the army, but Gaspar would always make fun of the army in the end—if the army wanted to commit some act of violence against him, or torture him, they would sink him and drown him with a stick, but, all of a sudden, he would pop up behind them, as if by magic. He had made fun of them; he had escaped.

"The people told many stories of torture and how Gaspar would make fun of the army, and it gave them great pride. They would tell these tales as a means of self-identification, and as a way of keeping their community pride in the face of invasion. It was a form of escape, because this magical person managed to do what they could not. He made fun of the army, he gave it a going over, and the army would die and Gaspar would survive."

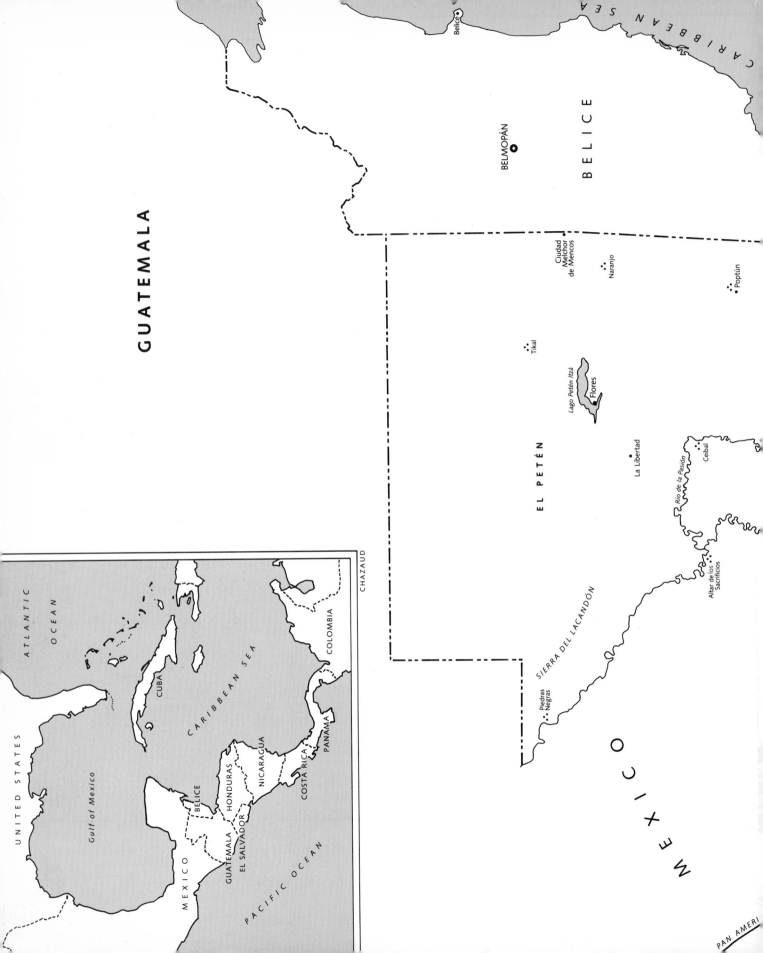

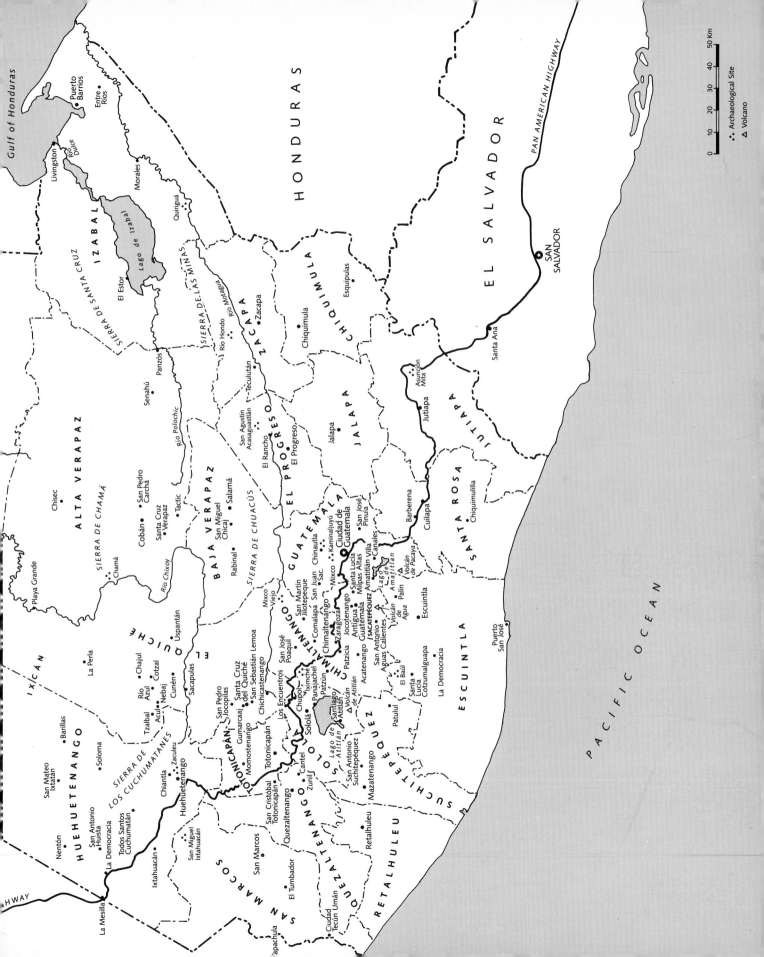

Index

torture, 126, 128, 140–41, 169
  secret houses for, 224–25
  see also repression
tourists and tourist industry, 78, 90, 136, 161, 163
Trotter, John Clinton, 202
Tuiz Ramírez, Basilio, 235
Turcios Lima, Luis, 23, 137
Tzacol refugee camp (Cobán), 119, 172, 179
Ubico, Jorge, 21
Unidad Revolucionaria Nacional Guatemalteca
  (URNG), 80
Union of the National Center (UCN), 159, 200,
  201, 218
unions, 21, 25, 28, 240
  repression against, 73, 76, 202, 240
United Front of the Revolution (FUR), 72
United Fruit Company (UFCO), 21, 103
United Nations:
  High Commissioner for Refugees (UNHCR), 118
  Human Rights Commission, 182, 183
  Special Rapporteur, 182, 183
  World Food Program (FAO), 119
U.S. Chamber of Commerce (Guatemala), 102
U.S. Congress, 103, 114
  observers at 1985 elections, 204
U.S. Embassy (Guatemala), 25, 81, 103, 125, 135
  concession of army culpability for repression, 73
  and GAM, 161
  and G-2, 200
  investigations of human rights abuses, 208
  MilGroup, 135
  and 1985 election, 201, 204–5
  officials' comments on PAC system, 164, 166
  position on massacres, 135

report on guerilla strength, 158
on Special Tribunals, 119
visa lines at, *97*
U.S. House of Representatives, Foreign Affairs
  Committee, 159
U.S. Special Forces Advisors, 24, 25, 125
U.S. State Department, 28
  and AID literacy program, 58
  Country Reports on Human Rights, 15, 46,
    48, 64, 69, 72, 76, 80, 81, 102, 163, 166,
    185, 206, 234, 235
  and GAM, 161
  and government repression in Guatemala, 13,
    25, 108, 158, 234
  and Mejía Víctores, 153–54
  and military aid, 16, 80–81, 119, 177, 205,
    242, 243
  and 1954 coup, 21, 23
  on Penados, 208
  and Ríos Montt, 110, 114
  travel advisory for Guatemala, 73, 164
  on unions in Guatemala, 202
University of San Carlos (USAC), 71, 102, 158,
  164, 187
  demonstrations at, 200, *215*
  Humanities Department student cafeteria, *93*
  repression against, 73, 76, *93*
Urízar, Juan Pablo, 193

Vagrancy Law, 21
van den Berghe, Pierre, 27
Vásquez, Ismael, 202
Vásquez Velásquez, Debora Carolina, 233
Vatican II, 40, 44

Verapaces, 29, 121
Verbena cemetery morgue, *207*, 218
"Victory 82," 114, 118
villages:
  description of, 34–35
  model, 18, 154–55, 183, 184, 185, 235–36
Villagrán Kramer, Francisco, 71–72, 205
Villegas, Armando, 232, 237

wages, rural, 50
Wall Street Journal (newspaper), 183, 237
Walters, Vernon, 80
Washington Office on Latin America (WOLA),
  28, 204
weapons, U.S., 80–81, *115*, 119
West Germany, 243
White Hand death squad, 24, 223
"Why I Am Against Communism" (booklet), 162
Wohlers Rivas, Eduardo, 168
Workers Day demonstration (May 1, 1980), 76

Xeatsán Bajo village (Patzún, Chimaltenango), 193
Xesic II, Quiché, 77

Ydígoras Fuentes, Miguel, 23, 42
Yon Sosa, Marco Antonio, 23
Yos Muxtay, Rafael, 227
Yujá Xona, Gregorio, 102

Zacapa, 23, 25
Zacualpa, Quiché, 98
Zash, Anthony, 203
Zelada Carillo, Ramón, 159